Barcelona

DIRECTIONS

WRITTEN AND RESEARCHED BY

Jules Brown

ROUGH GUIDES

NEW YORK • LONDON • DELHI

www.roughguides.com

Contents

Introduction to

Barcelona

It's tempting to say that there's nowhere quite like Barcelona – there's certainly not another city in Spain to touch it for sheer style, looks or energy. The glossy mags and travel press dwell enthusiastically on its outrageous architecture, designer shopping, hip bars and vibrant cultural scene, but Barcelona is more than just this year's fad. It's a confident, progressive city, one that is tirelessly self-renewing while preserving all that's best about its past.

The province of Catalunya (Catalonia in English), of which Barcelona is the capital, has a historical identity going back as far as the ninth century, and

▼ Casa Brunos Quadros, Ramblas

through the long period of domination by outside powers, as well as during the Franco dictatorship, it proved impossible to stifle the Catalan spirit. The city reflects this independence, being at the forefront of Spanish political activism, radical design and architecture, and commercial dynamism.

This is seen most perfectly in the glorious *modernista* (Art Nouveau) buildings that stud the city's streets and avenues. Antoni Gaudí is the most famous of those who have left their mark on Barcelona in this way: his Sagrada Família church is rightly revered, but just as fascinating are the (literally) fantastic houses, apartment buildings and parks that he and his contemporaries designed.

The city also boasts a medieval old town – full of pivotal buildings from an earlier age of expansion – and a stupendous artistic legacy, from national (ie, Catalan) collections of Romanesque, Gothic and contemporary art to major galleries containing the life's work of the Catalan

◀ Geese at La Seu

artists Joan Miró and Antoni Tàpies (not to mention a celebrated showcase of the work of Pablo Picasso).

Barcelona is a surprisingly easy place to find your way around, with the greater city, in effect, a series of self-contained neighbourhoods stretching out from the harbour, flanked by a brace of parks and girdled by the wooded Collserola mountains. You could see most of the major sights in a long weekend, though it pays to get off the beaten track when you can. Designer boutiques in gentrified old-town

When to visit

The best times to go to Barcelona are late **spring** and early **autumn**, when the weather is still comfortably warm, around 21–25°C, and walking the streets isn't a chore. In **summer**, the city can be unbearably hot and humid with temperatures averaging 28°C (but often a lot more). August sees the climate at its most unwelcoming, while many shops, bars and restaurants close as local inhabitants head out of the city in droves. It's worth considering a **winter** break, as long as you don't mind the prospect of occasional rain. It's generally still warm enough to sit out at a café, even in December when the temperature hovers around 13°C.

◀ Mercat de la Boqueria

▲ Sagrada Família

quarters, street opera singers belting out an aria, bargain lunches in workers' taverns, neighbourhood funicular rides, unmarked gourmet restaurants, craft outlets and workshops, restored medieval palaces, suburban walks and specialist galleries – all are just as much Barcelona as the Ramblas or Gaudí's Sagrada Família.

Barcelona
AT A GLANCE

THE RAMBLAS

One of the city's most famous sights, the kilometre-long tree-lined avenue, filled with pedestrians, pavement cafés and performance artists, is the hub of any visit.

▲ La Ribera

LA RIBERA

The easternmost old-town neighbourhood, home to the Picasso museum, is also a fashionable boutique-and-bar destination.

EL RAVAL

Still on the cusp between edginess and artiness, this western old-town neighbourhood contains both the flagship museum of contemporary art and the pick of the latest designer shops, bars and restaurants.

▲ Las Ramblas human statue

BARRI GÒTIC

The Gothic Quarter is the medieval nucleus of the city – a labyrinth of twisting streets and historic buildings, including La Seu (the cathedral) and the palaces and museums around Plaça del Rei.

▼ Barri Gòtic

◀ Port Vell

PORT VELL

The spruced-up Old Port harbour area features high-profile visitor attractions like the aquarium and Maremàgnum retail-and-leisure centre.

BARCELONETA

The former fishing quarter beyond Port Vell boasts the city's most concentrated batch of seafood restaurants, and marks the start of a series of beaches running up past the Port Olímpic.

▲ Dreta de l'Eixample

EIXAMPLE

The gridded nineteenth-century uptown district contains some of Europe's most extraordinary architecture – including Gaudí's Sagrada Família.

GRÀCIA

The nicest of the suburbs on the northern edge of the city centre is a noted nightlife destination, with some offbeat bars, independent cinemas and great restaurants contained within its charming streets and squares.

▲ Barceloneta beach

MONTJUÏC

Barcelona's best art museums and gardens, and the main Olympic stadium, are sited on the fortress-topped hill to the southwest of the centre.

▼ Montjuïc castle

Ideas

The big six

Gaudí's greatest fantasies to Picasso's earliest works, Gothic towers to Romanesque frescoes, ceramic dragons to human statues – Barcelona's must-see attractions glory in their extraordinary diversity. All are easily experienced in a long weekend, and with no charge to see three of them there's no excuse for missing out on the city's weird and wonderful highlights.

▲ La Seu

Pride of the Gothic era, the city's majestic medieval cathedral anchors the old town.

P.58 ▸ BARRI GÒTIC

▼ The Ramblas

The city's iconic central thoroughfare is the setting for one of Europe's greatest free shows, as buskers, stallholders, hawkers, eccentrics, locals and tourists collide to gleeful effect.

P.51 ▸ ALONG THE RAMBLAS

▶ Parc Güell

Gaudí's most playful instincts assert
themselves in Barcelona's unrivalled public
park, where contorted stone pavilions,
gingerbread buildings and surreal ceramics
combine unforgettably.

▼ Sagrada Família

If there's a more famous unfinished church
in the world, Barcelona would like to know
about it – the temple dedicated to the
"Sacred Family" is the essential pilgrimage
for Gaudí fans.

▼ Museu Picasso

Trace the genesis of the artist's genius in the
city that Picasso liked to call home.

▼ Museu Nacional d'Art de Catalunya (MNAC)

The National Museum of Art celebrates the
grandeur of Romanesque and Gothic art, two
periods in which Catalunya's artists were
pre-eminent in Spain.

Children's Barcelona

There's plenty for children to do, much of it free (for under 4s) or inexpensive (for under 12s). The main problem is transport, as many metro stations (except on lines 1 and 2) have stairs or escalators – adults often face a stiff climb with the pushchair. Disposable nappies, baby food and formula milk are widely available in pharmacies and supermarkets, though baby-changing areas are rare, except in department stores and shopping centres.

▼ Font Màgica

The lights and music cut in on cue several nights a week at Montjuïc's long-standing sound-and-light show – one for all the family.

P.111 ▶ MONTJUÏC

▼ Plaça de Vicenç Martorell

While children play in the traffic-free square's playground, parents can rest at the excellent café.

P.82 ▶ EL RAVAL

▲ Parc d'Atraccions

On the heights of Tibidabo, overlooking the
city, this terrific amusement park mixes old-
fashioned rides with high-tech experiences.

P.170 ▸ TIBIDABO AND PARC
DEL COLLSEROLA

▲ Parc Zoològic

From dolphins to big cats, Barcelona's zoo
packs the world's fauna into the rolling
grounds of the city's nicest park.

P.108 ▸ PARC DE LA
CIUTADELLA

▲ L'Aquàrium

Come face to face with sharks and other sea
creatures in Port Vell's highest-profile (and
highest-priced) all-weather family attraction.

P.74 ▸ PORT VELL AND
BARCELONETA

▶ Poble Espanyol

See Spain in a day in the "Spanish Village",
an outdoor museum of reconstructed
buildings, artisans' workshops and cafés
that makes a great family day out.

P.113 ▸ MONTJUÏC

Stay in style

As befits Spain's style and design capital, Barcelona has a wide array of chic hotels to suit the most fashionable visitor. Even city B&Bs and budget hotels aren't strangers to boutique style. Barcelona doesn't really have an off season – though prices do come down sometimes in August or at weekends, even in the top-rated establishments. Wherever you stay, it's essential to book well in advance.

▼ the5rooms

Bed-and-breakfast "Barcelona-style" means fashionable rooms in an elegant home-from-home.

P.194 ▸ ACCOMMODATION

▼ Arts Barcelona

A beachfront beauty with the designer touch, five-star comforts and a terrific pool – this is widely considered to be Barcelona's top hotel.

P.191 ▸ ACCOMMODATION

▲ Neri

From the tranquil roof terrace to the designer interior, this dramatic renovation of an old-town palace makes a stylish base in the Barri Gòtic.

P.189 ▸ ACCOMMODATION

◀ Gat Raval

Cool rooms in a cool neighbourhood – the Gat Raval offers boutique style at bargain prices.

P.190 ▸ ACCOMMODATION

▼ Claris

Rooftop pool, beautiful rooms, and talked-about restaurant and bar, right in the heart of the modern city.

P.192 ▸ ACCOMMODATION

On the move

Most of Barcelona's old-town areas are only accessible on foot, but for outlying sights you can let public transport take the strain. In fact, just reaching Montjuïc and Montserrat is more than half the fun, as you have to rely on cable cars and funicular railways to climb the steep gradients. Reaching Tibidabo is even more of an adventure, with train, tram and funicular all required before getting to the top.

▲ Tramvia Blau

It's worth trying to coincide with the antique tram service that forms part of the approach to Tibidabo.

P.172 ▸ TIBIDABO AND PARC DEL COLLSEROLA

▲ Telefèric de Montjuïc

This is the speediest way to the castle ramparts, with some of the best views of the city.

P.118 ▸ MONTJUÏC

▶ Trasbordador Aeri

The cross-harbour cable car is an iconic Barcelona ride, but wait for a clear day for the best views.

P.76 ▶ PORT VELL AND
BARCELONETA

▼ Sightseeing tour buses

Barcelona's tour buses loop around the city stopping at every major sight and attraction – the ticket lets you jump on and off when you like.

P.202 ▶ ESSENTIALS

▼ Las Golondrinas

To appreciate Barcelona the maritime city, jump on one of the daily sightseeing boats that depart from near the Columbus monument.

P.203 ▶ ESSENTIALS

▼ Cremellara de Montserrat

The towering heights of Montserrat, an hour from Barcelona, can be reached by rack railway as well as by cable car – a dramatic ride in any weather.

P.175 ▶ MONTSERRAT

Festive Barcelona

Traditionally, each neighbourhood celebrates with its own festival, though the major ones – like Gràcia's Festa Major (August) and the Mercè (September) – have become city institutions. There is always a parade (often with grotesque giant figures with papier-mâché heads), music and dancing, while traditional Catalan celebrations are characterized by the *correfoc* ("fire-running"), where drummers, dragons and devils cavort in the streets, and by the *castellers*, the red-shirted human tower-builders.

▲ Barcelona Festival

The summer's foremost arts and music festival centres its performances on Montjuïc's open-air Greek theatre.

P.115 › MONTJUÏC

▼ Castle-building, Catalan-style

Competing teams of human tower-builders draw crowds at every traditional festival, piling person upon person to achieve a chaotic perfection.

P.204 › ESSENTIALS

▲ Traditional dance

Every traditional festival is celebrated by dancing the sardana, the Catalan national dance, which dates back centuries – it's also danced outside the cathedral every weekend.

`P.64` ▸ BARRI GÒTIC

▲ Fira de Santa Llúcia

The first three weeks in December are devoted to the annual Christmas fair, held in front of La Seu – no one else back home will have gifts like these.

`P.204` ▸ ESSENTIALS

▲ Sónar

The electronic music and multimedia art world parties hard every June as Barcelona turns techno.

`P.204` ▸ ESSENTIALS

▼ Festa de la Mercè

The city's biggest annual festival is dedicated to merrymaking and mayhem on a lavish scale.

`P.204` ▸ ESSENTIALS

Shops and markets

Barcelona is great for shopping, especially for designer clothes, handcrafted accessories or stylish household items. The sharpest designers congregate in the Eixample and La Ribera; the secondhand/vintage and independent music scene focuses on El Raval, while it's the Barri Gòtic for boutiques, antiques and gifts. Opening hours are Monday to Saturday 10am to 1.30/2pm, 4.30 to 7.30/8pm, though department stores and malls open until 10pm, while smaller shops vary their hours considerably.

▲ Secondhand style

Vintage and "pre-loved" clothes all end up in the secondhand shops along the funky Carrer de la Riera Baixa.

P.84 ▶ EL RAVAL

▼ Book and coin market

Join the crowds on Sunday morning at the Mercat de Sant Antoni, good fun whether you're browsing or buying.

P.86 ▶ EL RAVAL

▼ Designer fashion

Some of the hottest European designers call Barcelona home – check out the hip boutiques and craft shops in the Barri Gòtic.

P.66 ▶ BARRI GÒTIC

▲ Els Encants

Haggle hard and pick up a bargain at the city's biggest flea market, held every Monday, Wednesday, Friday and Saturday.

P.144 ▶ SAGRADA FAMÍLIA AND GLÒRIES

▼ Mercat de la Concepció

Fantastic flowers, available 24 hours a day, in an uptown market just a little way off the beaten track.

P.135 ▶ DRETA DE L'EIXAMPLE

▼ Mercat de la Boqueria

The city's finest food market is a show in its own right, busy with locals and tourists from dawn to dusk.

P.52 ▶ ALONG THE RAMBLAS

Parks and gardens

It's not hard to find a bit of traffic-free space in Barcelona, from a quiet neighbourhood corner to a formal park. Some places, like Parc Güell and Parc de la Ciutadella, will be high on any visiting list, but to escape the crowds try hiking in the Collserola hills, just a fifteen-minute train ride away. Nearly all outdoor spaces have a kiosk-café, and many have a children's play area.

▼ Parc Joan Miró

An urban park whose concrete piazza and towering Miró sculpture are tempered by a shaded garden with children's playground.

P.150 ▶ ESQUERRA DE L'EIXAMPLE

▼ Parc de la Ciutadella

Enjoy the summer breeze as you paddle about the park at the eastern edge of the old town.

P.105 ▶ PARC DE LA CIUTADELLA

▲ Parc Güell

The city's most extraordinary park, festooned with ceramic decoration, is the product of architect Antoni Gaudí's surreal flight of fancy.

▼ Jardins de Mossèn Costa i Llobera

The huge cactus stands on the slopes of Montjuïc are a local secret, best enjoyed as the day's shadows lengthen.

▲ Jardí Botànic de Barcelona

Barcelona's extensive botanical gardens spread across a hillside above the Olympic stadium.

▶ Parc del Collserola

On the hottest of days a welcome breeze and pine-shaded springs reward hikers in the wooded hills above Barcelona.

The modernista trail

Barcelona's presiding architectural genius, Antoni Gaudí i Cornet, changed the way people looked at urban architecture and, with his *modernista* contemporaries – notably Josep Puig i Cadafalch and Lluís Domènech i Montaner – also changed the way Barcelona looked. Their style, a sort of Catalan Art Nouveau, erupted in the 1870s and 1880s, and following the *modernista* trail around the city shows you some of Europe's most extraordinary buildings.

▲ Almirall

A beautiful piece of *modernista* design also just happens to be a great city-centre bar.

P.89 ▸ EL RAVAL

▼ Casa Batlló

Self-guided tours through Gaudí's emblematic Casa Batlló end with a flourish on the startling roof terrace.

P.131 ▸ DRETA DE L'EIXAMPLE

▲ Hospital de la Santa Creu i de Sant Pau

Tour the ornate pavilions of the city's most innovative public hospital – and find out more about the city's architectural heritage at its Modernista Centre.

P.83 ▶ SAGRADA FAMÍLIA AND GLÒRIES

▲ Hotel España

Some of the greatest *modernista* names came together to decorate this famous nineteenth-century hotel, which has a particularly splendid dining room, perfect for lunch.

P.84 ▶ EL RAVAL

▶ La Pedrera

The "stone quarry" is the most eye-catching apartment building in the city, a sinuous structure with a fantasy roof terrace that hosts summer cocktail evenings.

P.133 ▶ DRETA DE L'EIXAMPLE

▲ Casa Amatller

Centrepiece of the famous Mansana de la Discòrdia, or "Block of Discord", a trio of elaborate mansions built for the city's nineteenth-century industrialists.

P.131 ▶ DRETA DE L'EIXAMPLE

Sports and recreation

A spin-off from the 1992 Olympics was an increased provision of sports and leisure facilities throughout Barcelona. The city beaches and swimming pools draw big summer crowds, while you can rent anything from roller blades to mountain bikes to explore the backstreets and promenades. However, ask a Catalan to recommend a spectator sport and there will be only one answer – football, as practised by the local heroes of FC Barcelona.

▲ City beaches

When the gallery-going, shopping and bar-hopping flags, spend the day at the beach – Barcelona has 5km of sand-fringed ocean.

P.124 ▸ PORT OLÍMPIC AND POBLE NOU

▶ Estadi Olímpic

The Olympic Stadium, remodelled for the
1992 Games, is at the heart of an Olympic
area that includes world-class swimming
and sports facilities.

P.116 ▶ MONTJUÏC

▲ Rent a bike

With around 150km of cycle paths, plus
beach promenades and forest trails,
renting a bike offers a different way to see
the city.

P.205 ▶ ESSENTIALS

▼ Camp Nou

The city's premier team, FC Barcelona,
plays in one of Europe's most magnificent
stadiums – you can take a tour as part of a
visit to the excellent football museum.

P.161 ▶ CAMP NOU, PEDRALBES
AND SARRIÀ-SANT
GERVASI

◀ Swimming at Montjuïc

The summer outdoor
pool at the Piscines
Bernat Picorell is
hugely popular
– there are full
indoor facilities too,
open year-round.

P.117 ▶ MONTJUÏC

Historic Barcelona

Any walk around the Old Town provides reminders of Barcelona's long history, with a street layout and surviving walls that go back to Roman times. But it's the fourteenth- and fifteenth-century Golden Age that lent the city its Catalan-Gothic lustre, when newly built churches, city hall, government palace and shipyards all testified to Barcelona's influence. Later, the eighteenth-century Bourbons reshaped the city again, building fortresses to subdue the unruly inhabitants.

▲ Museu Marítim

The engaging Maritime Museum is housed in the great medieval shipyards that underpinned Barcelona's early prosperity.

P.72 ▸ PORT VELL AND BARCELONETA

▲ Església de Santa María del Mar

Santa María was built in the roaring 1320s, with economic confidence at its height, making it the crowning glory of the Catalan-Gothic style of architecture.

P.62 ▸ LA RIBERA

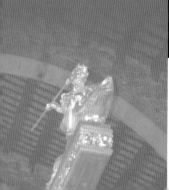

▶ Monestir de Pedralbes

Half an hour from the centre lies the Pedralbes monastery, boasting the city's most harmonious cloister.

▼ Museu d'Història de le Ciutat

The remains of Roman Barcelona – preserved under the old-town streets around Plaça del Rei – can be accessed through the fascinating city history museum.

▲ Església de Sant Pau del Camp

The city's oldest church, dating from the tenth century, provides a peaceful retreat in the modern Raval.

▼ Castell de Montjuïc

The hilltop Bourbon fortress offers an eagle's-eye view of the city.

Cafés

There are thousands of cafés, ranging from century-old coffee houses to unique neighbourhood haunts. Specialist places include a *forn* (bakery), *patisseria* (pastry shop) and *xocolateria* (specializes in chocolate), while a *granja* is more of a milk bar than a regular café, offering traditional delights like *orxata* (tiger-nut drink) and *granissat* (flavoured crushed ice). A café breakfast is typically a *flauta* (thin baguette sandwich), *ensaimada* (pastry spiral) or croissant.

▲ Textil Café

A relaxing museum café that's known for its good food.

P.102 ▶ LA RIBERA

▲ Café de l'Opera

House café for the opera house opposite, this is the most traditional of the city's watering holes.

P.56 ▶ ALONG THE RAMBLAS

▲ Granja M. Viader

For a taste of the old days, come for breakfast or a mid-morning chocolate drink in the city's oldest *granja* (milk bar).

P.87 ▸ EL RAVAL

◀ Laie Llibreria Café

Stop for breakfast, lunch or a read of the papers at Barcelona's best bookshop café.

P.137 ▸ DRETA DE L'EIXAMPLE

▼ Café Zurich

"Meet me at the Zurich" is an age-old Barcelona refrain.

P.56 ▸ ALONG THE RAMBLAS

Specialist museums

A selection of specialist collections adds to the city's extraordinary diversity. There are dedicated museums to the history of chocolate and the worlds of ceramics and textiles, while other collections zero in on Egyptian relics or the nuances of Catalan social history. Only CosmoCaixa (the Science Museum) and the unclassifiable Museu Frederic Marès are essential viewing, but visit one or two others to unpeel a layer of the city you might otherwise have missed.

▲ Museu Textil i d'Indumentaria

Textiles and clothing from Roman times to the present day illuminate one of the city's best-presented museums.

P.98 ▸ LA RIBERA

▲ Museu Frederic Marès

The "mad collector" to beat them all – don't miss Marès' extraordinary range of folkloric items, household utensils, toys and ephemera, contained within a lovely old-town palace with celebrated summer café.

P.62 ▸ BARRI GÒTIC

▼ Museu Egipci de Barcelona

Break off from the your Eixample shopping long enough to view this select showing of Egyptian antiquities.

P.132 ▶ DRETA DE L'EIXAMPLE

▲ CosmoCaixa

A museum with its own rainforest – only in Barcelona would a science museum go so far to entertain and inform.

P.172 ▶ TIBIDABO AND PARC DEL COLLSEROLA

◀ Museu de la Xocolata

Handcrafted chocolates, made on the premises, are the twist at this informative museum.

P.94 ▶ SANT PERE

▼ Museu de Ceràmica

The city's most comprehensive collection of ceramics is housed in one wing of a former royal palace.

P.165 ▶ CAMP NOU, PEDRALBES AND SARRIÀ-SANT GERVASI

On the waterfront

Dramatic changes over the last two decades have once again placed harbour and Mediterranean at the heart of Barcelona. The old docksides have been opened up as promenades and entertainment areas, and the city's once grimy beaches landscaped and prettified – it's as if a theatre curtain has been lifted to reveal that, all along, Barcelona had an urban waterfront of which it could be proud.

▲ Mirador de Colón

Take the elevator up to the viewing platform of the Christopher Columbus monument to survey the ever-developing waterfront.

P.72 ▸ PORT VELL AND BARCELONETA

▲ Santa Eulàlia

Step back to the days of sail with a tour of this historic schooner.

P.73 ▸ PORT VELL AND BARCELONETA

▼ Diagonal Mar

Jump on a metro or tram down to the Parc del Fòrum, at Diagonal Mar, to experience the city's latest dazzling waterfront development.

P.124 ▶ PORT OLÍMPIC AND POBLE NOU

▲ Luz de Gas

The floating bar (open summer only) is the best vantage-point for the comings and goings on the Port Vell promenade.

P.78 ▶ PORT VELL AND BARCELONETA

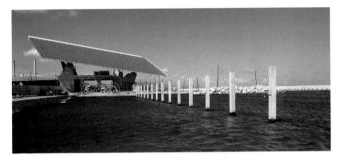

▼ Port Olímpic

The twin towers and packed marina dominate the Port Olímpic, whose restaurants and bars make it the city's liveliest resort area.

P.122 ▶ PORT OLÍMPIC AND POBLE NOU

▲ Port Vell

The "Old Port" area at the foot of the Ramblas has seen its former warehouses and cargo wharves transformed into a vibrant entertainment zone.

P.72 ▶ PORT VELL AND BARCELONETA

Out for lunch

Restaurants generally offer a lunchtime *menú del dia* (menu of the day), starting at about €8, rising to €12 in fancier places or at weekends. It's a real bargain, as dinner in the same restaurant might cost three times as much. Budget places often don't have a written menu, with the waiter simply reeling off the day's dishes. Lunch hours are 1–4pm, though locals don't eat until 2pm or later.

▲ L'Econòmic

Diners cram into this traditionally tiled lunch-only restaurant for excellent bargain meals, served Monday to Friday.

P.95 ▸ SANT PERE

▲ La Tomaquera

Food cooked on the chargrill (*a la brasa*) is the speciality here – not just chicken and steak but seasonal vegetables like artichokes and spring onions.

P.120 ▸ MONTJUÏC

▼ Taverna El Glop

This bustling Gràcia tavern is the favoured venue for a family lunch, especially at weekends when every table is occupied.

P.159 ▶ GRÀCIA AND PARC GÜELL

▼ Cuines Santa Caterina

Sant Pere's wonderful market is fast becoming a foodie haunt, so don't miss lunch at the designer market restaurant.

P.95 ▶ SANT PERE

▲ Café de l'Acadèmia

Many visitors' favourite old-town restaurant has a lovely terrace and offers up a set-price lunch that mixes contemporary and traditional Catalan flavours.

P.68 ▶ BARRI GÒTIC

▼ Flash, Flash

Tortillas, tortillas, tortillas, and not much else, served in this fun retro Gràcia landmark.

P.158 ▶ GRÀCIA AND PARC GÜELL

Galleries and artists

Barcelona has the world's finest collections of work by Catalan artists Joan Miró and Antoni Tàpies, while contemporary art of all kinds anchors the displays at MACBA and Caixa Forum. The Articket (€20) gives free admission into seven major art galleries, including all those covered here. The city also has dozens of private galleries, concentrated in La Ribera, El Raval and the Eixample – check *Guía del Ocio*'s "Arte" section for listings.

▲ Museu Picasso

The city's most visited art collection traces Picasso's career in its entirety.

P.95 ▶ LA RIBERA

▲ Museu d'Art Contemporani de Barcelona (MACBA)

Post-war contemporary art (Spanish, Catalan and international) has a home in El Raval's signature building.

P.79 ▶ EL RAVAL

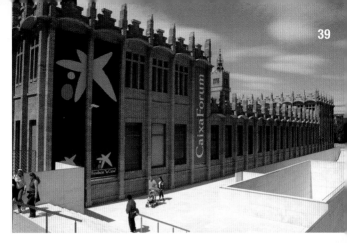

▲ Caixa Forum

There's always a show worth seeing in the city's premier arts and cultural centre – not to mention concerts, films, poetry readings and other events.

P.111 ▸ MONTJUÏC

▲ Fundacío Antoni Tàpies

Acquaint yourself with the work of the master Catalan abstract artist, contained within a striking Eixample mansion.

P.131 ▸ DRETA DE L'EIXAMPLE

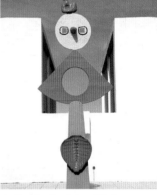

▲ Fundacío Joan Miró

There's no more beautiful gallery in the city than the house on the hill presenting the life's work of Joan Miró.

P.117 ▸ MONTJUÏC

◂ Museu Nacional d'Art de Catalunya (MNAC)

The glorious Romanesque frescoes, rescued from medieval Catalan churches, are the highlight of the national art museum.

P.113 ▸ MONTJUÏC

Music, dance and theatre

You can catch concerts, plays and performances at a wide variety of venues, and internationally renowned artists often appear in the city – particularly during the summer-long Barcelona Festival or at the annual festivals devoted to contemporary music (March/April), medieval and Baroque music (May) and jazz (Nov/Dec). City-sponsored productions are advertised at the Palau de la Virreina on the Ramblas (Wwww.bcn.es/cultura), and you can buy advance concert, theatre and show

▲ Teatre Nacional de Catalunya

The National Theatre – a remarkable modern take on a Greek temple – has a mission to promote Catalan-language productions.

P.145 ▶ SAGRADA FAMÍLIA AND GLÒRIES

▲ Gran Teatre del Liceu

The renowned Liceu is a city landmark, but book ahead if you want tickets, either for a night at the opera or the late-night recitals.

P.53 ▶ ALONG THE RAMBLAS

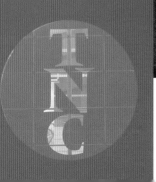

▼ L'Auditori

Barcelona's finest concert hall has a
year-round programme of classical and
contemporary music.

P.145 ▶ SAGRADA FAMÍLIA AND
GLÒRIES

▲ Sidecar

This rootsy Plaça Reial rock club presents
a varied roster of low-priced gigs and club
nights.

P.71 ▶ BARRI GÒTIC

▼ Palau de la Música Catalana

Concerts at this extravagant *modernista*-
designed concert hall are a treat, while the
popular daily guided tours are an added
attraction.

P.91 ▶ SANT PERE

▲ Jamboree/Tarantos

A longstanding favourite for flamenco, jazz,
funk and jam sessions – the after-show
dancing keeps on into the small hours.

P.71 ▶ BARRI GÒTIC

Out on the town

When it comes to a night's carousing, Barcelona offers style, tradition and kitsch in equal measures. From tapas-tasting to view-gazing, laid-back café-bar to full-on techno temple, bohemian boozer to cocktail emporium – you'll find it somewhere. For the latest listings buy the weekly *Guia del Ocio* (out every Thurs), which covers bars, venues and opening hours in its "Tarde Noche" section.

▲ Mirablau

The city does great views and great bars – Mirablau combines both to stunning effect.

P.173 ▸ TIBIDABO AND PARC DEL COLLSEROLA

▲ La Terrrazza

Montjuïc's outdoor dance club at the Poble Espanyol is one of the summer hotspots.

P.121 ▸ MONTJUÏC

▲ Dietrich

The city's thriving gay scene centres on a quarter known as the "Gaixample", where bars like Dietrich welcome partygoers with open arms.

P.152 ▶ ESQUERRA DE L'EIXAMPLE

▼ Moog

The Raval's techno club of choice, open from midnight for non-stop dancing.

P.90 ▶ EL RAVAL

▲ L'Ascensor

The old town has a great local bar seemingly on every corner, where you can drink and chew the fat until they throw you out at 3am.

P.70 ▶ BARRI GÒTIC

▲ Bosc de la Fades

There's kitsch, and then there's the "Forest of the Fairies", the rustic grotto-bar at the foot of the Ramblas.

P.57 ▶ ALONG THE RAMBLAS

City landmarks

By any standards Barcelona has its fair share of iconic locations and buildings, from the Ramblas to the Sagrada Família. Buildings associated with the International Exhibitions of 1888 and 1929, plus construction for the 1992 Olympics and 2004 Universal Forum, have helped to provide an extraordinary city backdrop. Meanwhile, contemporary architects have added towers, installations, squares and parks – some controversial, others much-loved landmarks – that bolster the city's reputation as an evolving urban experiment.

▲ Torre Agbar

The unmistakable "glowing cigar" – the Torre Agbar anchors the Glòries development site set to transform this sector of Barcelona.

P.144 ▸ SAGRADA FAMÍLIA AND GLÒRIES

▲ The Frank Gehry fish

Showpiece landmark of the Port Olímpic is the enormous glittering fish that straddles the promenade.

P.122 ▸ PORT OLÍMPIC AND POBLE NOU

▼ Clocktower, Plaça Rius i Taulet

Lunch or a drink under Gràcia's landmark clocktower is always a pleasure.

P.156 ▸ GRÀCIA AND PARC GÜELL

▲ Arc de Triomf

Barcelona's triumphant arch, relic of the 1888 Universal Exhibition, provides the gateway to the Parc de la Ciutadella area.

P.105 ▸ PARC DE LA CIUTADELLA

▼ Torre de Collserola

Norman Foster's communications tower is easily visible on the Barcelona skyline, and is just a short walk from the Tibidabo amusement park.

P.171 ▸ TIBIDABO AND PARC DEL COLLSEROLA

▲ Plaça de Catalunya

The whole city comes and goes through this pivotal square, where just-off-the-metro tourists mingle with office-workers, buskers, shoppers and café patrons.

P.49 ▸ ALONG THE RAMBLAS

Places

Along the Ramblas

No day in the city seems complete without a stroll along the Ramblas, Spain's most famous thorough-fare. Cutting through Barcelona's old town areas, and connecting Plaça de Catalunya with the harbour, it's at the heart of the city's life and self-image – lined with cafés, restaurants, souvenir shops, flower stalls and newspaper kiosks. The name, derived from the Arabic *ramla* (or "sand"), refers to the bed of a seasonal stream, which was paved over in medieval times. Decorative benches, plane trees and stately buildings were added in the nineteenth century as the Ramblas became the locals' perambulation of choice. Today, the show goes on, day or night, as street vendors, human statues, portrait painters, buskers and card sharps add to the colour and character of Barcelona's most enthral-ling street. There are metro stops at Catalunya (top of the Ramblas), Liceu (middle) and Drassanes (bottom), or you can walk the entire length in about twenty minutes.

Plaça de Catalunya

The huge square at the top of the Ramblas stands right at the heart of the city, with the old town and port below it, and the planned Eixample district above and beyond. It was laid out in its present form in the 1920s, centred on a formal layout of statues, fountains and trees, and is the focal point of local events and demonstrations – notably the mass gathering here on New Year's Eve. The most prominent monument is that dedicated to Francesc Macià, first president of the Generalitat (Catalan government), who died in office in 1933. For visitors, the square is known as the site of the main city tourist office – down the steps in the southeastern corner – while an initial orientation point is the white-faced El Corte Inglés department store on the eastern side of the square. Across on the southwest side

(over the road from the top of the Ramblas) is El Triangle shopping centre, incorporating not only a variety of stores and exhibition space but also the popular *Zurich* café in its ground floor.

The Ramblas itself actually comprises five separate named sections, though it's rare to hear them referred to as such. The northern stretch, for example,

▼ FLOWERS ON LAS RAMBLAS

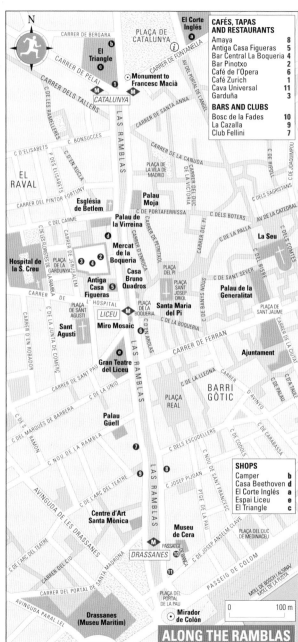

CAFÉS, TAPAS AND RESTAURANTS

Amaya	8
Antiga Casa Figueras	5
Bar Central La Boqueria	4
Bar Pinotxo	2
Café de l'Opera	6
Café Zurich	1
Cava Universal	11
Garduña	3

BARS AND CLUBS

Bosc de la Fades	10
La Cazalla	9
Club Fellini	7

SHOPS

Camper	b
Casa Beethoven	d
El Corte Inglés	a
Espai Liceu	e
El Triangle	c

ALONG THE RAMBLAS

A stroll down the Ramblas

There are tempting pavement cafés and restaurants all the way down the Ramblas, but the food can be indifferent, the prices high (and the drinks extortionate), so be warned. (For better value, go in the Boqueria market, where the traders eat.) The strolling crowds, too, provide perfect cover for pickpockets – keep an eye on wallets and bags as you watch the buskers and statues, or shop at the kiosks. And – however easy it looks to win – if you're going to play cards or dice with a man on a street, you've only yourself to blame.

nearest Plaça de Catalunya, is Rambla Canaletes, marked by an iron fountain – a drink from this supposedly means you'll never leave Barcelona.

Església de Betlem

Ramblas 107 ☎ 933 183 823. Daily 8am–6pm. It seems hard to believe, but the Ramblas was a war zone during the Spanish Civil War as the city erupted into factionalism in 1937. George Orwell was caught in the crossfire (an episode recorded in his *Homage to Catalonia*) and, with anarchists sacking the city's churches at will, the rich interior of the Baroque Església de Betlem (1681) was completely destroyed by fire. Only the main facade on c/del Carme survived the destruction: it still sports a fine sculpted portal and a relief depicting the Nativity.

Palau Moja

Ramblas 188 ☎ 933 162 740. Bookshop Mon–Fri 9am–8pm, Sat 9am–2pm & 4–8pm; Sala Palau Moja Tues–Sat 11am–8pm, Sun 11am–3pm. Gallery admission usually free. The arcaded Palau Moja dates from the late eighteenth century and still retains an exterior staircase and elegant great hall. The ground floor of the building, restored by the Generalitat, is now a cultural bookshop, while the palace's gallery, the Sala Palau Moja, is open for art

and other exhibitions relating to all things Catalan – the gallery entrance is around the corner in c/Portaferrissa. Take a look at the illustrated tiles above the fountain at the start of c/Portaferrissa, which show the medieval gate (the *Porta Ferriça*) and market that once stood here.

Palau de la Virreina

Ramblas 99 ☎ 933 017 775, ⓦ www .bcn.es/cultura. Galleries Tues–Fri 11am–2pm & 4–8.30pm, Sat 11am–8.30pm, Sun 11am–3pm; for current

▼ MONUMENT TO FRANCESC MACIÀ

▲ SCULPTED DOOR, ESGLÉSIA DE BETLEM

exhibitions see ⓦ www.bcn.es
/virreinaexposicions; information office
Mon–Sat 10am–8pm, Sun 11am–3pm.
The graceful eighteenth-century
Palau de la Virreina is set back
slightly from the Ramblas.
Once a private home, today
the building's two galleries
are used to house changing
exhibitions of contemporary
art and photography (admission
sometimes charged), while in
the courtyard you can usually
see the city's enormous Carnival
giants (*gegants*), representing
the thirteenth-century Catalan
king Jaume I and his wife
Violant. The ground floor of
the palace also contains the
Institut de Cultura's walk-in
information centre and ticket
office for cultural events run by
the Ajuntament (city council).
There's a shop too (Tues–Sat
10am–8.30pm), featuring locally
produced objets d'art and other
items relating to the city.

Mercat de la Boqueria

Ramblas 91 ☏ 933 182 584, ⓦ www
.boqueria.info. Mon–Sat 8am–8pm.
Other markets might protest,
but the city's glorious main food
market really can claim to be
the best in Spain. It's officially
called the Mercat Sant Josep,
though everyone knows it as
La Boqueria. Built on the site
of a former convent between
1836 and 1840, the cavernous
hall stretches back behind the
high wrought-iron entrance arch
facing the Ramblas. It's a riot of
noise and colour, as popular with
locals who come here to shop
daily as with snap-happy tourists.
Everything radiates out from the
central banks of fish and seafood
stalls – glistening piles of fruit
and vegetables, bunches of herbs
and pots of spices, baskets of wild
mushrooms, mounds of cheese
and sausage, racks of bread,
hanging hams, and overloaded
meat counters. If you're going to
buy, do some browsing first, as
the flagship fruit and veg stalls by
the entrance have much higher
prices than those further inside.

Ramblas statues

You can't move for human statues on the Ramblas. As fads and fashions change,
Greek statues and Charlie Chaplins have given way to the latest movie characters,
standing immobile on their little home-made plinths. Some join in the fun – "Mr
Burns" and "Lisa Simpson" posing jauntily for photographs, "Matador" swirling
a cape for the camera, "Ronaldinho" playing football keepy-uppy in front of an
appreciative crowd. Many are actors (or at least waiters who say they're actors),
and others make a claim to art – how else to begin to explain "Silver Cowboy",
lounging on the railings at Liceu metro, or "Tree Sprite", clinging chameleon-like
to one of the Ramblas plane trees. Then there's the plain weird, like "Cat in a
Dustbin", miaowing piteously out of sight only to emerge at the chink of a coin
in the hat.

You shouldn't miss seeing *Petras*, the wild mushroom and dried insect stall (it's at the back, by the *Garduña* restaurant). But if you really don't fancy chilli worms, ant candy and crunchy beetles, there are some excellent stand-up tapas bars in the market – the *Pinotxo* is the most famous.

Plaça de la Boqueria

The halfway point of the Ramblas is marked by Plaça de la Boqueria, which sports a large round **mosaic** by Joan Miró in the middle of the pavement. It's become something of a symbol for the city and is one of a number of public works in Barcelona by the artist, who was born just a couple of minutes' walk off the Ramblas in the Barri Gòtic. Close by, at Ramblas 82, the **Casa Bruno Quadros** – the lower floor is now the *Caixa Sabadell* – was built in the 1890s to house an umbrella store. Its unusual facade is decorated with a green dragon and Oriental designs, and scattered with parasols. On the other side of the Ramblas at no. 83, there are more *modernista* (Art Nouveau) flourishes on the **Antiga Casa Figueras** (1902),

which overdoses on stained glass and mosaics; it's now a renowned bakery-café.

Gran Teatre del Liceu

Ramblas 51–59 ⓦ www .liceubarcelona.com. Box office ⓣ 934 859 913; tours ⓣ 934 859 914, daily at 10am, 11.30am, noon, 12.30pm & 1pm. €4/8.50. Barcelona's celebrated opera house was first founded in 1847 and rebuilt after a fire in 1861 to become Spain's grandest theatre. Regarded as a bastion of the city's late nineteenth-century commercial and intellectual classes, the Liceu was devastated again in 1893 when an anarchist threw two bombs into the stalls during a production of *William Tell* – twenty people died. The Liceu then burned down for the third time in 1994, when a worker's blowtorch set fire to the scenery during last-minute alterations to an opera set. Fully restored once more, the lavishly decorated interior is accessible on tours, which depart from the opera house's modern extension, the Espai Liceu – you'll see and learn most on the guided 10am tour (the other, shorter, cheaper tours are self-guided).

▼ THE MIRÓ MOSAIC

▲ KIOSK ON LAS RAMBLAS

If you want to attend an opera or recital (including the popular late-night concerts or *sessions golfes*), you should check the website for details and make bookings well in advance.

Centre d'Art Santa Mònica

Ramblas 7 ☎933 162 810, ⓦwww.centredartsantamonica .net. Tues–Sat 11am–8pm, Sun 11am–3pm. Free. The Augustinian convent of Santa Mònica dates originally from 1626, making it the oldest building on the Ramblas. It was entirely remodelled in the 1980s, and now hosts regularly changing exhibitions of contemporary art on the ground floor. There's also a city information office at the centre, and a café-bar upstairs. Pavement artists and palm readers set up stalls outside on the Ramblas, augmented on weekend afternoons by a small street market selling jewellery, ethnic gear and ornaments.

Museu de Cera

Ramblas 4–6, entrance on Ptge. de Banca ☎933 172 649, ⓦwww .museocerabcn.com. July–Sept daily 10am–10pm; Oct–June Mon–Fri 10am–1.30pm & 4–7.30pm, Sat & Sun 11am–2pm & 4.30–8.30pm. €7.50. You'd have to be hard-hearted indeed not to derive some pleasure from the city's wax museum. Located in a nineteenth-century bank building, it presents an ever more ludicrous series of tableaux in cavernous salons and gloomy corridors, depicting recitals, meetings and parlour

▼ EL CORTE INGLÉS DEPARTMENT STORE

gatherings attended by an anachronistic – not to say perverse – collection of characters, from Hitler to Princess Diana. Needless to say, it's enormously amusing, but even if this doesn't appeal it is definitely worth poking your head into the museum's extraordinary grotto bar, the *Bosc de les Fades*.

Shops

Camper
C/Pelai 13–37, El Triangle, plus others throughout the city ☎902 364 598, ⓦwww .camper.com. Spain's most stylish, value-for-money shoe store opened its first shop in Barcelona in 1981. Providing hip, well-made, casual city footwear at a good price has been the cornerstone of its success.

Casa Beethoven
Ramblas 97 ☎933 014 826, ⓦwww .casabeethoven.com. Wonderful old shop selling sheet music, CDs and music reference books – not just classical, but also rock, jazz and flamenco.

El Corte Inglés
Pl. de Catalunya 14 ☎933 063 800, ⓦwww.elcorteingles.es. The city's biggest department store has nine retail floors, a good basement supermarket and – best of all – a top-floor café with terrific views.

Espai Liceu
Gran Teatre del Liceu, Ramblas 51–59 ☎934 859 913. The shop and café in the opera house extension boasts the widest range of opera CDs and DVDs in the city, as well as selling Liceu-branded

▲ ANTIGA CASA FIGUERAS

T-shirts, coffee mugs, ceramics and other souvenirs.

El Triangle
Pl. de Catalunya 4 ☎933 180 108. Shopping centre dominated by the flagship FNAC store, which specializes in books (good travel and English-language selections), music CDs and computer software. Also a Camper (for shoes), Sephora (cosmetics), Habitat, and various clothes shops, plus a café on the ground floor next to the extensive newspaper and magazine section.

Cafés

Antiga Casa Figueras
Ramblas 83 ☎933 016 027, ⓦwww.escriba.es. Mon–Sat 9am–3pm & 5–8.30pm. Pastries from the renowned Escribà family business in a *modernista*-designed pastry shop, with a few tables inside and out. Many people rate this as the best bakery in Barcelona.

Café de l'Opera

Ramblas 74 ☎933 177 585, ⓦwww
.cafeoperabcn.com. Daily 8.30am–
2am. Surprisingly – despite its
position, period feel and *terrassa*
tables – this venerable café-bar
is not a complete tourist-fest.
Long a favourite for pre- and
post-performance refreshments
at the opera house, this place
has a good range of cakes,
snacks and tapas, or a late-night
sangría de cava.

Café Zurich

Pl. Catalunya 1 ☎933 179 153,
ⓦwww.cafezurich.com. Mon–Fri
8am–11pm, Sat & Sun 10am–11pm,
June–Sept open until 1am. The
most famous meet-and-greet
café in town, right at the top
of the Ramblas underneath
El Triangle shopping centre.
It's good for croissants
and breakfast bocadillos
(sandwiches) and there's a huge
terrace, but sit inside if you
don't want to be bothered by
endless rounds of buskers and
beggars.

Cava Universal

Pl. Portal de la Pau 4 ☎933 026 184.
Daily 9am–10pm. A useful drinks
and snacks spot on the lower
Ramblas, with reasonable prices
and a sunny *terrassa* looking
directly onto the Columbus
monument.

Restaurants and tapas bars

Amaya

Ramblas 20–24 ☎933 026 138
(bar), ☎933 021 037 (restaurant),
ⓦwww.restauranteamaya.com. Bar
daily 10am–12.30am; restaurant
daily 1.30–4pm & 8.30pm–midnight.
A Ramblas fixture since
1941 – restaurant on one side,
tapas bar on the other, both
serving very good Basque
seafood specialities, including
octopus, baby squid, clams,
mussels, anchovies and prawns.
The bar offers the cheapest and
most enjoyable introduction
to the cuisine; otherwise, main

▲ AMAYA

dishes in the restaurant cost €14–20.

Bar Central La Boqueria

Mercat de la Boqueria, Ramblas 91; no phone. Mon–Sat 6.30am–4pm. The gleaming chrome stand-up bar in the central aisle is the venue for ultra-fresh market produce, served by black T-shirted staff who work at a fair lick. Breakfast, snack or lunch, it's all the same to them – salmon cutlets, sardines, calamari, razor clams, hake fillets, sausages, pork steaks, asparagus spears and the rest, plunked on the griddle and sprinkled with salt. Breakfast costs just a few euros; it's more like €5–15 for some tapas or a main dish and a drink.

Bar Pinotxo

Mercat de la Boqueria, Ramblas 91 ☎933 171 731. Mon–Sat 6am–5pm; closed Aug. The market's most renowned refuelling stop – just inside the main entrance on the right – attracts traders, chefs, tourists and celebs, who stand three deep at busy times. A *tallat* (small white coffee) and a grilled sandwich is the local breakfast of choice; otherwise let the cheery staff steer you towards the tapas and daily specials.

Garduña

Mercat de la Boqueria, c/Jerusalem 18 ☎933 024 323. Mon–Sat 1–4pm & 8pm–midnight. Tucked away at the back of the frenetic Boqueria market, this is a great place for lunch, when there's a good-value *menú del dia* – basically, you'll be offered the best of the day's produce at pretty reasonable prices, and if you're lucky you'll get an outdoor seat with market views.

Bars

Bosc de les Fades

Ptge. de Banca 5 ☎933 172 649. Mon–Thurs & Sun 10.30am–1am, Fri & Sat 10.30am–3am. Hidden in an alley by the wax museum, the "Forest of the Fairies" is festooned with gnarled plaster tree trunks, hanging branches, fountains and stalactites. It's a bit cheesy, which is perhaps why it's a huge hit with the twenty-something crowd who huddle in the grottoes and decorative side rooms.

La Cazalla

Ramblas 25; no phone. Mon–Sat 10am–3am. A historic remnant of the old days, the hole-in-the-wall *Cazalla* (under the arch, at the beginning of c/de l'Arc del Teatre) first opened its hatch in 1912. It was closed for some years, but it's now back in business offering stand-up coffee, beer and shots to an assorted clientele of locals, cops, streetwalkers and the occasional stray tourist.

Clubs

Club Fellini

Ramblas 27 ☎932 724 980, ⓦwww.clubfellini.com. Mon–Sat midnight–5am. Three *salas* – Mirror Room, Red Room and Bad Room – supply sounds from techno to soul for "night victims, modernos and freaks". If this sounds like you, look out for the flyers – the various club nights are heavily publicized.

Barri Gòtic

The highly picturesque Barri Gòtic, or Gothic Quarter, on the east side of the Ramblas, forms the very heart of Barcelona's old town. Its buildings date principally from the fourteenth and fifteenth centuries, when Barcelona reached the height of her medieval prosperity, and culminate in the extraordinary Gothic cathedral known as La Seu. Fanning out from here are arcaded squares and skinny alleys containing several fascinating museums and the surviving portions of the city's Roman walls. It will take the best part of a day to see everything – more if you indulge yourself in the abundant cafés, antique shops, boutiques and galleries. The main areas to explore lie north of c/de Ferran and c/de Jaume I, around the cathedral; and south from Plaça Reial and c/d'Avinyo to the harbour – the latter district is rather less gentrified than the cathedral area and you should take care at night in the poorly lit streets. Metros Liceu and Jaume I mark the east–west boundaries of the Barri Gòtic.

La Seu

Pl. de la Seu ☎ 933 151 554, ⓦ www .catedralbcn.org. Daily 8am–12.45pm & 5.15–7.30pm, cathedral and cloister free; otherwise 1–5pm, €4, includes entrance to all sections. Barcelona's cathedral is one of the great Gothic buildings of Spain. Located on a site previously occupied by a Roman temple, it was begun in 1298 and finished in 1448 – save the neo-Gothic principal facade, which was completed in the 1880s (and is currently obscured by scaffolding). La Seu is dedicated to Santa Eulàlia, who was martyred by the Romans for daring to prefer Christianity, and her ornate tomb rests in a crypt beneath the high altar. However, the most renowned part of the cathedral is its magnificent fourteenth-century **cloister**, which looks over a lush tropical garden complete with soaring palm trees and honking white geese. Don't leave without ascending to the

▲ LA SEU

roof (€2.20) – the elevator (*ascensor als terrats*) is just to the left of the crypt steps – which provides intimate views of the cathedral towers and surrounding Gothic buildings.

Performances of the Catalan national dance, the *sardana*, take place in front of the cathedral (Easter–Oct Sat at 6.30pm, & Sun at noon all year), while the wide, pedestrianized Avinguda de la Catedral hosts an antiques market every Thursday, and a Christmas craft fair every December. It's also worth looking in on the **Museu Diocesá** (Tues–Sat 10am–2pm & 5–8pm, Sun 11am–2pm, €5), which occupies the soaring spaces of a Roman tower that later formed part of the cathedral almshouse. It's been beautifully adapted to show its impressive collection of religious art and church treasures from around Barcelona.

Plaça del Rei

The most concentrated batch of historic monuments in the Barri Gòtic is the grouping around the Plaça del Rei. The square was once the courtyard of the palace of the counts of Barcelona, and across it stairs climb to the fourteenth-century **Saló del Tinell**, the palace's main hall. It was on the steps leading from the Saló del Tinell into the Plaça del Rei that Ferdinand and Isabella stood to receive Columbus on his triumphant return from his famous voyage of 1492. At one time the Spanish Inquisition met here, taking full advantage of the popular belief that the walls would move if a lie was spoken. Nowadays it hosts temporary

▲ BARRI GÒTIC STREET

exhibitions, while concerts are occasionally held in the hall or outside in the square. The palace buildings also include: the fourteenth-century **Capella de Santa Agata**, with its tall single nave and fine Gothic retable; and the Renaissance **Torre del Rei Martí**, which rises above one corner of the square. There's currently no public access to the tower, but the interiors of the hall and chapel can be seen during a visit to the Museu d'Història de la Ciutat.

Museu d'Història de la Ciutat

Pl. del Rei, entrance on c/del Veguer ☏ 933 151 111, ⓦ www.museuhistoria .bcn.es. April–Sept Tues–Sat 10am–8pm, Sun 10am–3pm; Oct–March Tues–Sat 10am–2pm & 4–7pm, Sun 10am–3pm. €5, first Sat afternoon of the month free. The crucial draw of the City History Museum is its amazing underground archeological section – nothing less than the extensive remains of the Roman city of Barcino. Descending in the elevator (the floor indicator shows "12 BC"), you are deposited onto walkways that run along the

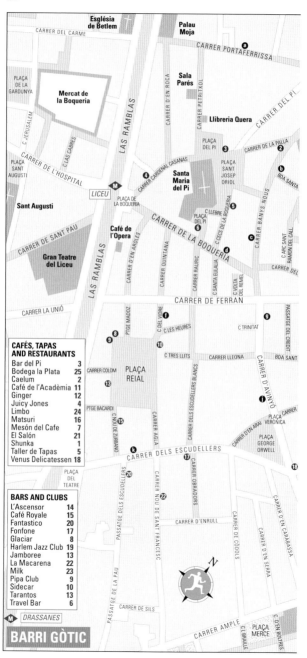

CAFÉS, TAPAS AND RESTAURANTS

Bar del Pi	3
Bodega la Plata	25
Caelum	2
Café de l'Acadèmia	11
Ginger	12
Juicy Jones	4
Limbo	24
Matsuri	16
Mesón del Cafe	7
El Salón	21
Shunka	1
Taller de Tapas	5
Venus Delicatessen	18

BARS AND CLUBS

L'Ascensor	14
Café Royale	15
Fantastico	20
Fonfone	17
Glaciar	8
Harlem Jazz Club	19
Jamboree	13
La Macarena	22
Milk	23
Pipa Club	9
Sidecar	10
Tarantos	13
Travel Bar	6

Ⓜ DRASSANES

BARRI GÒTIC

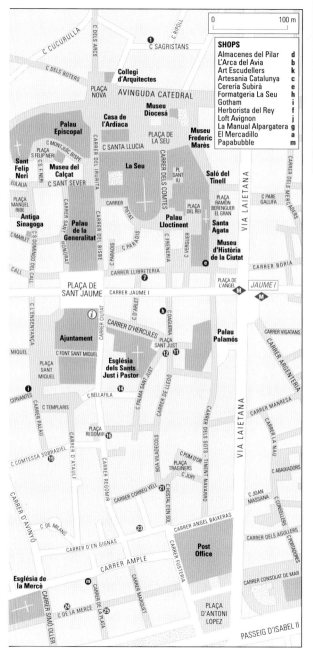

SHOPS

Almacenes del Pilar	d
L'Arca del Avia	b
Art Escudellers	k
Artesania Catalunya	c
Cereria Subirà	e
Formatgeria La Seu	h
Gotham	i
Herborista del Rey	f
Loft Avignon	j
La Manual Alpargatera	g
El Mercadillo	a
Papabubble	m

4000 square metres excavated thus far, stretching under Plaça del Rei and the surrounding streets as far as the cathedral. The remains date from the first century BC to the sixth century AD and, while not much survives above chest height, explanatory diagrams show the extent of the streets, walls and buildings – from lookout towers to laundries – while models, mosaics, murals and excavated goods help flesh out the reality of daily life in Barcino.

Note that your museum ticket also allows entry to the monastery at Pedralbes.

Museu Frederic Marès

Pl. de Sant Iu 5–6 ☎ 932 563 500, ⓦ www.museumares.bcn.es. Tues–Sat 10am–7pm, Sun 10am–3pm. €3, Wed afternoon & first Sun of month free.
Frederic Marès (1893–1991) was a sculptor, painter and restorer who more or less single-handedly restored Catalunya's decaying medieval treasures in the early twentieth century. The ground and basement floors of the museum consist of his personal collection of medieval sculpture – an important body of work that includes a comprehensive collection of wooden crucifixes showing the stylistic development of this form from the twelfth to the fifteenth centuries. However, it's the upper two floors, housing Marès' personal collectibles, which tend to make jaws drop. Entire rooms are devoted to keys and locks, pipes, cigarette cards and snuffboxes, fans, gloves and brooches, playing cards, draughtsmen's tools, walking sticks, dolls' houses, toy theatres, old gramophones and archaic bicycles – to list just a sample of what's on show. The large arcaded museum courtyard, studded with orange trees, is one of the most romantic in the old town, and the summer café here (*Café d'Estiu*; April–Sept 10am–10pm, closed Mon) is a perfect place to take a break from sightseeing.

Església de Santa María del Pi

Pl. Sant Josep Oriol ☎ 933 184 743, ⓦ www.parroquiadelpi.com. Mon–Sat 8.30am–1pm & 4.30–9pm, Sun 9am–2pm & 5–9pm. Five minutes' walk from the cathedral, the fourteenth-century church of Santa María stands at the heart of three delightful little squares. Burned out in 1936, but restored in the 1960s, the church boasts a Romanesque door but is mainly Catalan-Gothic in style. The rather plain interior only serves to set off some marvellous stained glass, the most impressive of which is contained within a ten-metre-wide rose window. The church flanks Plaça Sant Josep Oriol, the prettiest of the three adjacent squares and

▼ ARTISTS' MARKET, PLAÇA SANT JOSEP ORIEL

an ideal place to take an outdoor coffee, listen to the buskers and browse the weekend **artists' market** (Sat 11am–8pm, Sun 11am–2pm).

The church is named – like the squares on either side, Plaça del Pi and Placeta del Pi – after the pine tree that once stood here. A **farmers' market** spills across Plaça del Pi on the first and third Friday and Saturday of the month, selling honey, cheese, cakes and other produce, while **Carrer de Petritxol** (off Plaça del Pi) is the place to come for a cup of hot chocolate – *Dulcinea* at no. 2 is the traditional choice – and a browse around the street's commercial art galleries.

▲ SALA PARÉS

Sala Parés

C/de Petritxol 5–8 ☏ 933 187 020, ⓦ www.salapares.com. Mon 4–8pm, Tues–Sat 10.30am–2pm & 4–8pm, Sun Oct–June 11.30am–2pm; closed Aug. Possibly the most famous commercial art gallery in the city, established in the mid-nineteenth century, Sala Parés is well known as the site of Picasso's first solo exhibition. It still deals exclusively in nineteenth- and twentieth-century Catalan art, putting on around twenty exhibitions a year, including a bi-annual "Famous Paintings" exhibition of works by some of the best-known Spanish and Catalan artists.

Museu del Calçat

Pl. Sant Felip Neri 5 ☏ 933 014 533. Tues–Sun 11am–2pm. €2.50. The former headquarters of the city's shoemakers' guild (founded in 1202) houses a one-room footwear museum, containing originals dating back to the 1600s as well as oddities like the world's biggest shoe, made for the city's Columbus statue. The museum flanks one side of Plaça Sant Felip Neri, whose church still bears the marks of bomb damage sustained during the Civil War. It's a pretty square with a central fountain, and in summer you can eat outside at the restaurant of the boutique *Hotel Neri*, where they set out tables and candles in the square.

Antiga Sinagoga

C/Marlet 5, corner with c/Sant Domènec del Call ☏ 933 170 790, ⓦ www.calldebarcelona.org. Mon–Fri 11am–6pm, Sat & Sun 11am–3pm; occasionally closed Sat for ceremonies. €2. Barcelona's medieval Jewish quarter lay just to the south of

▼ ANTIGA SINAGOGA

Plaça Sant Felip Neri, centred on c/Sant Domènec del Call (*Call* is the Catalan word for a narrow passage). A small synagogue existed here from as early as the third century AD until the pogrom of 1391, but even after that date the building survived in various guises and has since been sympathetically restored. Not many people stop by the synagogue – if you do, you'll get a personalized tour by a member of the local Jewish community, who might put you on the trail of Barcelona's largely hidden Jewish heritage. Rather belatedly, the city authorities have signposted some of the surrounding streets and other points of interest in what's known as "El Call Major".

Plaça de Sant Jaume

The spacious square at the end of the main c/de Ferran was once the site of Barcelona's Roman forum and marketplace; now it's at the heart of city and regional government business. Whistle-happy local police try to keep things moving in the *plaça*, while taxis and bike-tour groups weave between the pedestrians. It's also the traditional site of

demonstrations, gatherings and local festivals, during which you can almost guarantee an encounter with the Catalan folk dance, the **sardana**. Participants all hold hands in a circle, each puts something in the middle as a sign of community and sharing, and, since it is not over-energetic (hence the jibes of other Spaniards), old and young can join in equally.

Ajuntament de Barcelona

Pl. de Sant Jaume ☎ 934 027 000. Public admitted Sun 10am–2pm, entrance on c/Font de Sant Miquel. Free. On the south side of Plaça de Sant Jaume stands Barcelona's city hall, parts of which date from as early as 1373, though the Neoclassical façade was added when the square was laid out in the nineteenth century. On Sundays you're allowed into the building for a self-guided tour around the splendid marble halls, galleries and staircases. The highlights are the magnificent restored fourteenth-century council chamber, known as the **Saló de Cent**, and the dramatic historical murals in the **Saló de les Cròniques** (Hall of Chronicles).

▲ AJUNTAMENT DE BARCELONA

Palau de la Generalitat

Pl. de Sant Jaume ☎ 934 024 600.
Tours on 2nd and 4th Sun of the month
(not Aug), every 30–60min, 10am–2pm;
also on April 23, and Sept 11 & 24.
Passport or ID required. Free. The
traditional home of the Catalan
government presents its best – or
at least its oldest – aspect around
the side on c/del Bisbe, where
the early fifteenth-century facade
contains a medallion portraying
St George and the dragon.
(Incidentally, the enclosed Gothic
bridge across the narrow street
– the so-called Bridge of Sighs
– is an anachronism, added in
1928.) There's a beautiful cloister
on the first floor with superb
coffered ceilings, while opening
off this are the intricately worked
chapel and salon of Sant Jordi
(St George, patron saint of
Catalunya as well as England),
and an upper courtyard planted
with orange trees. You can visit
the interior on a one-hour
guided tour on alternate Sundays
(note only one or two tours each
day are in English), while the
Generalitat is also traditionally
open on public holidays,
particularly April 23 – the **Dia
de Sant Jordi** (St George's
Day). Celebrated as a nationalist
holiday in Catalunya, this is also
a kind of local Valentine's Day,
when men give their sweethearts
a rose and receive a book in
return (although, in recent years,
modernization has demanded
books for women and roses for
men as well). The Generalitat's
precincts are packed with book
stalls and rose sellers on this day,
with huge queues forming to get
in the building.

Església dels Sants Just i Pastor

Pl. de Sant Just 6 ☎ 933 017 433.
Open for Mass at 7.30pm (Sun at
noon) and occasional other times.

▲ IRON LAMPS AT PLAÇA REIAL

Plaça de Sant Just is a medieval gem, sporting a restored fourteenth-century fountain and flanked by unassuming palaces. Apart from the excellent *Café de l'Acàdemia*, which puts out dining tables on the square, the highlight here is the Església dels Sants Just i Pastor, whose very plain stone facade belies the rich stained glass and elaborate chapel decoration inside (enter from the back, at c/de la Ciutat; the main doors on Pl. de Sant Just are open less often). The name commemorates the city's earliest Christian martyrs.

Plaça Reial

The elegant nineteenth-century Plaça Reial is hidden behind an archway off the Ramblas. Laid out in around 1850, the Italianate square is studded with tall palm trees and decorated iron lamps (designed by the young Antoni Gaudí), bordered by pastel-coloured arcaded buildings, and centred on a fountain depicting the Three Graces. Taking in the sun at one of the benches or pavement cafés puts you in mixed company – punks, bikers, buskers, Catalan eccentrics, tramps and bemused tourists. It used to be a bit dodgy in Plaça Reial, but most of the really unsavoury characters have been driven off over the years as tourists have staked an increasing claim to the square. Don't expect to see too many locals until night falls, when the surrounding bars come into their own. If you pass through on a Sunday morning, look in on the **coin and stamp market** (10am–2pm).

Carrer d'Avinyó

Carrer d'Avinyó, running south from c/de Ferran towards the harbour, cuts through the most atmospheric part of the southern Barri Gòtic. It used to be a red-light district of some renown, and was frequented by the young Picasso, whose family moved into the area in 1895. It still looks the part – a narrow thoroughfare lined with dark overhanging buildings – but the funky cafés, streetwear shops and boutiques tell the story of its creeping social advancement. A few rough edges still show, particularly around **Plaça George Orwell**, a favoured hangout for the grunge and druggy crowd.

Carrer de la Mercè

In the eighteenth century, the neighbourhood known as La Mercè – just a block from the harbour – was an aristocratic address, home to the many nobles and merchants enriched by Barcelona's maritime trade. Most fashionable families took the opportunity to move north to the Eixample later in the nineteenth century, and the streets of La Mercè took on an earthier hue. Since then, Carrer de la Mercè and surrounding streets have been home to a

series of characteristic old-style taverns known as *tascas* or *bodegas* – a glass of wine from the barrel in *Bodega la Plata*, or a similar joint, is one of the old town's more authentic experiences.

At Plaça de la Mercè, the eighteenth-century **Església de la Mercè** is the focus of the city's biggest annual bash, the Festes de la Mercè every September, dedicated to the co-patroness of Barcelona, whose image is paraded from the church. It's an excuse for a solid week of merrymaking and mayhem, culminating in spectacular pyrotechnics along the seafront.

Shops

Almacenes del Pilar

C/Boqueria 43 ☎ 933 177 984, ⓦ www.almacenesdelpilar.com. Closed Aug. A world of frills, lace, cloth and material used in the making of Spain's traditional regional costumes. You can pick up a decorated fan for just a few euros, though quality items go for a whole lot more.

L'Arca del Avia

C/Banys Nous 20 ☎ 933 021 598, ⓦ www.larcadelavia.com. Closed Aug. Catalan brides used to fill up their nuptial trunk (*l'arca*) with embroidered bed linen and lace, and this shop is a treasure trove of vintage and antique textiles. Period (eighteenth-, nineteenth- and early twentieth-century) costumes can be hired or purchased as well – one of Kate Winslet's *Titanic* costumes came from here.

Art Escudellers

C/Escudellers 23–25 ☎ 934 126 801, ⓦ www.escudellers-art.com.

Enormous shop selling a wide range of ceramics, glass, jewellery and decorated tiles from different regions of Spain. Shipping can be arranged, and there's also a gourmet wine and food section.

▲ ESPADRILLES AT LA MANUAL ALPARGATERA

Artesania Catalunya

C/Banys Nous 11 ☎ 934 674 660, ⓦ www.artesania-catalunya.com. The local government's arts and crafts promotion board has an old-town showroom, where it's always worth looking in on the current exhibitions. Most of the work is contemporary in style, from basketwork to glassware, though traditional methods are still very much encouraged.

Cerería Subirà

Bxda. Llibreteria 7 ☎ 933 152 606. Barcelona's oldest shop (since 1760) has a beautiful interior, selling unique handcrafted candles.

Formatgeria La Seu

C/Daguería 16 ☎ 934 126 548, ⓦ www.formatgerialaseu.com. Closed Mon & Aug. The best farmhouse cheeses from independent producers all over Spain. The Scottish owner will introduce you into the world of cheese at one of the regular cheese-and-wine tastings, or you can simply try before you buy.

Gotham

C/Cervantes 7 ☎ 934 124 647, ⓦ www.gotham-bcn.com. The place to come for retro (1930s to 1970s) furniture, lighting and accessories, plus original designs.

Herborista del Rey

C/del Vidre 1 ☎ 933 180 512. An early nineteenth-century herbalist's shop, tucked off Plaça Reial, which stocks more than 250 medicinal herbs designed to combat all complaints.

Loft Avignon

C/d'Avinyó 22 ☎ 933 012 420. If ever a shop was an indicator of the changing neighbourhood, it's this – the once-seedy backstreet becoming a byword for where-it's-at-fashion by international designers.

La Manual Alpargatera

C/d'Avinyó 7 ☎ 933 010 172, ⓦ www.lamanualalpargatera.com. This traditional workshop makes and sells *alpargatas* (espadrilles) to order, as well as producing other straw, rope and basket work.

El Mercadillo

C/Portaferrissa 17 ☎ 933 018 913. Double-decker complex of shops selling urban, skate-, club- and beachwear – look out for the camel marking the entrance. There's a bar upstairs with a nice patio garden.

Papabubble

C/Ample 28 ☎ 932 688 625, ⓦ www.papabubble.com. Closed Aug. Groovy young things rolling out home-made candy to a chill-out soundtrack. Come and watch them at work, sample a sweetie, and take home a gorgeously wrapped gift.

▲ CARRER DE LA PALLA

Cafés

Bar del Pi

Pl. Sant Josep Oriol 1 ☎ 933 022 123.
Mon–Sat 9am–11pm, Sun 10am–10pm;
closed 2 weeks in Jan & Aug. Small
café-bar best known for its
terrace on one of Barcelona's
prettiest squares. Service can
be slow – not that anyone's in
a hurry in this prime people-
watching spot.

Caelum

C/Palla 8 ☎ 933 026 993. Mon noon–
8.30pm, Tues–Sun 10.30am–8.30pm.
Closed 2 weeks in Aug. The lovingly
packaged confections in this
upscale café-deli are made in
convents and monasteries across
Spain. Choose from *frutas de
almendra* (marzipan sweeties)
from Seville, Benedictine
preserves or Cistercian cookies.

Mesón del Cafe

C/Llibreteria 16 ☎ 933 150 754.
Mon–Sat 7am–11pm. Offbeat
locals' bar where you'll probably
have to stand to sample the
pastries and the excellent coffee
– including a cappuccino laden
with fresh cream.

Restaurants and tapas bars

Bodega la Plata

C/de la Mercè 28 ☎ 933 151 009.
Daily 10am–4pm & 8–11pm. A
classic taste of the old town,
with a marble counter open
to the street and dirt-cheap
wine straight from the barrel.
Anchovies are the speciality
(salted and laid over cut
tomatoes or deep-fried, like
whitebait), attracting an
enthusiastic local crowd, from
pre-clubbers to businessmen.

Café de l'Acadèmia

C/Lledó 1 ☎ 933 198 253.
Mon–Fri 9am–noon, 1.30–4pm &
8.45–11.30pm; closed 2 weeks in
Aug. Creative Catalan cooking
in a romantic stone-flagged
restaurant, with a lovely summer
terrassa in the medieval square
outside. Dishes range from
confit of *bacallà* (salt cod) with
spinach and pine kernels to
aubergine terrine with goat's
cheese, plus grills, fresh fish and
rice. Prices are very reasonable
(mains €11–17) and it's always
busy, so dinner reservations are
essential. A no-choice *menú del
dia* is a bargain for the quality; a
nice breakfast is served too.

Ginger

C/Palma Sant Just 1 ☎ 933 105 309.
Tues–Sat 7pm–3am; closed 2 weeks in
Aug. Cocktails and creative tapas
in a slickly updated 1970s-style
setting. It's a world away from
patatas bravas and battered squid
– think roast duck vinaigrette,
tuna tartare and vegetarian satay
for around €6–7.50 a pop.

Juicy Jones

C/Cardenal Casañas 7 ☎ 933
024 330. Daily 10am–midnight.

Certainly adds a dash of colour to the veggie-vegan dining scene – juices are squeezed and soy milkshakes whizzed at the front bar, while the restaurant is out back in a mural-and-graffiti-splashed cellar. There's a big list of salads and sandwiches, and a *menú del dia* that touches all corners of the world – say cashew, carrot and coriander soup followed by vegetable roulade with a tamarind sauce. A new outlet in the Raval (c/de l'Hospital 74) offers more space and more of the same.

Limbo

C/de la Mercè 13 ☎ 933 107 699. Mon–Fri 1.30–4pm & 8.30pm– midnight, Sat 8.30pm–midnight. Designer restaurant that manages an intimate feel within a cavernous, pale grey warehouse-style interior of exposed brick and wooden beams. The contemporary Mediterranean menu is market-led, so there's fresh pasta made daily or things like goat's cheese soufflé or tuna with caramelized onions. Most dishes cost between €7 and €18, though if you come for weekday lunch there's a really good-value *menú del dia*.

Matsuri

Pl. Regomir 1 ☎ 932 681 535, ⓦ www.matsuri-restaurante .com. Mon–Thurs 1.30–3.30pm & 8.30–11.30pm, Fri 1.30–3.30pm & 8.30pm–midnight, Sat 8.30pm– midnight. Creative Southeast Asian cuisine, concentrating on Thai-style noodles, salads and curries, though there's sushi too. Tastes are very definitely Catalan in execution – nothing too spicy or adventurous – but service is friendly and the Indonesian-style furniture and terracotta colours make for a relaxed meal. Around €25 a head.

El Salón

C/l'Hostal d'en Sol 6–8 ☎ 933 152 159. Mon–Sat 1.30–4.30pm & 8.30pm– midnight; closed 2 weeks in Aug. A really charming place for a cosy dinner, with candlelit tables in a Gothic dining room. Seasonal Mediterranean dishes are served in a relaxed bistro atmosphere, with summer offerings like rocket salad with pears or lamb with mustard-and-honey sauce. Salads and starters average €7–10 and mains €12–16, though there's also a bargain lunchtime *menú del dia*.

Shunka

C/Sagristans 5 ☎ 934 124 991. Tues– Fri 1.30–3.30pm & 8.30–11.30pm, Sat & Sun 2–4pm & 8.30–11.30pm; closed 2 weeks in Aug. The locals think this is the best Japanese restaurant in the old town – it's certainly always busy, so advance reservations are essential. The open kitchen and bustling staff are half the show, while the food – from sushi to udon noodles – is really good. Around €30.

Taller de Tapas

Pl. Sant Josep Oriol 9 ☎ 933 018 020, ⓦ www.tallerdetapas.com. Mon–Sat 9.30am–midnight, Sun noon–midnight, Fri & Sat until 1am. The fashionable "tapas workshop" sucks in tourists with its pretty location by the church of Santa Maria del Pi – there's a year-round outdoor terrace. The open kitchen turns out market-fresh tapas, with fish a speciality at dinner. Prices are on the high side, but the food is reliable. There's another branch in the Born at c/Argenteria 51.

Venus Delicatessen

C/d'Avinyó 25 ☎ 933 011 585.
Mon–Sat noon–midnight. Not a
deli, despite the name, but it's a
handy place for Carrer d'Avinyó
boutique shoppers, serving
Med-bistro cuisine throughout
the day and night. It's also good
for vegetarians, with things like
lasagne, couscous, moussaka and
salads mostly meat-free, and all
costing €5–9.

Bars

L'Ascensor

C/Bellafila 3 ☎ 933 185 347. Daily
6.30pm–3am. Sliding antique
wooden elevator doors signal
the entrance to this popular
local bar. It's not at all touristy,
and has a comfortable feel
– great for a late-night drink
and a natter.

Café Royale

C/Nou de Zurbano 3 ☎ 934 121 433.
Daily 7pm–2.30am. Sleek lounge
bar where all the beautiful
people get together to show off
their best moves to the Latin
jazz, soul and funky tunes.

Glaciar

Pl. Reial 3 ☎ 933 021 163. Mon–Thurs
4pm–2am, Fri & Sat 4pm–3am, Sun
9am–2am. At this traditional
Barcelona meeting point the
terrace seating is packed out
most sunny evenings and at
weekends.

Milk

C/Gignàs 21 ☎ 932 680 922, ⓦwww
.milkbarcelona.com. Mon–Sat
6.30pm–3am, Sun 11am–3am. Irish-
owned bar and bistro that's
carved a niche as a welcoming
neighbourhood hangout.
Nothing flashy, but decent
food and cocktails backed by a
funky soundtrack. Book at the

weekends if you want to eat,
and come early for the popular
Sunday brunch.

Pipa Club

Pl. Reial 3 ☎ 933 024 732, ⓦwww
.bpipaclub.com. Daily 10pm–3am.
Historically a pipe-smoker's
haunt, it's a wood-panelled,
jazzy, late-night kind of place
– ring the bell for admission and
make your way up the stairs.

Travel Bar

C/Boqueria 27 ☎ 933 425 252,
ⓦwww.travelbar.com. Mon–Thurs &
Sun 9am–2am, Fri & Sat 9am–3am.
Backpacking Catalans have
brought their experiences home
to provide a bar where travellers
can hang out and meet like-
minded souls, sign up for tours,
check their email and generally
chill out.

Clubs

Fantastico

Ptge. dels Escudellers 3 ☎ 933 175
411, ⓦwww.fantasticoclub.com.
Wed–Sat 11pm–3am. A cheery dive
for the pop, electro and indie
crowd who want to listen to the
Kaiser Chiefs, Arctic Monkeys,
The Killers, The Pigeon
Detectives and the like.

Fonfone

C/dels Escudellers 24 ☎ 933 171 424,
ⓦwww.fonfone.com. Daily 10pm–
3am. Attracts a young crowd
for fast, hard music, though it
changes mood midweek with
satin soul, disco and best-of-
1980s nights.

Harlem Jazz Club

C/Comtessa de Sobradiel 8 ☎ 933 100
755. Closed Aug. For many years,
the hot place for jazz, though
don't let the name mislead you
– every jazz style gets an airing

here, from African and Gypsy to flamenco and fusion. There's live music nightly at 11pm and 12.30am (weekends 11.30pm & 1am). Usually free midweek, otherwise cover charge up to €10.

Jamboree/Tarantos

Pl. Reial 17 ☎933 191 789, ⓦwww .masimas.com. The two sister clubs at the same address offer jazz sessions at Jamboree (from 9pm; from €8) and short, exuberant flamenco tasters at Tarantos (performances at 8.30pm, 9.30pm & 10.30pm; €6), and you can stay on for the club, playing funk, swing, hip-hop and R&B from around midnight until 5am. It's one of the city's best nights out.

La Macarena

C/Nou de Sant Francesc 5; no phone, ⓦwww .macarenaclub.com. Mon–Thurs & Sun midnight–4am, Fri & Sat midnight– 5am. Once a place where flamenco tunes were offered up to La Macarena, the Virgin of Seville. Now it's a heaving, funky, electronic temple with a tolerant crowd – they have to be, as there's not much space. Entry free until around 1am, then €5.

▲ OUTSIDE TARANTOS

Sidecar

Pl. Reial 7 ☎933 021 586, ⓦwww .sidecarfactoryclub.com. Tues–Sun 8pm–4.30am. Hip music club – pronounced "See-day-car" – with nightly gigs (usually at 10.30pm) and DJs (from 12.30am) that champion rock, pop, fusion and urban styles. Local *mestiza* (ie Barcelona fusion) acts play here regularly, so this is the place to check out the latest Catalan hip-hop, rumba and flamenco sounds. Entry from €5–7, with some gigs up to €15.

PLACES

Barri Gòtic

Port Vell and Barceloneta

Barcelona has an urban waterfront that merges seamlessly with the old town, providing an easy escape from the claustrophobic medieval streets. The harbour at the bottom of the Ramblas has been thoroughly overhauled in recent years and Port Vell (Old Port), as it's now known, presents a series of heavyweight tourist attractions, from sightseeing boats to a maritime museum – not to mention the shops, bars and restaurants of the entertainment centre called Maremàgnum. By way of contrast, Barceloneta – the wedge of land to the east, backing the marina – retains its eighteenth-century character, and the former fishing quarter is still the most popular place to come and eat paella, fish and seafood. Metro Drassanes, at the bottom of the Ramblas, is the best starting point for Port Vell; Barceloneta has its own metro station.

Mirador de Colón

Pl. Portal de la Pau ☎ 933 025 224. June–Sept daily 9am–8.30pm; Oct–May daily 10am–6.30pm. €2.50, or €6.70 combination ticket with Museu Marítim. The striking monument at the foot of the Ramblas commemorates the visit made by Christopher Columbus to Barcelona in June 1493, when the Italian-born navigator was received in style by the Catholic monarchs Ferdinand and Isabella. Columbus tops a grandiose iron column, 52m high, guarded by lions, around which unfold reliefs telling the story of his life and travels – here, if nowhere else, the old mercenary is still the "discoverer of America". You can ride the lift up to the enclosed viewing platform at Columbus's feet, from where the 360-degree views are terrific. Meanwhile, from the quayside in front of the Columbus monument, Las Golondrinas sightseeing boats depart on regular trips throughout the year around the inner harbour.

▼ MIRADOR DE COLÓN

Museu Marítim

Avgda. de les Drassanes ☎ 933 429 920, ⊛ www.museumaritimbarcelona .org. Daily 10am–8pm. €6.50, free on afternoon of 1st Sat of month; combination tickets available with Golondrinas sightseeing boats and Columbus monument. Barcelona's unique medieval shipyards, or Drassanes, date from the thirteenth century and were in continuous use – fitting and arming Catalunya's war fleet or trading vessels – until well into the eighteenth century. Today, the huge, stone-vaulted buildings make a fitting home for the enjoyable Maritime Museum, whose centrepiece is a full-scale copy of a sixteenth-century royal galley which was originally constructed here. This is surrounded by different thematic sections covering Catalunya's relationship with the sea, which contain sailing boats, figureheads, old maps and charts, navigation instruments and other nautical bits and pieces. You'll get the most out of a visit if you pick up the audio guide (included in the entrance fee). There's also a good restaurant at the museum, while the café puts out tables in the pretty courtyard – on summer evenings this becomes a popular patio lounge-bar.

▲ DETAIL FROM PORT DE BARCELONA BUILDING

PLACES

Port Vell and Barceloneta

Santa Eulàlia

Moll de la Fusta; no phone. May–Oct Tues–Fri noon–7.30pm, Sat & Sun 10am–7pm, Nov–April closes at 5.30pm. €2.40, free with Museu Marítim ticket. The three-masted ocean-going schooner *Santa Eulàlia* is a flagship showpiece of the nearby Museu Marítim. Dating from 1908, and previously named the *Carmen Flores*, it once made the run between Barcelona and Cuba, but was subsequently acquired by the museum and fully restored. A short tour lets you walk the deck and shows off the interior.

Maremàgnum

Moll d'Espanya ☎ 932 258 100, ⓦ www.maremagnum.es. Daily 10am–10pm. From near the Columbus statue, the wooden Rambla de Mar swing bridge strides across

▲ MAREMÀGNUM

the harbour to Maremàgnum on Moll d'Espanya. It's a typically bold piece of Catalan design, the soaring glass lines of the leisure complex tempered by the surrounding undulating wooden walkways. Inside are two floors of gift shops and boutiques, plus a range of cafés and restaurants with harbourside seating. Outside, benches and park areas provide scintillating views back across the harbour to the city.

L'Aquàrium

Moll d'Espanya ☎ 932 217 474, ⓦ www.aquariumbcn.com. Daily: July & Aug 9.30am–11pm; Sept–June 9.30am–9pm, until 9.30pm at weekends. €16. Adjacent to Maremàgnum,

Port Vell's high-profile aquarium drags in families and school parties throughout the year to see "a magical world, full of mystery". Or, to be more precise, to see 11,000 fish and sea creatures in 35 themed tanks representing underwater caves, tidal areas, tropical reefs, the planet's oceans and other maritime habitats. It's vastly overpriced, and despite the claims of excellence it offers few new experiences, save perhaps the eighty-metre-long walk-through underwater tunnel which brings you face to face with gliding rays and cruising sharks. Some child-centred displays and activities, and a nod towards ecology and conservation matters, pad out the

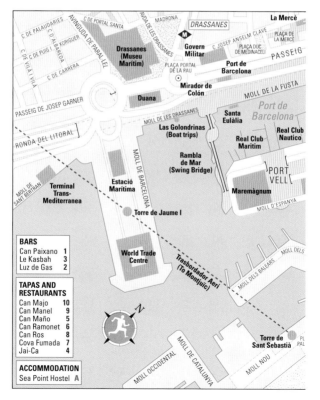

attractions, before you're tipped out in the aquarium shop so they can part you from even more of your money.

IMAX Port Vell

Moll d'Espanya ℡ 932 251 111, ⓦ www.imaxportvell.com. Screenings 11am–10.30pm, later at weekends. Tickets €7.50 or €11 depending on the film. Barcelona's IMAX theatre stands next to the aquarium, with three screens showing films virtually hourly in 3D or in giant format. The themes are familiar – the mysteries of the human body, forces of nature, heroic exploration, alien adventure, etc. – but you'll find that the films are in Spanish or Catalan only.

Museu d'Història de Catalunya

Palau de Mar, Pl. de Pau Vila 3 ℡ 932 254 700, ⓦ www.mhcat.net. Tues & Thurs–Sat 10am–7pm, Wed 10am–8pm, Sun and public hols 10am–2.30pm. €3; first Sun of month and public hols free. The only surviving warehouse on the Port Vell harbourside is known as the Palau de Mar, home to an enterprising museum tracing the history of Catalunya from the Stone Age to the twentieth century. There are temporary shows on the ground floor, while a lift takes you up to the permanent displays: second floor for year dot to the Industrial Revolution, and third for periods

PLACES Port Vell and Barceloneta

PORT VELL AND BARCELONETA

▲ MARISCAL CRAYFISH, PORT VELL

and events up to 1980 (though later coverage is planned). You can pick up full English notes at the desk, and there's plenty to get your teeth into, whether it's poking around the interior of a Roman grain ship or comparing the rival nineteenth-century architectural plans for the Eixample. On the fourth floor, the café-bar boasts a glorious view from its huge terrace of the harbour, Tibidabo, Montjuïc and the city skyline – you don't need a museum ticket to visit this.

The seafood restaurants in the **Palau de Mar** arcade below the museum are some of the most popular in the city, especially at weekends. Here you overlook the packed **marina**, where Catalans park their yachts like they park their cars – impossibly tightly – fronted in summer by hawkers spreading blankets on the ground to sell jewellery and sunglasses.

Barceloneta

There's no finer place for lunch on a sunny day than the Barceloneta neighbourhood, bound by the harbour on one side and the Mediterranean on the other. Laid out in 1755 as a classic eighteenth-century grid, its long, narrow streets are still very much as they were planned, broken at intervals by small squares – like Plaça de la Barceloneta, with its eighteenth-century fountain and Neoclassical church of

Sant Miquel del Port. There's also a stylish local market, the **Mercat de la Barceloneta** (open from 7am, closed Mon & Sat afternoons), with a couple of excellent restaurants, while Barceloneta's famous seafood restaurants are found scattered right across the tight grid of streets but most characteristically lined along the harbourside **Passeig Joan de Borbó**.

Passeig Marítim

A double row of palms backs the sweeping stone esplanade that runs from Barceloneta's beach, Platja de Sant Sebastià, as far as the Port Olímpic. It's a fifteen-minute walk from Barceloneta to the port, but some do it much quicker than that – the Passeig Marítim is a notable track for bladers, skaters and joggers, who have one of the Med's best views for company.

On the way, just before the hospital and port, you'll pass the **Parc de la Barceloneta**, a rather plain expanse enlivened only by its whimsical *modernista* water tower (1905), rising like a minaret above the palms.

Trasbordador Aeri

Torre de Sant Sebastiá, Barceloneta ☎ 932 252 718. Daily 10.30am–7pm, June–Sept until 8pm. €9 one-way, €12.50 return. The most thrilling ride in the city centre is across the inner harbour on the cable car, which sweeps over the water from the foot of Barceloneta to Montjuïc. The views are stunning, and you can pick out with ease the familiar towers of La Seu and Sagrada Família, while the trees lining the Ramblas look like the forked tongue of a serpent. Departures are every fifteen minutes, though in summer and at weekends you may have to wait for a while at the top of the towers for a ride as the cars only carry about twenty people at a time.

Restaurants and tapas bars

Can Majo

C/Almirall Aixada 23 ☎ 932 215 818. Tues–Sat 1–4pm & 8–11pm, Sun 1–4pm. You can sit almost on the beach at this quality seafood restaurant – the summer *terrassa* is ringed by a blue picket fence, and the whole world saunters by as you tuck into reliably good rice, *fideuà* (noodles with seafood), *suquet* (fish stew) or grilled fish. The menu changes daily according to what's off the boat; expect to spend €40–50 a

Plats del Dia	
Pebrot del Padro	8.00 €
Camarons	20.00 €
Xipirons a l'andalusa	15.50 €
"Tallarinas"	17.00 €
"Berberechos"	12.00 €
"Percebes"	22.00 €
Ostres *per peça*	2.80 €
Gambes Grossa de Palamós	18.00 €
Calamarsets de platja planxa	15.00 €
Cloisses gallegues mitjana a la marinera	18.00 €
Turbot al forn	23.50 €
Llagosta Mediterrani *(per Kg)*	130.00 €
Paella de marisc i Llamàntol del Pais *(minim 2 persones)*	35.00 €
Arrós melós de escamarlans *(minim 2 persones)*	22.00 €

Vi recomenat	
Viña del Vero Gewüztraminer	15.88 €

Can Majó

▲ MENÙ DEL DIA

head (and make a reservation if you want an outside table at the weekend).

Can Manel

Pg. Joan de Borbó 60 ☎ 932 215 013. Daily 1–4pm & 8pm–midnight. An institution since 1870, which fills very quickly because the food is both good and reasonably priced. If you want lunch outside on the shaded terrace, get there by 1.30pm. Paella, *fideuà* (noodles with seafood) and *arròs a banda* (rice with seafood) are staples – from around €13 per person – while the catch of the day, usually simply grilled, ranges from cuttlefish (around €10) to sole, bream or hake (up to €22).

Can Maño

C/Baluard 12 ☎ 933 193 082. Mon–Fri 8am–5.30pm & 8–11pm, Sat noon–5pm; closed Aug. There's rarely a tourist in sight in this old-fashioned locals' diner, jam-packed with formica tables. Fried or grilled fish is the thing here (sardines, mullet, calamari), supplemented by a few daily seafood specials and basic meat dishes. Expect rough house wine and absolutely no frills, but it's an authentic experience, which is likely to cost you less than €12 a head.

Can Ramonet

C/Maquinista 17 ☎ 933 193 064. Daily 1–4pm & 8pm–midnight; closed Sun dinner & Aug. Reputedly the oldest restaurant in the port area, it has the added attraction of a shady *terrassa* in front of the neighbourhood market. The food is pretty good, though with fish and seafood mains running at around €17–25 meals can soon turn out to be quite pricey. You can always opt instead for the rustic front bar, where the tapas (from €8) are piled high on wooden barrels – the *pernil* (cured ham) is a house speciality.

Can Ros

C/Almirall Aixada 7 ☎ 932 215 049. Daily 1–5pm & 8pm–midnight; closed Wed. This has long been one of the best places to sample paella, *arròs negre* ("black rice", ie made with cuttlefish ink) or a *fideuà* (noodles) with clams and shrimp, all of which cost around €12 – as almost everywhere, rice servings are for a minimum of two people. The only drawback is there's no outside seating, and the tables are packed in close together, but it's a comfortable, no-hurry kind of place.

Cova Fumada

C/Baluard 56 ☎ 932 214 061. Mon–Fri 9am–3pm & 6–8pm, Sat 9am–3pm; closed Aug. Come for a gregarious lunch in this busy traditional bar (it's behind the brown wooden doors on the market square, there's no sign). The seafood is straight from the market, and if you want the house speciality ask for the *bombas* (spicy fried meatballs).

Jai-Ca

C/Ginebra 13 ☎ 932 683 265. Daily 10am–11pm. A classic tapas bar.

▼ PLAÇA DE LA BARCELONETA

Scrutinize the platters on the bar or just check what your neighbour's having – a bundle of *navajas* (razor clams), say, or some plump anchovies or fried shrimp. Meanwhile, the fryers in the kitchen work overtime, turning out crisp baby squid and little green peppers scattered with salt. Take your haul to a tile-topped cane table, or outside onto the tiny street-corner patio.

Bars

Can Paixano

C/de la Reina Cristina 7 ☎ 933 100 839. Mon–Sat 9am–10.30pm; closed 2 weeks in Aug. A must on everyone's itinerary is this counter-only joint where the drink of choice – all right, the only drink – is *cava* (Catalan champagne) by the glass or bottle with little sandwiches, and that's your lot. It's very, very popular, so you'll probably have to fight your way in.

Le Kasbah

Pl. Pau Vila, behind Palau de Mar ☎ 932 380 722, ⊛ www.ottozutz.com. Tues–Sun 10pm–3am. The *terrassa* is the big summer draw here, when nothing but a reviving cocktail and a breath of fresh air will do, though the funky, sort-of-Oriental interior has a certain chilled-out charm.

Luz de Gas

Moll del Diposit, in front of Palau de Mar ☎ 932 097 711, ⊛ www.luzdegas .com. March–Oct daily noon–3am. Sip a chilled drink on the polished deck of the moored boat, and soak up some great marina and harbour views. Queues form on hot days, when every parasol-shaded seat is taken, but it's especially nice at dusk as the city lights begin to twinkle.

El Raval

The old-town neighbourhood of El Raval, on the west side of the Ramblas, was traditionally known as a red-light area. It still has some very seedy corners (particularly south of Carrer de Sant Pau), though it's changing rapidly, notably in the "upper Raval" around Barcelona's contemporary art museum, MACBA, from which ripple out cutting-edge galleries, see-and-be-seen restaurants and fashionable bars. Historically, El Raval (from the Arabic word for suburb) stood outside the medieval city walls, housing hospitals, churches, monasteries and noxious businesses like slaughterhouses (*tallers*, hence the street name Carrer dels Tallers) that had no place in the more refined Gothic quarter. Throughout most of the twentieth century, the neighbourhood was notorious for its sleazy Barri Xinès (China Town), though regeneration has cleaned up large parts of El Raval, and now a younger, artier, more affluent population rubs shoulders with the area's Asian and North African immigrants and the older, traditional residents. Metros Catalunya, Liceu, Drassanes and Paral.lel serve the neighbourhood.

Museu d'Art Contemporani de Barcelona (MACBA)

Pl. dels Àngels 1 ☎934 120 810, ⓦwww.macba.es. Mid-June to mid-Sept Mon & Wed 11am–8pm, Thurs & Fri 11am–midnight, Sat 10am–8pm, Sun & public hols 10am–3pm; rest of the year closes weekdays 7.30pm; closed Tues all year. €4 or €7.50 depending on exhibitions visited, Wed €3. Anchoring the northern reaches of the Raval is the iconic Museu d'Art Contemporani de Barcelona (MACBA), whose stark main facade is entirely constructed of glass. Once inside, you go from the ground to the fourth floor up a series of swooping ramps, which afford continuous views of the square below – usually full of careering skateboarders. The collection represents the main movements in art since 1945, mainly (but not

exclusively) in Catalunya and Spain, and is shown in rotating exhibitions, so, depending on when you visit, you may catch works by major names

▼ SKATEBOARDING OUTSIDE MACBA

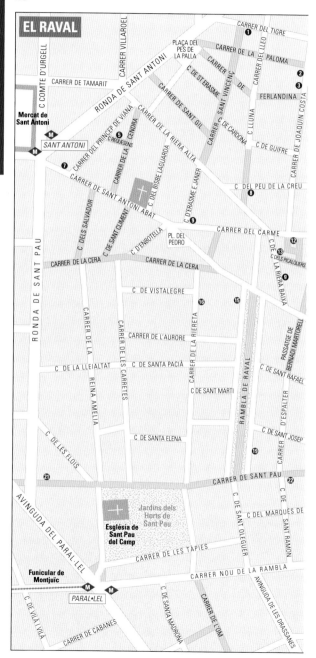

EL RAVAL

CARRER DEL TIGRE ❶
CARRER DE LA LLEO
CARRER DEL PALOMA ❷
❸
FERLANDINA
CARRER VILLAROEL
CARRER DE JOAQUIN COSTA
PLAÇA DEL PES DE LA PALLA
CARRER
C. DE ST EBASME
CARRER
SANT VINCENÇ DE
C DE GUIFRE
C LLUNA
CARRER DE CARDONA
C COMTE D'URGELL
CARRER DE TAMARIT
RONDA DE SANT ANTONI
CARRER DE SANT GIL
CARRER DE SANT ANTONI
CARRER DE LA RIERA ALTA
Mercat de Sant Antoni
M SANT ANTONI
M
❺ C REQUESENS
CARRER DEL PRINCEP DE VIANA
CARRER DE LA CENDRA
❼
CARRER DE SANT ANTONI ABAT
CARRER DE LA
C DEL BISBE LAGUARDA
D'ERASME E JANER
C. DEL PEU DE LA CREU ❽
❾
CARRER DEL CARME ⓬
⓭
C. DE LA RIERA BAIXA
C DELS PICALQUERS ❾
C DELS SALVADOR
C DE SANT CLIMENT
C. D'ENBOTELLA
PL. DEL PEDRO
CARRER DE LA CERA
CARRER DE LA CERA
RONDA DE SANT PAU
C. DE VISTALEGRE
⓰ ⓯
CARRER DE L'AURORE
CARRER DE LA RIERETA
PASSATGE DE BERNADI MARTORELL
C. DE SANT RAFAEL
CARRER DE LA REINA AMELIA
CARRER DE LES CARRETES
C. DE SANTA PACIÀ
C DE SANT MARTI
RAMBLA DE RAVAL
D'ESPALTER
C. DE SANT JOSEP
C. DE LA LLEIALTAT
CARRER
C. DE SANTA ELENA
⓳
C. DE LES FLOIS
㉑
CARRER DE SANT PAU ㉒
Jardins dels Horts de Sant Pau
Església de Sant Pau del Camp
C. DE SANT OLEGUER
C DEL MARQUES DE
C DE SANT RAMON
AVINGUDA DEL PARAL·LEL
CARRER DE LES TAPIES
CARRER NOU DE LA RAMBLA
Funicular de Montjuïc
M M PARAL·LEL
C. DE VILA I VILA
C. DE SANTA MADRONA
CARRER DE L'OM
AVINGUDA DE LES DRASSANES
CARRER DE CABANES

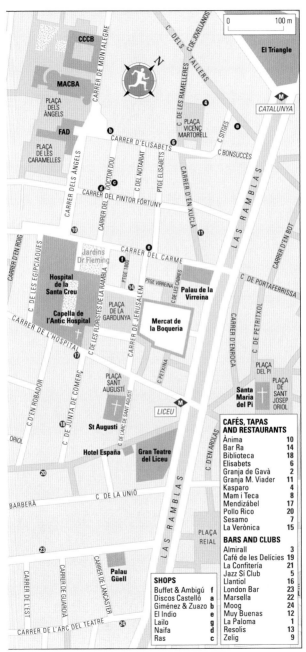

0   100 m

El Triangle

CCCB

MACBA

PLAÇA
DELS
ÀNGELS

FAD

PLAÇA
DE LES
CARAMELLES

C DE LES RAMELLES

CARRER DE MONTALEGRE

C DELS TALLERS

C DE JOVELLANOS

CATALUNYA

PLAÇA
VICENÇ
MARTORELL

CARRER D'ELISABETS

CARRER DELS ÀNGELS

C SITGES

C BONSUCCÉS

LAS RAMBLAS

CARRER D'EN BOT

CARRER DEL DOCTOR DOU

CARRER DEL NOTARIAT

PTGE ELISABETS

CARRER D'EN XUCLÀ

CARRER DEL PINTOR FÓRTUNY

CARRER DEL CARME

CARRER D'EN ROIG

Jardins
Dr Fleming

PTGE TBÓ

PTGE VIRREINA

C DE LES CARBRES

**Palau de la
Virreina**

C DE PORTAFERRISSA

CARRER D'EN ROCA

C DE PETRITXOL

**Hospital
de la
Santa Creu**

C DE LES EGIPCÍAQUES

C DE LES FLORISTES DE LA RAMBLA

PLAÇA
DE LA
GARDUNYA

**Mercat de
la Boqueria**

C D'ETXINA

PLAÇA
DEL PI

**Capella de
l'Antic Hospital**

CARRER DE L'HOSPITAL

CARRER DE JERUSALEM

**Santa
Maria
del Pi**

PLAÇA
DE
SANT
JOSEP
ORIOL

C D'EN ROBADOR

C DE JUNTA DE COMERÇ

PLAÇA
SANT
AUGUSTÍ

C DE L'ARC DE SANT AGUST

LICEU

C D'EN AROLAS

ORIOL

St Augustí

Hotel España

**Gran Teatre
del Liceu**

C DE LA UNIÓ

LAS RAMBLAS

PLAÇA
REIAL

BARBERÀ

CARRER DE LANCASTER

CARRER DE GUARDIA

**Palau
Güell**

CARRER DE L'EST

CARRER DE L'ARC DEL TEATRE

CAFÉS, TAPAS AND RESTAURANTS
Ànima	10
Bar Ra	14
Biblioteca	18
Elisabets	6
Granja de Gavà	2
Granja M. Viader	11
Kasparo	4
Mam i Teca	8
Mendizábel	17
Pollo Rico	20
Sesamo	7
La Verònica	15

BARS AND CLUBS
Almirall	3
Café de les Delícies	19
La Confitería	21
Jazz Sí Club	5
Llantiol	16
London Bar	23
Marsella	22
Moog	24
Muy Buenas	12
La Paloma	1
Resolis	13
Zelig	9

SHOPS
Buffet & Ambigú	f
Discos Castelló	a
Giménez & Zuazo	b
El Indio	e
Lailo	g
Naifa	d
Ras	c

such as Joan Miró or Antoni Tàpies, or coincide with shows by contemporary Catalan conceptual artists. Probably the best way to acquaint yourself with the collection is to take the free guided tour (in English on Mon at 6pm, otherwise daily at 6pm, Sun and public hols at noon, plus night tours in summer). There's also a good museum shop, selling everything from designer espresso cups to art books, and a café around the back that's part of the CCCB (contemporary culture centre).

Foment de les Artes Décoratives (FAD)

Pl. dels Àngels 5–6 ☎ 934 437 520, ⊛ www.fadweb.org, ⊛ www. tallersoberts.org. Tues–Fri 11am–8pm, Sun 11am–4pm. Free. A section of the former Convent dels Àngels now houses the headquarters of the Foment de les Artes Décoratives (FAD) – a decorative art and design organization founded in 1903 – whose exhibition spaces (including the former convent chapel) are dedicated to industrial and graphic design, crafts, architecture, contemporary jewellery and fashion. FAD also coordinates the annual **Tallers Oberts** (or "Open Workshops"; usually over two weekends in May), when visitors can tour craft outlets in the old town and join in craft sessions and workshops.

Centre de Cultura Contemporània de Barcelona (CCCB)

C/Montalegre 5 ☎ 933 064 100, ⊛ www.cccb.org. Tues–Sun 11am–8pm, Thurs until 10pm. €4.40 or €6 depending on exhibitions visited. The city's contemporary culture centre (CCCB) hosts temporary art and city-related exhibitions as well as supporting a cinema and a varied concert programme. The imaginatively restored building is a prime example of the juxtaposition of old and new; originally built in 1714 on the site of a fourteenth-century convent, it was for hundreds of years an infamous workhouse and lunatic asylum. In the entrance to the centre, in what is now called the Plaça de les Dones, you can see the old tile panels and facade in a pretty patio presided over by a small statue of Sant Jordi, patron saint of Catalunya. At the back of the building the *C3* café-bar makes the most of its *terrassa* on the modern square joining the CCCB to the MACBA. It's open until late for dinner, drinks and music, while a relaxed meal can also be had just up the street in the arcaded and tiled patio, the **Pati Manning** (c/ Montalegre 7), where a daytime café serves a good-value *al fresco* lunch.

Plaça de Vicenç Martorell

One of Barcelona's nicest traffic-free squares lies just off

The beat from the street

Mestiza – the Barcelona sound – is a cross-cultural musical fusion whose heartland is the immigrant melting-pot of the Raval. Parisian-born Barcelona resident Manu Chao kick-started the whole genre, but check out the Carrer dels Tallers music stores for CDs by the other flag-bearers – Cheb Balowski (Algerian-Catalan fusion), Ojos de Brujo (Catalan flamenco and rumba), GoLem System (dub/reggae) and Macaco (rumba, raga, hip-hop).

▲ ORANGE TREES IN THE COURTYARD OF HOSPITAL DE LA SANTA CREU

the Ramblas, a few minutes' walk from MACBA. There are not many places in the old town where children can play safely, so the small playground here (with swings and a slide) is all the more welcome for local families. What's more, it's overlooked by a first-rate café, the *Kasparo*, whose arcade tables are busy from morning to night – a real find if you're looking for a break from sightseeing. Meanwhile, around the corner, the narrow **Carrer del Bonsuccés**, **Carrer Sitges** and **Carrer dels Tallers** house a concentrated selection of the city's best independent music stores and urban and streetwear shops.

Hospital de la Santa Creu

Entrances on c/del Carme and c/de l'Hospital. Daily 10am–dusk. Free. La Capella exhibition information on ⓦ www.bcn.es/virreinaexposicions. This attractive complex of Gothic buildings was founded as the city's main hospital in 1402, a role it maintained until 1930. The spacious fifteenth-century hospital wards were subsequently converted for cultural and educational use, including the Catalan national library, the Biblioteca de Catalunya. Visitors can wander freely through the pleasant medieval cloistered garden (access from either street), and there's a rather nice café-*terrassa* at the c/de l'Hospital side. Meanwhile just inside the c/del Carme entrance (on the right) are some superb seventeenth-century decorative tiles and a Renaissance courtyard. The hospital's former chapel, **La Capella**, entered separately from c/de l'Hospital, is a well-regarded exhibition space featuring a changing programme of works by young Barcelona artists.

Rambla de Raval

The most obvious manifestation of the changing character of El Raval is the palm-lined boulevard that has been gouged through the former tenements and alleys, providing a huge new pedestrianized area between c/de l'Hospital and c/de Sant Pau. The *rambla* has a distinct character that's all its own, dotted with kebab shops, curry

▲ GIANT CAT SCULPTURE, RAMBLA DE RAVAL

restaurants, halal butchers, telephone offices and grocery stores, as well as an increasing number of rather fashionable cafés and bars – a popular target for locals and tourists alike. Come on Saturday and there's an all-day street market.

Just off the top of the *rambla* – tucked off c/de l'Hospital – the narrow **Carrer de la Riera Baixa** is at the centre of the city's secondhand/vintage clothing scene. A dozen funky little independent clothes shops provide the scope for an hour's browsing.

Hotel España

C/de Sant Pau 9–11 ☎ 933 181 758, Ⓦ www.hotelespanya.com. Some of the most influential names in Catalan *modernista* architecture and design came together at the turn of the twentieth century to transform the dowdy *España* hotel (originally built in 1860) into one of the city's most lavish addresses. With a tiled dining room designed by Domènech i Montaner, a bar with an amazing marble fireplace by Eusebi Arnau, and a ballroom whose marine murals were executed by Ramon Casas, the hotel was the fashionable sensation of its day. It's been well looked after ever since, and you can have a good nose around for the price of lunch or even stay here overnight – though the guest rooms are nowhere near as impressive as the public areas.

Palau Güell

C/Nou de la Rambla 3–5. El Raval's outstanding building is the Palau Güell (1886–90), an extraordinary townhouse designed by the young Antoni Gaudí for wealthy industrialist Eusebi Güell i Bacigalupi. At a time when architects sought to conceal the iron supports within buildings, Gaudí turned them to

▼ DETAIL FROM HOTEL ESPAÑA

▲ ROOF DETAIL, PALAÜ GUELL

his advantage, displaying them as decorative features in the grand rooms on the main floor, which are lined with dark marble hewn from the Güell family quarries. Columns, arches and ceilings are all shaped, carved and twisted in an elaborate style that was to become the hallmark of Gaudí's later works, while the roof terrace culminates in a fantastical series of chimneys decorated with swirling patterns made from fragments of glazed tile, glass and earthenware. Unfortunately, guided tours of the building have been suspended while renovation work is carried out, and Palau Güell is not expected to be open to the public until at least 2008.

Església de Sant Pau del Camp

C/de Sant Pau 101 ☎934 410 001. Mon 5–8pm, Tues–Fri 10am–1.30pm & 5–8pm, Sat 10am–1.30pm. Admission to cloister €2. The name of the church of Sant Pau del Camp (St Paul of the Field) is a graphic reminder that it once stood in open fields beyond the city walls. One of the most interesting churches in Barcelona, Sant Pau was a Benedictine foundation of the tenth century, built after its predecessor was destroyed in a Muslim raid of 985 AD, and constructed on a Greek cross plan. Above the main entrance are curious, primitive thirteenth-century carvings of fish, birds and faces, while other animal forms adorn the double capitals of the charming twelfth-century cloister. Inside, the rather plain church is enlivened only by tiny arrow-slit windows, and small stained-glass circles high up in the central dome.

Mercat de Sant Antoni

C/del Comte d'Urgell 1 ☎934 234 287. Mon–Thurs & Sat 7am–2.30pm & 5.30–8.30pm, Fri 7am–8.30pm. The neighbourhood's major produce market makes a nice contrast to the Boqueria – there are not nearly so many tourists for a start – and, unlike many of the other city markets, it's surrounded by enclosed aisles packed with stalls selling cheap shoes, underwear, T-shirts, children's clothes, bed linen, towels and other household

▼ SANT PAU DEL CAMP

goods. Come on Sunday and there's a **book and coin market** (9am–2pm) instead, with collectors and enthusiasts getting here early to pick through the best bargains. The traditional place to take a break from market shopping is *Els Tres Tombs*, the restaurant-bar across the road. Open from 6am until late, it draws a good-natured mix of locals, market traders, students and tourists. Incidentally, there are plans to remodel the market entirely between 2008 and 2010, though its external character should be retained and a temporary market building will be installed.

Shops

Buffet & Ambigú

Ptge. 1800 s/n ☎ 932 430 178, ⓦ www.catalogobuffet.com. To keep on top of Spain's charge to the

▼ SHOP FACADE, EL INDIO

summit of modish European cuisine, pay a visit to the "gastronomic library", hidden up a dark covered passageway behind *Bar Ra*. Thousands of cookbooks, many in English, chart the recipes, exploits and philosophies of the latest chefs and restaurants, including several Barcelona hot spots.

Discos Castelló

C/del Tallers 3 ☎ 933 182 041; no.7 ☎ 933 025 946; no.9 (Overstocks) ☎ 934 127 285; and no.79 ☎ 933 013 575; ⓦ www.discoscastello.es. You could spend half a day flitting from shop to shop, each with its own speciality and vibe: classical recordings at no.3, a bit of everything at no.7, hip-hop, alternative rock, *mestiza*, hardcore and electronica at no.9, and jazz and 70s pop-rock at no.79.

Giménez & Zuazo

C/Elisabets 20 ☎ 934 123 381, ⓦ www.boba.es. Two collections a year of cutting-edge women's fashion that's funky and informal.

El Indio

C/del Carme 24 ☎ 933 175 442. The most traditional place in town to buy linen, pillows, blankets, sheets and tablecloths – the *modernista* facade, long cutting counters, wood panels and marble floor survive from its nineteenth-century glory days.

Lailo

C/de la Riera Baixa 20 ☎ 934 413 749. Secondhand and vintage clothes shop with a massively wide-ranging stock. If you're serious about the vintage scene, this is your first stop – and if you don't find what you want just move on down the street to the neighbouring boutiques.

Naifa

C/Dr. Joaquim Dou 11 ☎933 024 005.
Original, colourful, informal
– and very reasonably priced –
men's and women's collections.

Ras

C/Dr. Joaquim Dou 10 ☎934 127
199, ⓦwww.rasbcn.com. Opens
1pm, closed Mon. Specializes
in books and magazines on
graphic design, architecture,
photography and contemporary
art. Temporary exhibitions at the
back are always worth a look.

Cafés

Granja de Gavà

C/Joaquim Costa 37 ☎933 175 883.
Mon–Fri 8am–1am, Sat 8am–2.30am.
Traditionally tiled café with arty
airs – witness the daubs on the
walls, the 3m-high woman on
the bar and the weekly poetry
readings. It's a relaxed spot,
proclaiming "No TV, just good
music", and serves up breakfast,
sandwiches, shakes, juices, crepes
and salads.

Granja M. Viader

C/Xuclà 4–6 ☎933 183 486. Mon
5–8.45pm, Tues–Sat 9am–1.45pm
& 5–8.45pm. The oldest *granja*
(milk bar) in town, inventor of
"Cacaolat" (a popular chocolate
drink), but you could also try
mel i mató (curd cheese and
honey), *llet Mallorquina* (fresh
milk with cinnamon and lemon
rind) or a thick hot chocolate
topped with fresh cream.

Kasparo

Pl. Vicenç Martorell 4 ☎933 022 072.
Daily 9am–10pm, until midnight in
summer; closed 2 weeks in Jan. A
place to relax, in the arcaded
corner of a quiet square, with
outdoor seating year-round.
There's muesli, Greek yoghurt

▲ VINTAGE CLOTHES, CARRER DE RIERA
BAIXO

and toast and jam for early
birds. Later, sandwiches, tapas
and assorted *platos del dia*
(dishes of the day) are on offer
– things like hummus and bread,
vegetable quiche, couscous or
pasta.

Mendizábal

C/Junya de Comerç 2, no phone. Daily
10am–midnight, June–Sept until 1am.
This cheery stand-up counter
opposite the Hospital de la
Santa Creu dispenses juices,
shakes, beer and sandwiches to
passing punters. The lucky ones
grab a table over the road in the
shady little square.

Restaurants and tapas bars

Ànima

C/dels Àngels 6 ☎933 424 912. Daily
1–4pm & 9pm–midnight. Sleek, arty
joint attracting a young crowd,
who come for the seasonally
influenced fusion cooking
– courgette flowers and mussels

tempura followed by monkfish with a garlic and pistachio crust are typical summer dishes, with most mains around €14. It's a nice place for lunch, especially if you can get a table outside.

Bar Ra

Pl. de la Garduña 3 ☎615 959 872, ⓦ www.ratown.com. Mon–Sat 9am–2am. Extremely hip place behind the Boqueria market, with a groove-ridden music policy and a sunny *terrassa*. "It's not a restaurant," they proclaim, but who are they kidding? Breakfast runs from 10am, there's a *menú del dia* served every day (weekends as well) from 1–4pm, with dinner from 9pm until midnight. The menu is eclectic to say the least – Thai spring rolls to Catalan sausage – but with the market on the doorstep it's all good stuff.

Biblioteca

C/Junta del Comerç 28 ☎934 126 261, ⓦ www.bibliotecarestaurant. com. Mon–Fri 8pm–midnight, Sat 1–3.30pm & 8pm–midnight; closed 2 weeks in Aug. One of the most agreeable places to sample what Barcelona tends to call "creative cuisine". The name is a nod to the library of cookbooks, all inwardly digested it seems, since fish might be cooked Japanese- or Basque-style, clams paired with cured ham, lamb given the local treatment (with parsnip and turnip), or venison pie served with purée of the day. Meals cost around €40, and clued-up English-speaking staff make it a hassle-free dining experience. Reservations advised.

Elisabets

C/d'Elisabets 2 ☎933 175 826. Mon–Sat 8am–11pm; closed Aug.

Reliable Catalan home cooking at cramped tables in the brick-walled rear dining room, or snacks and drinks at the bar. The hearty lunch (1–4pm) is hard to beat for price, otherwise there's a big choice of tapas and *bocadillos* (sandwiches).

Mam i Teca

C/de la Lluna 4 ☎934 413 335. Mon, Wed–Fri & Sun 1–4pm & 8.30pm–midnight, Sat 8.30pm–midnight. An intimate (code for very small) place for superior tapas and fine wines, run by a wine-loving gourmet. All the meat is organic, the regional cheeses are well chosen, and market-fresh ingredients go to make up things like daily pasta dishes, a platter of grilled vegetables or a serving of lamb cutlets. Finish with chocolate truffles or home-made ice cream. There are only three or four tables, or you can perch at the bar.

Pollo Rico

C/de Sant Pau 31 ☎934 413 184. Daily 10am–midnight; closed Wed. Barcelona's original "greasy spoon" has been here forever and if you're in the mood for good spit-roast chicken and a glass of rot-gut wine, served quick-smart at the bar, this is the place. The upstairs dining room is a tad more sophisticated (only a tad) – either way, you'll be hard pushed to spend €12 from a long menu of Spanish/ Catalan staples.

Sesamo

C/Sant Antoni Abat 52 ☎934 416 411, ⓦ www.sesamo-bcn.com. Mon & Wed–Sat 1–5pm & 8pm–1am, Sun 8pm–1am. Innovative yet inexpensive vegetarian cooking that relies on fresh, mostly organic ingredients and influences from all over the globe. The set lunch is a steal, though even eating *à la carte* at night you're unlikely to top €25. Meals are served 1–3.30pm and 9–11.30pm; outside kitchen times, you can drop in for a drink.

La Verònica

Rambla de Raval 2–4 ☎ 933 293 303. Daily noon–1am; closed 2 weeks in Aug. Relocated from its original home in the Barri Gòtic, funky pizzeria La Verònica fits right into the new-look Rambla de Raval. There are loads of crispy pizzas (mostly vegetarian, all between €9 and €12) and inventive salads, enjoyed by a resolutely young and up-for-a-night-out crowd.

Bars

Almirall

C/de Joaquin Costa 33 ☎ 933 189 917. Daily 7pm–3am. Dating from 1860, Barcelona's oldest bar – check out the *modernista* doors and counter – is a venerated leftist hangout.

Café de les Delícies

Rambla de Raval 47 ☎ 934 415 714. Daily 6pm–2am, Fri & Sat until 3am. One of the first off the blocks in this revamped neighbourhood, and still perhaps the best; cute, cosy, mellow and arty, with a summer terrace and food for sharing.

La Confitería

C/de Sant Pau 128 ☎ 934 430 458. Mon–Sat 8pm–3am, Sun 7pm–2am. This old *modernista* bakery and sweet shop – carved wood bar, faded tile floor, murals, antique chandeliers – is now a popular meeting point, with a friendly, relaxed atmosphere.

London Bar

C/Nou de la Rambla 34 ☎ 933 185 261. Tues–Sun 7pm–4am; closed 2 weeks in Aug. Opened in 1910, this well-known *modernista* hangout attracts a mostly tourist clientele these days, but it's still worth looking in at least once. It puts on gigs at the back most nights, and you can always count on getting a one-for-the-road drink in the small hours.

Marsella

C/de Sant Pau 65 ☎ 934 427 263. Mon–Thurs 10pm–2am, Fri & Sat 10pm–2am; closed 2 weeks in Aug. Authentic, atmospheric, sleaze-period bar – named for the French port of Marseilles – where absinthe is the drink of choice. If there's a place where the spirit of the old Barri Xines lives on, this is it.

Muy Buenas

C/del Carme 63 ☎ 934 425 053. Tues–Sat 9am–3am. Arguably the Raval's nicest watering

▼ LA CONFITERÍA

hole, with eager-to-please staff making things go with a swing. A long marble trough does duty as the bar, and the beer's pulled from antique beer taps.

Resolis

C/Riera Baixa 22 ☎ 934 412 948. Mon–Sat 11am–1am. The team behind Ànima restaurant rescued this decayed, century-old bar and turned it into a cool hangout with decent tapas. They didn't do much – a lick of paint, polish the panelling, patch up the brickwork – but now punters spill out of the door onto "secondhand clothes street" and a good time is had by all.

Zelig

C/del Carme 116 ☎ 934 415 622. Tues–Sun 7pm–2am, Fri & Sat until 3am. The photo-frieze on granite walls and a fully stocked cocktail bar make it very much of its *barri*, but *Zelig* stands out from the crowd. It offers a chatty welcome, a tendency towards 1980s sounds and a slight whiff of camp.

Clubs

Jazz Sí Club

C/Requesens 2 ☎ 933 290 020, ⓦ www.tallerdemusics.com. Good, inexpensive (€4–7) gigs in a small club associated with the music school. Every night from around 8 or 9pm there's something different, from rock,

blues, jazz and jam sessions to the popular weekly Cuban (Thursday) and flamenco (Friday) nights.

Llantiol

C/Riereta 7 ☎ 933 299 009, ⓦ www .llantiol.com. Closed Mon. Local-language theatre isn't at all accessible to non-speakers, but you might give this idiosyncratic café-cabaret a try – the varied shows feature a mix of mime, song, clowns, magic and dance. Shows (€9–12) normally begin at 9pm and 11pm (6pm & 9pm on Sun, with an additional late-night Saturday special).

Moog

C/Arc del Teatre 3 ☎ 933 017 282, ⓦ www.masimas.com. Daily midnight–5am. Influential club playing techno, electro, drum 'n' bass, house, funk and soul to a cool but up-for-it crowd. Admission €9.

La Paloma

C/Tigre 27 ☎ 933 016 897, ⓦ www .lapaloma-bcn.com. The fabulous 1903-era ballroom and concert venue was a city mainstay for years, where old and young alike were put through their rumba and cha-cha-cha steps, with DJs kicking in after midnight on an assorted roster of rowdy club nights. Problems with the city council led to closure in 2007, but it's hoped it's not permanent – check the website for the latest details.

Sant Pere

Perhaps the least visited part of the old town is the medieval *barri* of Sant Pere, the area that lies immediately east of Via Laietana and the Barri Gòtic and north of Carrer de la Princesa. It has two remarkable buildings – the *modernista* concert hall known as the Palau de la Música Catalana and the stylishly designed neighbourhood market, Mercat Santa Caterina. There's been much regeneration in the *barri* over recent years: new boulevards are being opened up, and a slew of cool bars and restaurants has emerged, some of them destinations in their own right. To walk through the neighbourhood, you can start at Metro Urquinaona, close to the Palau de la Música Catalana, with Metro Jaume I marking the southern end of Sant Pere.

Palau de la Música Catalana

C/Sant Pere Més Alt ☎ 902 442 882, ⓦ www.palaumusica.org. Box office open Mon–Sat 10am–9pm. Guided tours daily 10am–3.30pm, plus July–Sept 10am–7pm, in English on the hour. €9. Happen upon *modernista* architect Lluís Domènech i Montaner's stupendous concert hall from narrow c/Sant Pere Més Alt and it barely seems to have enough space to breathe. Built in 1908, the bare brick structure is smothered in tiles and mosaics, with the highly elaborate facade resting on three great columns, like elephant's legs. However, successive extensions and interior remodelling have since opened up the site – the Petit Palau offers a smaller auditorium space, while to the side an enveloping glass facade, courtyard and terrace restaurant provide the main public access. The concert season runs from October to June and includes performances by the Orfeo Català choral group and the

▲ PALAU DE LA MÚSICA CATALANA

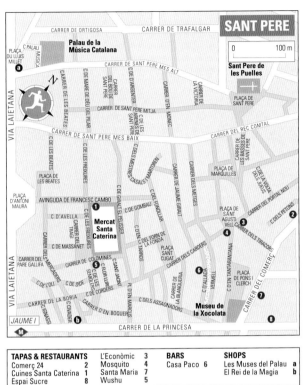

TAPAS & RESTAURANTS				BARS		SHOPS	
Comerç 24	2	L'Econòmic	3	Casa Paco	6	Les Muses del Palau	a
Cuines Santa Caterina	1	Mosquito	4			El Rei de la Magia	b
Espai Sucre	8	Santa Maria	7				
		Wushu	5				

Barcelona city orchestra, though there's a broad remit – you can catch anything here from flamenco to world music gigs. Half the enjoyment of any performance is experiencing the stunning interior. The dramatic tiled lobby provides a taster, which incorporates a bulbous stained-glass skylight capping the second-storey auditorium – which contemporary critics claimed to be an engineering impossibility. You can also see the interior on a guided tour, though visitor numbers are limited and you'll have to book in advance, either in person or by phone at the box office (entrance at c/Palau de la Música 4–6), or by calling at the nearby gift shop, Les Muses del Palau, c/Sant Pere Més Alt 1.

Església de Sant Pere de les Puelles

Pl. de Sant Pere ☎ 932 680 742. Mon–Sat 8.45am–1pm & 5–7.30pm, Sun 10am–2pm. Sant Pere's focal square is named, like the neighbourhood itself, for its monastic church, whose high walls and Gothic portal tower above the paved square's cast-iron drinking fountain. The church was rebuilt in 1147 on even older foundations, but has been restored inside over the centuries almost beyond interest. However, the three medieval

streets that converge at the church, carrers de Sant Pere Més Alt (upper), Mitja (middle) and Baix (lower), contain the bulk of the district's finest buildings and the nicest shops – a mixture of small boutiques and old family businesses.

Mercat Santa Caterina

Avgda. Francesc Cambò 16 ☎ 933 195 740, ⓦ www.mercatsantacaterina .net. Mon 8am–2pm; Tues, Wed & Sat 8am–3.30pm; Thurs & Fri 8am– 8.30pm. The very heart of the neighbourhood is the Mercat Santa Caterina, whose splendid restoration has retained its nineteenth-century balustraded walls and added slatted wooden doors and windows and a dramatic wave roof

(and how many other markets come with wireless Internet access?). During the renovation work, the foundations of a major medieval convent were discovered on the site – parts of the walls are now visible behind glass at the rear of the market. Santa Caterina is one of the best places in the city to come and shop for food, and its market restaurant and bar are definitely worth a special visit. In the surrounding streets, several other new bars and eating places have also opened.

Plaça de Sant Agusti Vell

The pretty, tree-shaded Plaça de Sant Agusti Vell is a nice target for lunch, with its amiable neighbourhood restaurants. It sits right in the middle of Sant Pere's most ambitious urban regeneration projects: work is under way to open up a couple of city blocks to the north, to be renamed the Jardins Pou de la Figuera. The southern extension, across c/dels Carders, was completed in the 1990s and has had time to settle in. Now, **Carrer d'Allada Vermell** is

one of the most agreeable old-town *ramblas*, its overarching trees and small children's playground interspersed with outdoor cafés and bars. Meanwhile, running down from Plaça de Sant Agustí Vell, **Carrer dels Carders** – once "ropemakers' street" – is now a funky retail quarter mixing grocery stores and cafés with shops selling streetwear, African and Asian arts and crafts, and jewellery.

Museu de la Xocolata

C/del Comerç 36 ☎ 932 687 878, ⓦ www.pastisseria.com. Mon & Wed–Sat 10am–7pm, Sun 10am–3pm. €3.90. Not many cities can boast a museum dedicated entirely to chocolate. Barcelona's is housed in the former Convent de Sant Agustí, whose thirteenth-century cloister, rediscovered when the building was renovated, can still be viewed. The museum itself plods through the history of chocolate, from its origins as a sacred and medicinal product of prehistoric Central America through to its introduction to Europe as a confection in the sixteenth century. Whether you choose to go in or not probably depends on how keen you are to see models of Gaudí buildings or religious icons sculpted from chocolate. Nonetheless, the museum café serves a fine cup of hot chocolate – and the choccie counter is something to behold too – while at the adjacent Escola de Pastisseria, glass windows allow you to look onto the students learning their craft in the kitchens.

Shops

Les Muses del Palau

C/Sant Pere Més Alt 1 ☎ 902 442 882. Your one-stop shop for anything related to the Palau de la Música and *modernisme* – branded gifts, jewellery and accessories, postcards and CDs.

El Rei de la Magia

C/Princesa 11 ☎ 933 193 920. Spain's oldest magic shop contains all the tricks of the trade, from rubber chickens to Dracula capes. They also do magic shows.

▲ CHOCOLATE AT THE MUSEU DE LA XOCOLATA

Restaurants and tapas bars

Comerç 24

C/Comerç 24 ☎ 933 192 102, ⓦ www
.carlesabellan.com. Tues–Sat 1.30–
3.30pm & 8.30pm–12.30am; closed 2
weeks in Aug. Chef Carles Abellan
presents "glocal" cooking (ie
global + local): dishes from
across the world, interpreted
locally by a master of invention.
In an oh-so-cool interior,
the meal comes tapas-style,
mixing flavours and textures
with seeming abandon but to
calculated effect (*foie gras* and
truffle hamburger, shot glasses
of frothy soup, tuna *sashimi* on
pizza). Prices are high (around
€70–80 a head), and reservations
are advised, though you can
have a cheaper, less formal meal
at Abellan's Eixample tapas bar,
TapaÇ24, where the food has
something of the same panache.

Cuines Santa Caterina

Mercat Santa Caterina, Avgda.
Francesc Cambó s/n ☎ 932 689
918. Bar daily 8am–midnight,
restaurant 1–4pm & 8–11.30pm. The
market restaurant is ravishingly
designed, with big windows
and refectory tables set under
soaring wooden rafters. The
food touches all bases – pasta to
sushi, Catalan rice dishes to Thai
curries – and though portions
aren't enormous, they're not
expensive either (most things
cost €9–12). Or you can just
drink and munch superior tapas
at the horseshoe bar, watching
the market go about its frenetic
business.

Espai Sucre

C/de la Princesa 53 ☎ 932 681 630,
ⓦ www.espaisucre.com. Tues–Thurs 9–
11.30pm, Fri & Sat sittings at 8.30pm
& 11pm; closed Aug. The "Sugar
Space" takes the current fad for
food deconstruction off at a
tangent by serving pretty much
just dessert – inspired creations
by Jordi Butrón, who assembles
flavours and textures with the
skill of a magician. There's a
three-course or five-course
seasonally changing pudding
menu, with wines available to
match, plus a small selection
of savoury "mains" to pad out
the experience. And check the
website for a schedule of dessert
demos and hands-on courses.

L'Econòmic

Pl. de Sant Agusti Vell 13 ☎ 933 196
494. Mon–Fri 12.30–4.30pm; closed
Aug. The beautifully tiled dining
room dates back to 1932, and
makes the perfect surroundings
for a hearty lunch, served up,
as the name implies, for a very
reasonable price – around €10
for a seasonally influenced
three-course meal and wine.
You may have to wait under
the arches outside for a table to
become available.

Mosquito

C/dels Carders 46 ☎ 932 687
569, ⓦ www.mosquitotapas.com.
Tues–Sun 5pm–1am, Fri & Sat until
2.30am. Delicious pan-Asian
tapas, including things like
Balinese chicken wings, Thai
or Singapore noodles, crispy
spinach *pakoras* or potato *chaat*.
There's a sushi/sashimi menu
too, and if you factor in the
friendly service, Fair Trade
coffee, world music and very
reasonable prices you've got a
winning combination.

Santa Maria

C/Comerç 17 ☎ 933 151 227,
ⓦ www.santamaria.biz. Tues–Sat 1.30–
3.30pm & 8.30pm–12.30am; closed
2 weeks in Aug. Paco Guzmán's

▲ CASA PACO

Tues–Sat 1–11pm. If you're only going to eat one non-Catalan meal in Barcelona, this is where you should come – an Aussie-owned Asian wok bar, turning out super-authentic *pad Thais*, Malaysian *laksas*, Vietnamese rice paper rolls, red and green curries, Chinese noodles and the like. An appetizer, main course and wine comes to under €25. There are only a handful of tables, so you might want to reserve for busy (ie, late-evening) periods, though note that there's continuous food service all day so it's one place in Barcelona you don't have to wait until 10pm for your dinner.

new-wave tapas bar has a glass-fronted kitchen turning out taste sensations – like Catalan sushi, octopus confit, frogs' legs in soy and ginger, yucca chips, or quail with salsa. Under €40 a head should see you right, finishing on a high note with the famous "Dracula" for dessert – a shot glass of strawberry and vanilla cream flavours that sets off crackles in your head.

Wushu

C/Colomines 2 ☎ 933 107 313, ⓦ www.wushu-restaurant.com.

Bars

Casa Paco

C/d'Allada Vermell 10 ☎ 935 073 719. Mon–Thurs & Sun 9am–2am, Fri & Sat 9am–3am, Oct–March opens 6pm. The *barri*'s signature bar is this cool-but-casual music joint that's a hit on the weekend DJ scene. There's a great *terrassa* under the trees, and if you can't get a table here there are half a dozen other *al fresco* bars down the traffic-free boulevard. The associated *Pizza Paco* across the way (also with its own *terrassa*) means you don't have to go anywhere else for dinner.

La Ribera

The traditional highlights of the old artisans' quarter of La Ribera are the graceful church of Santa María del Mar and the Museu Picasso, the latter Barcelona's single biggest tourist attraction. More recently, the neighbourhood has also become the location of choice for designers and craftspeople, whose boutiques and workshops lend it an air of creativity. Art galleries and applied art museums occupy the medieval mansions of Carrer de Montcada – the neighbourhood's most handsome street – while the *barri* is at its most hip in the area around the Passeig del Born, whose cafés, restaurants and bars make it one of the city's premier nightlife centres. The most direct access point for La Ribera is Metro Jaume I.

Museu Picasso

C/de Montcada 15–23 ☎ 932 563 000, ⓦ www.museupicasso.bcn.es. Tues–Sun 10am–8pm. €6, special exhibitions €5, museum and exhibitions €8.50, first Sun of the month free. Despite containing none of his best-known works, Barcelona's celebrated Picasso Museum provides a fascinating opportunity to trace the artist's development from his paintings as a young boy to the mature works of later years. The early drawings are particularly interesting, in which Picasso – still signing with his full name, Pablo Ruiz Picasso – attempted to copy the nature paintings in which his father specialized. Paintings from his art-school days in Barcelona (1895–97) show tantalizing glimpses of the city that the young Picasso was beginning to explore, while works in the style of Toulouse-Lautrec, like the menu Picasso did for *Els Quatre Gats* tavern in 1900, reflect his

Picasso in Barcelona

Although born in Málaga, **Pablo Picasso** (1881–1973) spent much of his youth – from the age of 14 to 23 – in Barcelona. The time Picasso spent here encompassed the whole of his Blue Period (1901–04) and provided many of the formative influences on his art. Not far from the Museu Picasso you can still see many of the buildings in which Picasso lived and worked, notably the Escola de Belles Arts de Llotja (c/Consolat del Mar, near Estació de França), where his father taught drawing and where Picasso himself absorbed an academic training. The apartments where the family lived when they first arrived in Barcelona – Pg. d'Isabel II 4 and c/Reina Cristina 3, both near the Escola – can also be seen, though only from the outside, while Picasso's first real studio (in 1896) was located over on c/de la Plata at no.4. A few years later, many of his Blue Period works were finished at a studio at c/del Comerç 28. His first public exhibition was in 1901 at the extravagantly decorated *Els Quatre Gats* tavern (c/Montsió 3, Barri Gòtic; ⓦ www.4gats.com); you can still have a meal there today.

▲ PICASSO T-SHIRTS

interest in Parisian art. Other selected works are from the famous Blue Period (1901–04) and Pink Period (1904–06), and from his Cubist (1907–20) and Neoclassical (1920–25) stages. The large gaps in the main collection only underline Picasso's extraordinary changes of style and mood, best illustrated by the jump to 1957, a year represented by his 44 interpretations of Velázquez's masterpiece *Las Meninas*.

The museum's minor works – sketches, drawings and prints – cover in detail most phases of the artist's career up until 1972, including his work as a ceramicist.

Provided you accept that the museum is always busy, and that no really famous Picassos are on show in the permanent collection, few should leave here disappointed. A free guided tour is the best way to get to grips with the collection – in English currently on Thursday at 6pm and Saturdays at noon. A café with a *terrassa* in one of the courtyards offers refreshments, and there is of course a shop, stuffed full of Picasso-related gifts.

Museu Textil i d'Indumentaria

C/de Montcada 12–14 ☎ 933 197 603, ⓦ www.museutextil.bcn.es. Tues–Sat 10am–6pm, Sun 10am–3pm. €3.50, first Sun of the month free; ticket also valid for Museu de Ceràmica and Museu de les Artes Decoratives in Pedralbes. The fourteenth-century Palau de Llió contains the extensive collections of the city's Textiles and Clothing Museum. Selected items, from late Roman fabrics to 1930s cocktail dresses – all beautifully presented – demonstrate the art and technique behind cloth-making, embroidery, lace and tapestry work. The upper floor concentrates on Spanish and Catalan designers of the 1970s to 1990s, with a room devoted to Pedro Rodríguez (1895–1990), the first *haute couture* designer to establish a studio in Barcelona. Special exhibitions at the museum are well regarded (for which there's usually a separate charge), while the courtyard *Textil Café* is one of the nicest in the old town. In the associated shop, funky jewellery, silk ties, candles, kitchen aprons, bags and other design-led gifts and trinkets abound.

Museu Barbier-Mueller

C/de Montcada 14 ☎ 933 104 516. Tues–Fri 11am–7pm, Sat 10am–7pm, Sun 10am–3pm. €3, first Sun of the month free. A fascinating collection of Pre-Columbian art is housed in the renovated sixteenth-century Palau Nadal, next door to the Textiles and Clothing Museum. Temporary exhibitions – all beautifully presented – highlight wide-ranging themes, and draw on a peerless collection of sculpture, pottery, jewellery and textiles as well as everyday items, from decorated Mongolian belt-buckles to carved African furniture. Afterwards, have a browse in the museum shop, which has a wide range of artefacts, including wall hangings, jewellery, terracotta pots and figurines. And if you're looking for a Panama hat, this is the place.

Església de Santa María del Mar

Pl. de Santa Maria 1, at Pg. del Born ☎933 102 390. Daily 9am–1.30pm & 4.30–8pm; Sun choral Mass at 1pm.

The Ribeira's flagship church was begun on the order of King Jaume II in 1324, and finished in only five years. Built on what was the seashore in the fourteenth century, Santa María was at the heart of the medieval city's maritime and trading district (c/Argentería,

for example, is named after the silversmiths who once worked there, and it came to embody the commercial supremacy of the Crown of Aragon, of which Barcelona was capital). It's an exquisite example of Catalan-Gothic architecture, with a wide nave and high, narrow aisles, and for all its restrained exterior decoration is still much dearer to the heart of the average local than the cathedral, the only other church in the city with which it compares. The Baroque trappings were destroyed during the Civil War, which is probably all to the good since the long-term

CAFÉS, TAPAS & RESTAURANTS				CLUBS & BARS			
Àbac	18	Casa Delfín	12	Berimbau	10	Mudanzas	15
La Bascula	3	Euskal Etxea	8	Espai Barroc	5	El Nus	4
Café del Born	13	Mar de la Ribera	11	La Fianna	6	La Vinya del Senyor	14
Rosal	9	Salero	17				
Textil Café	2	Senyor Parellada	1				
Cal Pep	16	El Xampanyet	7				

▲ SANTA MARÍA DEL MAR

restoration work has concentrated on showing off the simple spaces of the interior; the stained glass, especially, is beautiful.

Behind the church is the square known as **Fossar de les Moreres**, which marks the spot where, following the defeat of Barcelona on September 11, 1714, Catalan martyrs fighting for independence against the King of Spain, Felipe V, were executed. A red steel scimitar with an eternal flame commemorates the fallen.

Passeig del Born

Fronting the church of Santa María del Mar is the fashionable Passeig del Born, once the site of medieval fairs and tournaments and now an avenue lined with a parade of plane trees shading a host of classy bars and shops. Cafés at the eastern end put out tables in front of the old Mercat del Born (1873–76), once the biggest of Barcelona's nineteenth-century market halls. It was the city's main wholesale fruit and veg market until 1971, and was then due to be demolished, though it was saved by local protest, with the idea of turning it into a library and cultural centre. Work has been going on for years, hampered by the excavation of eighteenth-century shops, factories, houses and taverns that were found under the market. The archeological remains should be retained, and visible, once the project is complete. Boutiques and craft workshops hide in the narrow medieval alleys on either side of the *passeig* – carrers Flassaders and Vidreria, in particular, are noted for clothes, shoes, jewellery and design galleries. At night the Born becomes one of Barcelona's biggest bar zones, as spirited locals frequent a panoply of drinking haunts – from old-style cocktail lounges to thumping music bars.

Shops

Almacen Marabi

C/Flassaders 30, no phone, ⓦwww .almacenmarabi.com. Mariela Marabi, originally from Argentina, makes handmade felt finger dolls, mobiles, puppets and animals of extraordinary invention. Her eye-popping workshop also has limited-edition pieces by other selected artists and designers.

▲ NARROW PASSAGES AT PASSEIG DEL BORN

▲ CAFÉ ON PASSEIG DEL BORN

Atalanta Manufactura

Pg. del Born 10 ☏ 932 683 702.
Boutique-*atelier* making
naturally dyed and painted silk
and linen artefacts, including
lovely scarves and wall hangings.

La Botifarreria de Santa Maria

C/Santa Maria 4 ☏ 933 199 123. If
you ever doubted the power of
the humble Catalan pork sausage,
drop by this designer temple-
deli where otherwise beautifully
behaved locals jostle at the
counter for the day's home-made
botifarra, plus rigorously sourced
hams, cheese, pâtés and salamis.
There are even *Botifarreria* T-shirts
for true disciples.

Casa Gispert

C/Sombrerers 23 ☏ 933 197 535,
🌐 www.casagispert.com. Roasters
of nuts, coffee and spices for
over 150 years – it's a truly
delectable store with some
tantalizing smells, and there are
gourmet deli items available too.

Custo Barcelona

Pl. de les Olles 7 ☏ 932 687 893,
🌐 www.custo-barcelona.com. Where
the stars get their T-shirts.

Hugely colourful (and highly
priced) designer Ts, tops and
sweaters for men and women.
Also at Ramblas 109, at c/de
Ferran 36 in the Barri Gòtic,
and at L'Illa shopping.

Czar

Pg. del Born 20 ☏ 933 107 222. A
galaxy of running shoes, pumps,
bowling shoes and baseball
boots – if your Starsky and
Hutch Adidas SL76s have worn
out, they'll sell you another pair.

U-Casas

C/Espaseria 4 ☏ 933 100 046, 🌐 www
.casasclub.com. Casas has four
lines of shoe stores across Spain,

▼ BACKSTREET ART SHOP

with the U-Casas brand at the young and funky end of the market. Never mind the shoes, the stores are pretty spectacular, especially here in the Born where an enormous shoe-shaped bench-cum-sofa takes centre-stage. Other branches are at c/Tallers 2 (Raval), c/Portaferrissa 25 (Barri Gòtic) and L'Illa and Maremàgnum shopping centres.

Vila Viniteca

C/Agullers 7 & 9 ☎ 932 683 227, ⓦ www.vilaviniteca.es. A very knowledgeable specialist in Catalan and Spanish wines. Pick your vintage and then nip over the road for the gourmet deli part of the operation.

Cafés

Café del Born

Pl. Comercial 10 ☎ 932 683 272. Mon–Thurs & Sun 9am–1am, Fri & Sat 9am–3.30am. No gimmicks, no dodgy art and no fusion food – just a successful neighbourhood café-bar with wooden floors, a high ceiling and a simple Mediterranean menu. Sunday brunch is popular.

Rosal

Pg. del Born 27; no phone. Daily 9am–2am. The *terrassa* at the end of the Born gets the sun all day, making it a popular meeting place, though it's also packed on summer nights.

Textil Café

C/de Montcada 12–14 ☎ 932 682 598, ⓦ www.textilcafe.com. Tues & Wed 10am–8.30pm, Thurs 10am–midnight, Fri & Sat 10am–1am, Sun 10am–midnight, Tues–Thurs in winter daytime only. Everyone loves this relaxed boho café, set inside the shady, cobbled medieval courtyard of the Textile and Clothing

Museum. The food's great for sharing – there's hummus, tzatziki, guacamole, baba ganoushe and tapenade, as well as things like quiche, salads, chilli, lasagne and big sandwiches. And there's also a lunchtime or evening *menú del dia*.

Restaurants and tapas bars

Àbac

C/del Rec 79 ☎ 933 196 600, ⓦ www.restaurantabac.com. Mon 8.30–11pm, Tues–Sat 1.30–4.30pm & 8.30–11pm; closed 2 weeks in Jan and 3 weeks in Aug. The minimalist domain of chef Xavier Pellicer, who refines Catalan food in ever more imaginative ways – for example, the signature dish of lamb cooked in vanilla milk. Of course it all comes at a price (more than €100 a head) but it's rated as one of the city's best gourmet experiences.

La Bascula

C/Flassaders 30 ☎ 933 199 866. Tues–Sat 1pm–midnight. A hippy-chic makeover for an old backstreet chocolate factory. It's a welcoming veggie place, serving speciality pastas, gourmet sandwiches, *empanadas* (stuffed pastries), crepes, dipping platters, salads and the like, and there are dozens of organic teas, coffees, wines, juices and shakes.

Cal Pep

Pl. de les Olles 8 ☎ 933 107 961. Mon 8pm–midnight, Tues–Sat 1.30–4pm & 8pm–midnight; closed Aug. There's no equal in town for fresh-off-the-boat and out-of-the-market tapas, and if you don't want to queue, get there on opening for a seat at the counter. Prices can be high for what's effectively a bar meal (up to €40), but it's definitely worth it for the likes of fried shrimp, hot green peppers, grilled sea bass, Catalan sausage, and baby squid and chickpeas – all overseen by Pep himself, bustling up and down the counter.

Casa Delfin

Pg. del Born 36 ☎ 933 195 088. Mon–Sat 8am–5pm; closed Aug. Old-school paper-tablecloth bar-restaurant, right at the end of the main drag, that offers a cheap and cheerful *menú del dia* – up to ten fish and ten meat choices, from grills to stews, topped off by home-made desserts or fruit. Add a coffee and the whole blowout shouldn't top €15.

Euskal Etxea

Pl. de Montcada 1–3 ☎ 933 102 185. Mon 6.30pm–midnight, Tues–Sat noon–4pm & 6.30pm–midnight; restaurant opens 1.30pm & 8.30pm. The bar at the front of the local Basque community centre is great for *pintxos*-picking – these pint-sized tapas, held together by a stick, are displayed along the counter, so just point to what you want (and keep the sticks so the bill can be tallied at the end). There's a pricier restaurant out back with more good Basque specialities.

Mar de la Ribera

C/Sombrerers 7 ☎ 933 151 336. Mon 8–11.30pm, Tues–Sat 1–4pm & 8–11.30pm. A cosy little place serving simple Galician-style seafood at prices (€6–12) that encourage large, leisurely meals. Try the mixed fried fish and paella, or any of the fish steaks and fillets – hake, salmon, tuna, sole, calamari – dressed with oil, garlic and chopped parsley, accompanied by platters of tasty grilled vegetables.

Salero

C/Rec 60 ☎ 933 198 022. Mon–Sat 1.30–4pm & 8.30pm–midnight; closed 2 weeks in Aug. A crisp, modern space fashioned from a former salt-cod warehouse – if white is your colour, you'll enjoy the experience. The food's Mediterranean-Asian, presenting delights like an aubergine curry with coconut or a *mee goreng* (fried noodle) of the day, with most dishes costing €10–16.

Senyor Parellada

C/Argenteria 37 ☎ 933 105 094. Daily 1–4pm & 8.30pm–midnight. An utterly gorgeous renovation of an eighteenth-century building has kept the arcaded interior and splashed the walls yellow. Food is Catalan through and through – cuttlefish and cod, home-style cabbage rolls, duck with figs, a papillote of beans with herbs – served from a long menu that doesn't bother dividing starters from mains. Most dishes cost between €8 and €15, while more than a dozen puds await those who struggle through.

▼ CARRER DE LA MONTCADA

El Xampanayet

C/de Montcada 22 ☎ 933 197 003.
Tues–Sat noon–4pm & 6.30–11pm,
Sun noon–4pm; closed Aug.
Traditional blue-tiled bar doing
a roaring trade in sparkling *cava*
and cider. Salted anchovies are
the house speciality, but there's
also marinaded tuna, spicy
mussels, sliced meats and cheese.
As is often the way, the drinks
are cheap and the tapas turn out
to be rather pricey, but there's
usually a good buzz about the
place.

Bars

Berimbau

Pg. del Born 17 ☎ 933 195 378. Daily
6pm–2.30am. The oldest Brazilian
bar in town, still a great place
for authentic sounds and killer
cocktails.

Espai Barroc

Palau Dalmases, c/de Montcada 20
☎ 933 100 673. Tues–Sat 8pm–2am,
Sun 6–10pm. One of a series
of handsome mansions along
c/de Montcada, Palau Dalmases
is open in the evenings as a
rather grand bar. You can sip
wine, champagne or Cognac

▼ BUBBLY CAVA

in the refined surroundings
or, once a week, enjoy the
billowing strains of live opera
(Thurs at 11pm; €20, first
drink included).

La Fianna

C/Banys Vells 19 ☎ 933 151 810,
🌐 www.lafianna.com. Mon–Wed &
Sun 6pm–1.30am, Thurs–Sat 6pm–
2.30am. Flickering candelabras,
parchment lampshades, rough
plaster walls and deep colours
set the Gothic mood in this
stylish mansion lounge-bar.
Relax on the chill-out beds and
velvet sofas, or book ahead to
eat – the fusion-food restaurant
is open from 8.30pm, or it's a
popular Sunday brunch spot.

Mudanzas

C/Vidrieria 15 ☎ 933 191 137. Daily
10am–2.30am. Locals like the
relaxed feel (especially if you
can hide yourself away in the
upper room), while those in
the know come for the wide
selection of rums from around
the world.

El Nus

C/Mirallers 5 ☎ 933 195 355. Daily
except Wed 7.30pm–2.30am. Still
has the feel of the shop it once
was, down to the antique cash
register, though now it's a kind
of jazz-bar-cum-gallery – a
quiet, faintly old-fashioned, late-
night place.

La Vinya del Senyor

Pl. Santa Maria 5 ☎ 933 103 379.
Tues–Thurs noon–1am, Fri & Sat
noon–2am, Sun noon–midnight.
Nook-and-cranny wine bar
with tables right outside the
lovely church of Santa María
del Mar. The wine list runs to
novel length – a score of them
available by the glass – and there
are oysters, smoked salmon and
other classy tapas.

Parc de la Ciutadella

For time out from the old town's historic intrigues and labyrinthine alleys, retreat to the city's favourite green space, Parc de la Ciutadella, on the eastern edge of La Ribera. It holds a full set of attractions – the Catalan parliament building (not open to the public), plant houses, museums and a zoo – though on lazy summer days there's little incentive to do any more than stroll the shady garden paths and pilot rowboats across the placid ornamental lake. The park dates from the demolition in 1869 of a Bourbon citadel, erected here in the mid-eighteenth century after Barcelona's resistance during the War of the Spanish Succession. Ciutadella was subsequently chosen as the site of the 1888 Universal Exhibition – from which period dates a series of buildings and monuments by the city's pioneering *modernista* architects. The park's main gates are on Passeig de Picasso (a short walk from La Ribera), and there's also an entrance on Passeig de Pujades (Metro Arc de Triomf); for direct access to the zoo, use Metro Ciutadella-Vila Olímpica.

Arc de Triomf

Pg. Lluís Companys. The giant brick arch at the northern end of Passeig Lluís Companys announces the architectural splendours to come in the Ciutadella park itself. Roman in scale, yet reinterpreted by its *modernista* architect, Josep Vilaseca i Casanovas, as a bold statement of Catalan intent, it's studded with ceramic figures and motifs and topped by two pairs of bulbous domes. The reliefs on the main facade show the city of Barcelona welcoming visitors to the 1888 Universal Exhibition, which was held in the park to the south.

Cascada

Parc de la Ciutadella. Park open daily 8am–dusk. Perhaps the

▼ ARC DE TRIOMF

most notable of the park's structures is the monumental fountain in the northeast corner. It was designed by Josep Fontseré i Mestrès, the architect chosen to oversee the conversion of the former citadel grounds into a park, and he was assisted by the young Antoni Gaudí, then a student: the Baroque extravagance of the Cascada's statuary (notably its dragons) is suggestive of the flamboyant decoration that was later to become Gaudí's trademark. The best place to contemplate the fountain's tiers and swirls is from the small open-air café just to the south. Here you'll also find a lake, where for a few euros you can rent a rowboat and paddle about among the ducks.

Museu de Zoologia

Pg. de Picasso ☎ 933 196 912, ⊛ www.bcn.es/museuciencies. Tues–Sun 10am–2.30pm, Thurs & Sat until 6.30pm. €3.50, first Sun of the month free. The city's Natural Science Museum divides its collections between two buildings in Ciutadella park. Most eye-catching is

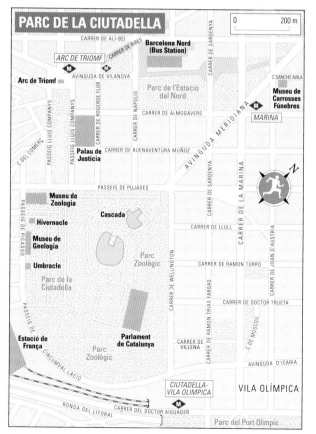

▲ CASCADA

that housing the zoological museum – a red-brick, castle-like design by Domènech i Montaner, intended for use as the Universal Exhibition's café-restaurant. Dubbed the "Castell dels Tres Dragons", it became a centre for *modernista* arts and crafts, and many of Domènech's contemporaries spent time here experimenting with new materials and refining their techniques. The museum itself presents a rather dry series of displays about Iberian fauna, though temporary popular-science exhibitions spark more interest. You can liven up a visit for the under-12s by asking for the free educational activities kit.

Hivernacle and Umbracle

Pg. de Picasso. Both open daily 8am–dusk. Free. The two unsung glories of Ciutadella are its plant houses, arranged either side of the Geological Museum. The imposing Umbracle (palm-house) is a handsome structure with a barrelled wood-slat roof supported by cast-iron pillars, which allows shafts of light to play across the assembled palms and ferns. Both materials and concept are echoed in the larger Hivernacle (conservatory), whose enclosed greenhouses are separated by a soaring glass-roofed terrace. A refined café-bar at the Hivernacle is the best stop in the park for drinks or a meal.

▼ MUSEU DE ZOOLOGIA

Museu de Geologia

Pg. de Picasso ☎ 933 196 895, ⓦ www.bcn.es/museuciencies. Tues–Sun 10am–2.30pm, Thurs & Sat until 6.30pm. €3.50, first Sun of the month free. The other building of the Natural Science Museum was actually the first public museum to be founded in Barcelona, the city's Geological Museum, which opened in 1882. In many ways it's a period piece, with nineteenth-century cases of exhibits housed in a classical pedimented building. There are rocks and minerals on one side, and fossils on the other, with many of the exhibits found in Catalunya, from fluorescent rocks to mammoth bones.

Parc Zoològic

C/de Wellington ☎ 932 256 780, ⓦ www.zoobarcelona.com. Daily: June–Sept 10am–7pm; March–May & Oct 10am–6pm; Nov–Feb 10am–5pm. €15. The city zoo takes up most of the southeastern part of the Parc de la Ciutadella. It's far too crowded, both with animals and visitors, and far too expensive, but nonetheless it's hugely popular with families, as there are mini-train and pony rides, a petting zoo and daily dolphin shows alongside the main animal attractions. These include the jungle bird aviary, permanent gorilla exhibition and comprehensive collection of reptiles. Notable endangered species found at the zoo include the Iberian wolf, and big cats such as the Sri Lanka leopard, snow leopard and the Sumatran tiger. However, the zoo's days here in its current form are numbered – the powers that be perhaps having finally appreciated the irony of its juxtaposition next to the parliament building, and grown weary of explaining to visiting dignitaries the source of the strong smell pervading the area. There are advanced plans to move the marine animals at

▲ UMBRACLE

least to a new coastal zoo and wetlands area at the Diagonal Mar seashore (possibly by 2010).

Museu de Carrosses Fúnebres

C/Sancho de Ávila 2 ☎ 934 841 700. Mon–Fri 10am–1pm & 4–6pm, Sat & Sun 10am–1pm. Free. Present yourself at the front desk of the Serveis Funeraris (funerary services) de Barcelona (by the blue Banc Sabadell sign) for one of the city's more esoteric attractions. You'll be escorted into the bowels of the building and the lights will be thrown on to reveal a staggering set of 22 funerary carriages, each parked on its own cobbled stage, complete with ghostly attendants, horses and riders suspended in frozen animation. Used for city funeral processions from the end of the nineteenth century onwards, most of the carriages and hearses are extravagantly decorated in gilt, black or white. Old photographs show some of the carriages in use in the city's streets, while showcases highlight antique uniforms, mourning wear and formal riding gear.

▲ STROLLING IN PARC DE LA CIUTADELLA

Cafés

Hivernacle

Pg. de Picasso ☎ 932 954 017. Daily 10am–midnight. A quiet, relaxing *terrassa* set amongst the palm trees inside the nineteenth-century glass conservatory. It's a genteel stop for daytime drinks, fancy tapas or fine Catalan dining, with live music and jazz nights a couple of times a week.

Montjuïc

You'll need to reserve at least a day to see Montjuïc, the steep hill and park rising over the city to the south-west. It takes its name from the Jewish community that once settled on its slopes, and there's been a castle on the heights since the mid-seventeenth century. But it's as a cultural leisure park that contemporary Montjuïc is positioned, anchored around the heavyweight art collections in the Museu Nacional d'Art de Catalunya (MNAC). This is supplemented by works in two other superb galleries, namely contemporary art in the Caixa Forum and that of the famous Catalan artist Joan Miró in the Fundació Joan Miró. In addition, there are several other minor museums on the hill plus the substantial open-air collections of the Poble Espanyol (Spanish Village), quite apart from the arenas associated with the 1992 Olympics. Metro Espanya provides easy access to Caixa Forum, Poble Espanyol and MNAC; the Trasbordador Aeri (cross-harbour cable car from Barceloneta) and Funicular de Montjuïc (from Metro Paral.lel) drop you a short walk from the Fundació Joan Miró, while the Olympic area can be reached by escalators behind MNAC.

Plaça d'Espanya

When Montjuïc was chosen as the site of the International Exhibition of 1929, its slopes were laid with gardens, terraces, fountains and monumental buildings. Gateway to the Exhibition was the vast Plaça d'Espanya, based on plans by noted architect Josep Puig i Cadalfach. Arranged around a huge Neoclassical fountain, the square is unlike any other in Barcelona, and a radical departure from the *modernisme* so in vogue elsewhere in the contemporary city. Striking twin towers, 47m high, stand at the foot of the imposing Avinguda de la Reina Maria Cristina, which heads up towards Montjuïc, the avenue lined by huge exhibition halls still used for trade fairs. At the end of the avenue monumental steps (and modern escalators) ascend the hill to the Palau Nacional (home of MNAC), past water cascades and under the flanking walls,

▲ BUS MONTJUÏC TURISTIC

▲ FONT MÀGICA FROM THE STEPS OF MNAC

busts and roofline "kiosks" of two grand Viennese-style pavilions.

Bus Montjuïc Turístic

Blue route from Pl. d'Espanya, red route from Pl. Portal de la Pau ☎ 934 414 982. Daily June 26 to Sept 15, otherwise weekends only. Departures every 40min, 10am–9pm. €3. Montjuïc's open-top bus service runs on two routes, one starting at Plaça d'Espanya (Metro Espanya), the other at the foot of the Ramblas at Plaça Portal de la Pau (Metro Drassanes). The service covers every major sight on the hill, including out-of-the-way attractions like the castle and botanic gardens. There are five connecting stops, so you can switch routes, and the all-day ticket lets you get on and off at will. The other bus service on Montjuïc is the city bus designated "PM" (city transport tickets valid on this), covering much the same route, while the sightseeing Bus Turístic (see p.000) also stops at the main Montjuïc attractions. There are stops for all these services right outside the upper station of the Funicular de Montjuïc.

Font Màgica

Pl. de Carles Buigas. May–Sept Thurs–Sun 8pm–midnight, music starts 9.30pm; Oct–April Fri & Sat only at 7pm, 7.30pm, 8pm & 8.30pm. Free. On selected evenings, the fountain at the foot of the Montjuïc steps becomes the centrepiece of an impressive if slightly kitsch sound-and-light show – the sprays and sheets of brightly coloured water appear to dance to the strains of Holst and Abba.

Caixa Forum

Avgda. del Marquès de Comillas 6–8 ☎ 934 768 600, ⓦ www.fundacio .lacaixa.es. Tues–Sun 10am–8pm. Free. The former Casamarona textile factory (1911) at the foot of Montjuïc conceals a terrific arts and cultural centre. The exhibition halls were fashioned from the former factory buildings, whose external structure was left untouched – original girders, pillars and stanchions, factory brickwork and crenellated walls appear at every turn. The Casamarona tower, etched in blue and yellow tiling, rises high above the walls, as readily

TAPAS		CLUBS	
Inopia	2	Sala Apolo	3
		Tablao de Carmen	1
		La Terrrazza	1

ACCOMMODATION
Hotel AC Miramar   A

recognizable as the huge Miró
starfish logos emblazoned
across the building. The centre's
celebrated contemporary art
collection focuses on the
period from the 1980s to the
present, with hundreds of artists
represented, from Antoni Abad
to Rachel Whiteread. Works
are shown in partial rotation,
along with temporary touring
exhibitions, and there's also a
library and resource centre, the
Mediateca multimedia space,
regular children's activities, and
a 400-seat auditorium with a
full programme of music, art,
poetry and literary events. The
café–restaurant is a nice spot,
too – an airy converted space
within the old factory walls,
serving sandwiches, snacks and
lunch.

Pavelló Mies van der Rohe

Avgda. del Marquès de Comillas
☎ 934 234 016, ⓦ www.miesbcn
.com. Daily 10am–8pm; guided
visits Wed & Fri 5–7pm. €3.50. The
1986 reconstruction by Catalan
architects of the Pavelló Mies
van der Rohe recalls part of the
German contribution to the
1929 International Exhibition.
Originally designed by Mies
van der Rohe, and used as a
reception room during the
Exhibition, it's considered a
major example of modern
rationalist architecture. The
pavilion has a startlingly beautiful
conjunction of hard straight lines
with watery surfaces, its dark-
green polished onyx alternating
with shining glass. It's open to
visitors, but unless there's an
exhibition in place (a fairly

regular occurrence) there is little to see inside, though you can buy postcards and books from the small shop and debate quite how much you want a Mies mousepad or a "Less is More" T-shirt.

Poble Espanyol

Avgda. del Marquès de Comillas ☎ 935 086 330, ⓦ www.poble-espanyol .com. Mon 9am–8pm, Tues–Thurs 9am–2am, Fri & Sat 9am–4am, Sun 9am–midnight. €7.50, combined ticket with MNAC €12. The Spanish Village – a hybrid open-air park of reconstructed famous or characteristic Spanish buildings – is the most extraordinary relic of the 1929 International Exhibition. "Get to know Spain in one hour" is what's promised and it's nowhere near as cheesy as you might think. It works well as a crash-course introduction to regional architecture – everything is well labelled and at least reasonably accurate. The echoing main square is lined with cafés, while the surrounding streets, alleys and buildings contain around forty workshops, where you can see engraving, weaving, pottery and other crafts. Inevitably, it's all one huge shopping experience – castanets to Lladró porcelain, religious icons to Barcelona soccer shirts – and prices are inflated, but children will love it (and you can let them run free as there's no traffic). Get to the village as it opens if you want to enjoy it in relatively crowd-free circumstances – once the tour groups arrive, it becomes a bit of a scrum. You could, of course, always come at the other end of the day, when the village transforms into a vibrant and exciting centre of Barcelona nightlife, its clubs among the hippest in the city.

Museu Nacional d'Art de Catalunya (MNAC)

Palau Nacional ☎ 936 220 376, ⓦ www.mnac.es. Tues–Sat 10am–7pm, Sun & hols 10am– 2.30pm. €8.50, ticket valid 48hr, first Sun of the month free; special exhibitions, varied charges apply. Catalunya's national art gallery occupies the towering Palau Nacional, set back on Montjuïc at the top of the long flight of steps from the fountains. It's one of Barcelona's essential visits – and one of Spain's great museums – showcasing a thousand years of Catalan art in stupendous surroundings. For first-time visitors it can be difficult to know where to start, but if time is limited it's recommended you concentrate on the medieval collection, which is split into two main sections, one dedicated to Romanesque art and the other to Gothic – periods in which Catalunya's artists were pre-eminent in Spain.

▼ POBLE ESPANYOL

▲ ASCLEPIOS AT MUSEU D'ARQUEOLÒGIA

The collection of Romanesque frescoes in particular is the museum's pride and joy. Removed from churches in the Catalan Pyrenees, they are presented in a reconstruction of their original setting, so you can see their size and where they would have been placed in the church buildings. Many of the Renaissance and Baroque works on display have come from private collections bequeathed to the museum, notably the celebrated Thyssen-Bornemisza bequest. Then, in a final flourish, MNAC ends on a high note with its unsurpassed nineteenth- and twentieth-century Catalan art collection (until the 1940s – everything from the 1950s and later is covered by MACBA in the Raval). It's particularly strong on *modernista* and *noucentista* painting and sculpture, the two dominant schools of the period, while there are some fascinating diversions into subjects like *modernista* interior design, avant-garde sculpture and historical photography.

Blockbuster exhibitions, and special shows based on the museum's archives, are very popular (and separate charges apply). There's also a café-bar, gift shop and art bookshop, and a superior museum restaurant called *Oleum* (Tues–Sun lunch only) that has extraordinary city views.

Museu Etnològic

Pg. Santa Madrona 16–22 ☎ 934 246 807, ⓦ www.museuetnologic.bcn .es. June–Sept Tues–Sat noon–8pm, Sun 11am–3pm, Oct–May Tues & Thurs 10am–7pm, Wed & Fri–Sun 10am–2pm. €3. The Ethnological Museum boasts extensive cultural collections from across the globe. This sort of gathering of artefacts is too often a dull exercise, but the museum instead puts on excellent rotating exhibitions, which usually last for a year or two and focus on a particular subject or geographical area. Refreshingly, pieces close to home aren't neglected either and the Spanish collections range across every province in the country, with exhibitions occasionally honing in on the minutiae of rural life and work in Catalunya, for example, or examining medieval carving or early industrialization. In addition, the museum has opened up its reserved rooms, where the conservers and staff have generally worked, so that you can delve about among the storage cabinets, piled high with everything from African masks to Spanish fans.

Museu d'Arqueològia

Pg. Santa Madrona 39–41 ☎ 934 246 577, ⓦ www.mac.es. Tues–Sat 9.30am–7pm, Sun & hols 10am–2.30pm. €2.40. Montjuïc's archeological collection spans the centuries from the Stone Age to the time of the Visigoths, with the Roman and Greek periods particularly well represented. Finds from Catalunya's best-preserved archeological site – the Greek remains at Empúries on the Costa Brava – are particularly notable, while an upper floor interprets life in Barcino (Roman Barcelona) through a collection of tombstones, statues, inscriptions and friezes found all over the city.

Teatre Grec and the Barcelona Festival

Pg. Santa Madrona 38 ☎ 933 161 000, ⊕ www.barcelonafestival.com. Centrepiece of Barcelona's annual summer cultural festival is this reproduction of a Greek theatre cut into a former quarry on the Montjuïc hillside. The festival starts in the last week of June (and runs throughout July and August), and incorporates drama, music and dance – with some of the most atmospheric works performed here in the Greek theatre, from Shakespearean productions to shows by Catalan avant-garde performance artists like La Fura del Baus. There are also concerts, plays and dance productions at other city venues, featuring local unknowns to international superstars – in total, around fifty different events held over a six-week period. There's more information (and ticket bookings) at the Palau de la Virreina on the Ramblas.

La Ciutat del Teatre

Mercat de les Flors ☎ 934 261 875, ⊕ www.mercatflors.org; Teatre Lliure ☎ 932 289 747, ⊕ www.teatrelliure .cat; Institut del Teatre ☎ 932 273 900, ⊕ www.institutdelteatre.org. Downhill from the Palau Nacional, just to the east, steps descend the hillside to the theatre area known as La Ciutat del Teatre ("Theatre

City"), which occupies a corner at the back of the old working-class neighbourhood of Poble Sec. The theatre buildings sit in a tight huddle off c/de Lleida, with the **Mercat de les Flors** – once a flower market, now centre for dance and the "movement arts" – and progressive **Teatre Lliure** ("Free Theatre") occupying the spaghetti-western-style Palau de l'Agricultura premises built for the 1929 Exhibition. Both have a full programme of theatre and dance, while Mercat de les Flors hosts an annual nonstop two-day performing arts festival (the Mataró de l'Espectacle, or "Entertainment Marathon") in June.

The sleek **Institut del Teatre**, meanwhile, brings together the city's major drama and dance schools, and various conservatories, libraries and study centres.

Poble Sec

The neighbourhood of Poble Sec, or "dry village" (so-called because it had no water supply until the nineteenth century), is a complete contrast to the

▲ POBLE SEC BALCONIES

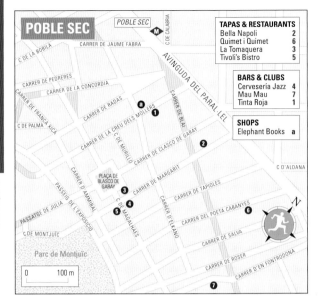

landscaped slopes of Montjuïc. There's nothing specific to see here, but the grid of steep streets is lined with down-to-earth grocery stores, bakeries, local shops and good-value restaurants. Asian immigrants have stamped their mark on many of the neighbourhood stores, while Poble Sec is also becoming a bit of a "new Raval" as a few fashionable bars have opened recently – the pedestrianized Carrer de Blai is a good target for an evening drink and stroll. The neighbourhood has its own metro station, or it's an easy walk from El Raval, while the Montjuïc funicular has its lower station on the southern fringe of the neighbourhood at Metro Paral.lel.

Estadi Olímpic

Museu Olímpic i de l'Esport, Avgda. de l'Estadi 21 ☎ 934 262 089, ⓦ www .fundaciobarcelonaolimpica.es. Mon & Wed–Sun 10am–8pm, Oct–March until 6pm. €8. The 65,000-seater Olympic Stadium was the venue for the opening and closing ceremonies of the 1992 Barcelona Olympics. The stadium itself was built originally for the 1929 Exhibition, and though completely refitted, the architects left the Neoclassical facade untouched. In front of the stadium a vast *terrassa* provides one of the finest vantage points in the city. Long water-fed troughs break the concrete and marble expanse, while the confident, space-age curve of Santiago Calatrava's communications tower dominates the skyline.

Around the other side, just across the road from the stadium, the history of the Games themselves – and Barcelona's successful hosting – are covered in the Olympic and Sports Museum. It's a fully interactive experience, with lots of equipment and memorabilia on display, but at the price it's probably one for hardcore Olympics fans only.

Piscines Bernat Picornell

Avgda. de l'Estadi 30–38 ☏ 934 234 041, ⓦ www.picornell.com. Mon–Fri 7am–midnight, Sat 7am–9pm, Sun 7.30am–4pm. Outdoor pool €4.90; indoor €8.90, includes gym and sauna. Remodelled and expanded for the Olympics, the city's favourite indoor swimming pools are open all year, while the outdoor pools are open to the public in summer only (June–Sept daily 9am–9pm). During the summer Grec festival, the pool hosts a popular film-and-swim session – one of Barcelona's more offbeat cultural events.

Fundació Joan Miró

Parc de Montjuïc ☏ 934 439 470, ⓦ www.bcn.fjmiro.es. Tues–Sat 10am–7pm, July–Sept until 8pm, Thurs 10am–9.30pm, Sun & hols 10am–2.30pm. €7.50, exhibitions €4. Barcelona's most adventurous art museum houses the life's work of Joan Miró (1893–1983), one of the greatest Catalan artists. His friend, the architect Josep-Luis Sert, designed the impressive white building set in lovely gardens overlooking the city, inside which is a permanent collection of paintings, graphics, tapestries, sculptures, sketches and notes, most donated by Miró himself and covering the period from 1914 to 1978. The paintings and drawings in particular are instantly recognizable, among the chief links between Surrealism and abstract art. You'll notice his designs all over his native city, most notably the starfish logo of the savings bank, Caixa de Pensions, and the pavement mosaic in the middle of the Ramblas. The foundation also displays works by other artists in homage to Miró, with the single most compelling exhibit being Alexander Calder's Mercury Fountain, which he built for the Republican pavilion at the Paris Universal Exhibition of 1936–37 – the same exhibition for which Picasso painted *Guernica*.

▼ PISCINES BERNAT PICORNELL

▲ COMMUNICATIONS TOWER, MONTJUÏC

The museum lies just a few minutes' walk from the Montjuïc funicular and cable-car stations. It sponsors excellent temporary exhibitions, film shows, lectures and children's theatre, while summer music nights (usually June and July) are a feature every year. There's also a library, with books and periodicals on contemporary art, a bookshop selling posters, and a café-restaurant (lunch 1.30–3pm, otherwise drinks, pastries and sandwiches) with outdoor tables on a sunny patio – you don't have to pay to get into the museum to use this.

Funicular de Montjuïc

Inside Metro Paral.lel, Avgda. del Paral. lel Ⓦwww.tmb.net. Every 10min daily 9am–10pm (Oct–March until 8pm). €1.30, city transport tickets and passes valid. The quickest way to reach the lower heights of Montjuïc is to take the funicular, which departs from inside the station at Metro Paral.lel and takes a couple of minutes to ascend the hill. At the upper station you can switch to the Montjuïc cable car or the Montjuïc bus services, or you're only a few minutes' walk from the Fundació Joan Miró.

Telefèric de Montjuïc

Avgda. de Miramar Ⓦwww .tmb.net. Daily service, June–Sept 10am–9pm; April, May & Oct 10am–7pm; Nov–March 10am–6pm. €5.70 one-way, €7.90 return. The Montjuïc cable car whisks you up to the castle and back in stylish little gondolas with panoramic windows, dangling passengers precariously over the landscaped grounds below. It's an exciting ride and the views, of course, are stupendous. There's an intermediate station halfway up, called Mirador, where you can get out for more sweeping views.

Jardins de Mossèn Costa i Llobera

C/de Miramar. Daily 10am–sunset. Free. The cross-harbour cable car from Barceloneta drops you close to a precipitous cactus garden which looks out over the port. Steep steps lead down into flourishing stands of Central and South American, Indian and African cacti, some over 6m high. It's a dramatic scene, rarely experienced by most visitors to Montjuïc, though the people lounging on the steps and in the shade of the bigger specimens suggest it's something of an open secret among the locals.

Castell de Montjuïc

Carretera de Montjuïc ☎933 298 613. Grounds: daily 7am–8pm; free. Museu Militar: mid-March to mid-Nov Tues–Sun 9.30am–8pm; mid-Nov to mid-March Tues–Sun 9.30am–5pm; €2.50. Marking the top of the hill and the end of the line – Barcelona's castle served as a military base and prison for many decades, and it was here that the last president of the prewar Catalan government, Lluís Companys, was executed on Franco's orders on October 15, 1940. As army (and therefore state) property, it has occupied an anachronistic position in the Catalan capital since autonomy, though moves are afoot to turn the fortress over to the city. In the meantime, the castle's old-fashioned military museum struggles on, though it's the building itself, and its dramatic location, that merits a visit. You can walk along the ramparts for free, and there's a little outdoor café within the walls. However, you have to pay to go inside the inner keep, where there's another café, a *mirador* (viewpoint) and an extensive parade ground, beyond which the **Museu Militar** presents endless swords, guns, medals, uniforms, maps and photographs.

Below the castle walls, a panoramic pathway – the **Camí del Mar** – has been cut from the cliff edge, providing scintillating views, first across to Port Olímpic and the northern beaches and then southwest as the path swings around the castle. The path is just over 1km long and ends at the back of the castle battlements near the Mirador del Migdia, where there's an open-air café (weekends from 10am) and a place that rents out bikes for use on the surrounding wooded trails.

Jardí Botànic de Barcelona

C/Dr Font i Quer 2 ☎934 264 935, ⓦwww.jardibotanic.bcn.es. June–Aug daily 10am–8pm, April, May & Sept Mon–Fri 10am–6pm, Sat, Sun & hols 10am–8pm; Oct–March daily 10am–5pm. €3. Principal among Montjuïc's many gardens is the city's Botanical Garden, laid out on terraced slopes which offer fine views across the city. The Montjuïc buses run here directly, or the entrance is just a five-minute walk around the back of the Olympic

▼ VIEW FROM CASTELL DE MONTJUÏC

Stadium. It's a beautifully kept contemporary garden, where wide, easy-to-follow paths (fine for strollers) wind through landscaped zones representing the flora of the Mediterranean, Canary Islands, California, Chile, South Africa and Australia. Just don't come in the full heat of the summer day, as there's very little shade. Guided tours in Spanish/Catalan every weekend (except August) show you the highlights, but you get an English-language audio-guide and map included in the entry fee in any case.

Shops

Elephant Books

C/Creu dels Molers 12 ☎ 934 430 594, ⊛ www.lfantbooks.4t.com. Only stocks English-language books, with cheap prices for current novels, classics, children's books and secondhand.

Restaurants and tapas bars

Bella Napoli

C/Margarit 14 ☎ 934 425 056. Tues–Sun 1.30–4.30pm & 8.30pm–12.30am. Authentic Neapolitan pizzeria, right down to the cheery waiters and cheesy pop music. The pizzas – the best in the city – come straight from the depths of a beehive-shaped oven, or there's a huge range of pastas, risottos and veal *scaloppine*, with almost everything priced between €8 and €12.

Inopia

C/Tamarit 104 ☎ 934 245 231. Tues–Fri 7–11pm, Sat 1.30–3.30pm & 7–11pm. You'll have to make a special trip to this sleek, in-the-know tapas bar, stuck in sightseer's no-man's-land, but it's unquestionably worth it. It's the brainchild of Albert Adrià, brother of Ferran Adrià (of best-restaurant-in-the-world fame, *El Bulli*), and it's always standing-room only for the best "classic tapas" in town. Regional wines are very reasonably priced, and don't miss the signature-dish *patatas bravas* (spicy fried potatoes), the griddled tuna, the lamb brochettes or the *fritura de verdura* (vegetable tempura); you can eat and drink for around €25.

Quimet i Quimet

C/Poeta Cabanyes 25 ☎ 934 423 142. Tues–Sat noon–4pm & 7–11pm, Sun noon–4pm; closed Aug. Poble Sec's cosiest tapas joint – at busy times everyone has to breathe in to squeeze another punter through the door. The bottles are stacked five shelves high, while little plates of classy finger food are dished out from the minuscule counter – things like roast onions, marinaded mushrooms, stuffed cherry tomatoes, grilled aubergine or anchovy-wrapped olives.

La Tomaquera

C/Margarit 58; no phone. Tues–Sat 1.30–3.45pm & 8.30–10.45pm; closed Aug. Sit down in this chatter-filled tavern and the bread arrives with a dish of olives and two quail's eggs – and there any delicacy ends, as the sweaty chefs set to hacking steaks and chops from great sides and ribs of meat. It's not for the faint-hearted, but the grilled chicken will be the best you've ever had, and the entrecôtes are enormous. Locals limber up with pan-fried snails with *chorizo* and tomato. Most main dishes cost €7–11.

Tivoli's Bistro

C/Magalhaes 35 ☎ 934 414 017,
☻www.tivolisbistro.com. Tues
8.45–11pm, Wed–Sat 1.30–4pm &
8.45–11pm; closed mid-Aug to
mid-Sept. Home-style Thai
cuisine, toned down for local
tastes, but reasonably priced
and run by a nice Catalan-
Thai couple, who also organize
cooking classes. A set dinner
(around €25 per person, drinks
extra; dishes change monthly) is
delivered to your table, usually
incorporating a starter or two, a
red or green curry, a vegetable
and fish dish, and Thai noodles
or rice. Lunch is a simpler set
meal at around half the price.

Bars

Cervesería Jazz

C/Margarit 43 ☎ 934 433 259.
Mon–Sat 7pm–2.30am. Grab a stool
at the carved bar and shoot the
breeze over an imported beer
in this amiable neighbourhood
bar. The music policy embraces
reggae and other mellow sounds,
not just jazz.

Tinta Roja

C/Creu dels Molers 17 ☎ 934 433 243.
Wed, Thurs & Sun 8pm–1.30am, Fri &
Sat 8pm–3am; closed 2 weeks in Aug.
Highly theatrical tango bar with
a succession of crimson rooms
dripping with ornamentation
leading through to a stage at the
back. There's cabaret and live
music (tango, rumba, Cuban,
flamenco) – often free – a
couple of nights a week, though
special shows are €10.

Clubs

Mau Mau

C/Fontrodona 33 ☎ 934 418 015,
☻www.maumaunderground.com.
Thurs 11pm–2.30am, Fri & Sat
11pm–3am. Great underground
lounge-club, cultural centre
and chillout space, with comfy
sofas, nightly film and video
projections, exhibitions and
a roster of guest DJs. Strictly
speaking it's a private club, but
membership is only €5 and they
tend to let foreign visitors in
anyway.

Sala Apolo

C/Nou de la Rambla 113 ☎ 934
414 001, ☻www.sala-apolo.com,
☻www.nitsa.com. This old-time
ballroom is now a hip concert
venue with regular live gigs
and an eclectic series of club
nights, foremost of which is
the long-running techno/
electronica *Nitsa Club* (Fri &
Sat 12.30pm–6.30am).

Tablao de Carmen

Avgda. Marquès de Comillas, Poble
Espanyol ☎ 933 256 895, ☻www
.tablaodecarmen.com. Tues–Sun,
shows at 7.45pm & 10pm. The
Poble Espanyol's flamenco
club at least looks the real deal,
sited in a replica Andalucian
street and featuring a variety
of flamenco styles from both
seasoned performers and new
talent. Prices start at €35 for the
show and a drink, rising to €65
and upwards for the show plus
dinner. Advance reservations
required.

La Terrrazza

Avgda. Marquès de Comillas, Poble
Espanyol ☎ 932 724 980, ☻www
.laterrrazza.com. May–Oct Thurs–Sat
midnight–6am. Open-air summer
club that's *the* place to be in
Barcelona. Nonstop dance,
house and techno, though
don't get there until at least
3am and be prepared for the
style police. Admission usually
costs €15–20.

Port Olímpic and Poble Nou

The main waterfront legacy of the 1992 Olympics was the Port Olímpic, the sparkling marina development which lies fifteen minutes' walk along the promenade from Barceloneta. Locals have taken to this in a big way, making full use of the surrounding beaches and boardwalks, and descending in force at the weekends for a leisurely lunch or late drink in one of the scores of restaurants and bars. It's a pattern beginning to be repeated further north in the old working-class neighbourhood of Poble Nou, which overlays its traditional character with the buzz provided by one of Barcelona's hottest club and arts scenes. There are metro stations at Ciutadella-Vila Olímpica and Poble Nou, or bus #59 runs from the Ramblas through Barceloneta and out to Port Olímpic.

Port Olímpic

From any point along the Passeig Marítim, the soaring twin towers of the Olympic port impose themselves upon the skyline, while a shimmering golden mirage above the promenade slowly reveals itself to be a huge **copper fish** (courtesy of Frank Gehry, architect of the Bilbao Guggenheim). These are the showpiece manifestations of the huge seafront development constructed for the 1992 Olympics, which incorporated an athletes' village for the 15,000 competitors and

▼ PASSEIG MARÍTIM

support staff – the apartment buildings and residential complexes were converted into permanent housing after the Games. The port itself – site of many of the Olympic watersports events – is backed by the city's two tallest buildings, the **Torre Mapfre** and the steel-framed **Hotel Arts Barcelona**, both 154m tall. Two wharves contain the bulk of the action: the Moll de Mestral has a lower deck by the marina lined with bars and *terrassas*, while the Moll de Gregal sports a double-decker tier of seafood restaurants. The beach, meanwhile, turns into a full-on summer resort, backed by a series of class-conscious clubs along Passeig Marítim that appeal to the local rich kids and A-list celebs.

Rambla de Poble Nou

Further up the coast, pretty, traffic-free, tree-lined Rambla de Poble Nou runs inland through the most attractive part

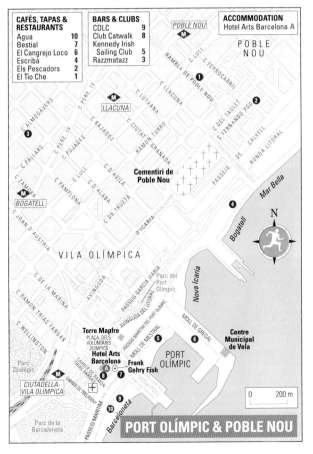

CAFÉS, TAPAS & RESTAURANTS		BARS & CLUBS	
Agua	10	CDLC	9
Bestial	7	Club Catwalk	8
El Cangrejo Loco	6	Kennedy Irish Sailing Club	5
Escribà	4	Razzmatazz	3
Els Pescadors	2		
El Tio Che	1		

ACCOMMODATION	
Hotel Arts Barcelona	A

PORT OLÍMPIC & POBLE NOU

0   200 m

▲ RAMBLA DE POBLE NOU

of nineteenth-century Poble Nou ("New Village") and is entirely modest in character – no card sharps or human statues here, just a run of neighbourhood shops and cafés frequented by locals out for their daily stroll. Stop off for a cold drink at *El Tio Che* or lunch at *Els Pescadors* – Poble Nou metro (yellow line 4) will save you the walk back to Ciutadella, Barceloneta or the city centre.

Cementiri de Poble Nou

Avgda. d'Icaria. Daily 8am–6pm. This vast nineteenth-century mausoleum has its tombs set in walls 7m high, tended by families who have to climb great stepladders to reach the uppermost tiers. With traffic noise muted by the high walls, and birdsong accompanying a stroll around the flower-lined pavements, quiet courtyards and chapels, this village of the dead is a rare haven of peace in the city.

City beaches

A series of city beaches reaches north from the Port Olímpic, along a five-kilometre stretch of sandy coast as far as the River Besòs. Split into different named sections (Nova Icària, Bogatell, etc), they are all furnished with boardwalks, showers and water fountains, while some also feature

Diagonal Mar

The waterfront north of Poble Nou has seen the latest city transformation, in the wake of the Universal Forum of Cultures Expo (held here in 2004). The district is promoted as **Diagonal Mar**, anchored by the Diagonal Mar shopping mall (Metro El Maresme Fòrum or tram T4) and with several classy hotels, convention centres and exhibition halls grouped nearby. The dazzling **Edifici Fòrum** building is the work of Jacques Herzog (architect of London's Tate Modern), the convention centre is the biggest in southern Europe, while the boast about the main open space is that it's the second-largest square in the world (150,000 square metres) after Beijing's Tiananmen Square. This immense expanse spreads towards the sea, culminating in a giant solar-panelled canopy that overlooks the new marina and landscaped beach and park areas. In summer, temporary bars, dance floors, open-air cinema and chill-out zones are established at the **Parc del Fòrum**, and the city authorities have shifted some of the bigger annual music festivals and events down here to inject a bit of life outside convention time. At other times it can still be a bit soulless, but it's definitely worth the metro or tram ride if you're interested in heroic-scale public projects.

climbing frames, public art and open-air cafés and bars. It's a pretty extraordinary facility for a major city, and gives Barcelona a real resort feel, especially in summer. But at any time of year, the merest hint of sun brings out the locals en masse, while weekends see scratch games of beach volleyball and football played up and down the coast. Save your swim for a pool, though – while the sands are regularly swept and replenished, the sea water's still not as clean as it could be.

Cafés

El Tio Che

Rambla Poble Nou 44–46 ☎ 933 091 872, ⊛ www.eltioche.com. Daily 10am–midnight; reduced hours in winter. A down-to-earth café in a down-to-earth neighbourhood, run by the same family for four generations. The specialities

▲ DOORMAN AT HOTEL ARTS

are orange or lemon *granissat* (crushed-ice) and their famous *orxata* (milky tiger-nut drink), but there are also *torrons* (almond fudge), hot chocolate, coffee, croissants and sandwiches.

▲ TRAM AT DIAGONAL MAR

Restaurants and tapas bars

Agua

Pg. Marítim 30 ☎ 932 251 272, ⓦ www.aguadeltragaluz.com. Daily 1.30–4pm & 8.30pm–midnight, Fri & Sat until 5pm & 1am. Much the nicest boardwalk restaurant on the beachfront strip, perfect for brunch, though if the weather's iffy you can opt for the sleek, split-level dining room. The menu is seasonal, contemporary Mediterranean – grills, rice dishes, pasta, salads and tapas – and the prices are pretty fair (meals around €25), so it's usually busy.

Bestial

C/Ramon Trias Fargas 2–4 ☎ 932 240 407, ⓦ www.bestialdeltragaluz .com. Daily 1–4pm & 8–11.30pm, Sat & Sun until 12.30am. Right beside Frank Gehry's fish (under the wooden bridge) you'll find a stylish terrace-garden in front of the beach, great for an *al fresco* lunch. Inside, the feel is sharp and minimalist, while the cooking's Mediterranean, mainly Italian, with dishes given an original twist. Rice, pasta and wood-fired pizzas are in the €9–14 range, with other dishes up to €21. At weekends, there's music and drinks until 2am.

El Cangrejo Loco

Moll de Gregal 29–30 ☎ 932 211 748, ⓦ www.elcangrejoloco.com. Daily 1pm–1am. The large outdoor terraces or huge picture windows at the "Crazy Crab" offer panoramas of the local coast and marina. The fish and shellfish are first-rate, with the catch changing daily, but a mixed fried-fish plate or broad beans with prawns are typically Catalan starters. Paella can be thoroughly recommended too, and the service is spot-on. Around €30 and upwards.

Escribà

Ronda del Litoral 42, Platja Bogatell ☎ 932 210 729, ⓦ www.escriba.es. Tues–Sat 11am–1am, Sun 11am–4pm;

restricted hours in winter. Glorified beach shack – a *xiringuito* in the parlance – that's enough off the beaten track (a 15min walk along the prom from the Port Olímpic) to mark you out as in the know. The paellas and *fideuàs* (from €13–16) fly out of the kitchen; daily fish specials are more like €20, and there's a ten percent terrace surcharge – but what the hell, the food and views are great. Desserts are sensational cakes and pastries from the Escribà family patisserie.

Els Pescadors

Pl. Prim 1 ☎ 932 252 018, ⓦ www .elspescadors.com. Daily 1–4pm & 8pm–midnight. It's a difficult call, but if you had to choose just one top-class fish restaurant in Barcelona, this would be it – it's hidden away in a pretty square in the back alleys of Rambla de Poble Nou, and lunch outside on a sunny day just can't be beaten (reservations advised). The daily changing menu runs to a dozen or more fresh fish dishes, and half-a-dozen others involving rice or *fideuà* (noodles), with a whole separate section for the house special salt-cod (try it with *samfaina*, like a Catalan ratatouille). Most dishes cost €10–25 and if you don't go mad you'll escape for about €50 a head.

Bars

Kennedy Irish Sailing Club

Moll de Mestral 26–27 ☎ 932 210 039, ⓦ www.kennedybcn.com. Daily 6pm–5am. Most of the Port Olímpic bars are indistinguishable – pumping sounds, backdrop video screens and preening youth – but Barcelona's "little bit of Ireland" provides a beer drinkers' haven between the disco bars. Guinness and Murphy's on tap, plus live music (pub rock, covers, Irish) Thursday to Sunday and big-screen sports.

Clubs

CDLC

Pg. Marítim 32 ☎ 932 240 470, ⓦ www.cdlcbarcelona.com. Daily noon–3am; food until midnight Mon–Wed, 1am Thurs–Sun. The seaside flagship of Barcelona's faddish dining-and-dancing club-restaurant scene, CDLC (that's the Carpe Diem Lounge Club) presents an east-west fusion – food and decor – beloved of the flash, famous or filthy rich.

Club Catwalk

C/Ramon Trias Fargas 2–4 ☎ 932 216 161, ⓦ www.clubcatwalk.net. Wed–Sun midnight–5am. Portside club of choice for the beautiful of Barcelona, playing house, funk, soul and r&b for well-heeled locals and visitors. It's under the landmark Hotel Arts Barcelona, and if you can persuade them to let you in admission costs €15–20.

Razzmatazz

C/dels Almogavers 122 & c/Pamplona 88 ☎ 932 720 910, ⓦ www .salarazzmatazz.com. Fri & Sat 1–5am. Razzmatazz hosts the biggest in-town rock gigs (concert hall capacity is 3000), while at weekends the former warehouse turns into "five clubs in one", spinning indie, rock, pop, techno, electro and more in variously named bars like "The Loft", "Pop Bar" or "Lolita". Entrance to all the bars, plus one drink, is €15.

Dreta de l'Eixample

The gridded nineteenth-century new-town area north of Plaça de Catalunya is the city's main shopping and business district. It was designed as part of a revolutionary urban plan – the Eixample in Catalan ("Extension" or "Widening") – that divided districts into regular blocks, whose characteristic wide streets and shaved corners survive today. Two parallel avenues, Passeig de Gràcia and Rambla de Catalunya, are the backbone of the Eixample, with everything to the east known as the Dreta de l'Eixample (the right-hand side). It's here, above all, that the bulk of the city's famous *modernista* (Catalan Art Nouveau) buildings are found, whose fanciful flourishes provide some of the most compelling urban images in Europe. However, any visit might equally concentrate on the Dreta's other undoubted pleasures – from museum and gallery visits to browsing in some of the city's most stylish shops. Start your exploration from either Metro Passeig de Gràcia or Metro Diagonal.

Passeig de Gràcia

The prominent showy avenue, which runs northwest from Plaça de Catalunya as far as the

▼ PASSEIG DE GRÀCIA

southern reaches of Gràcia, was laid out in its present form in 1827. As the Eixample became *the* fashionable part of town in which to live, the avenue developed as a showcase for the talents of *modernista* architects who were eagerly commissioned by status-conscious merchants and businessmen. Walk the length of Passeig de Gràcia from Plaça de Catalunya to Avinguda Diagonal (a 25min stroll) and you'll pass some of the city's most extraordinary architecture, notably the famous group of three buildings (casas Lleó Morera, Amatller and Batlló) known as the Mansana de la Discòrdia, or "Block of Discord", as they show off wildly varying manifestations of the *modernista* style and spirit. Further up is Antoni Gaudí's iconic apartment building La Pedrera while, in between, wrought-iron Art Nouveau street lamps, fashion stores, classy tapas bars and a designer hotel or two set the tone for this resolutely upscale avenue.

Casa Lleó Morera

Pg. de Gràcia 35. No public access. Domènech i Montaner's Casa Lleó Morera (1906) is the least extravagant of the buildings in the so-called Mansana de la Discòrdia and has suffered more than the others from "improvements" wrought by subsequent owners, which included removing the ground-floor arches and sculptures. A Loewe leather clothes and accessories store occupies the ground floor, while the main entrance to the building is resolutely guarded to prevent more than a peek inside. This is a pity because it has a rich Art Nouveau interior, flush with ceramics and exquisite stained glass.

Museu del Perfum

Pg. de Gràcia 39 ☏ 932 160 121, ⊛ www.museodelperfume.com. Mon–Fri 10.30am–1.30pm & 4.30–8pm, Sat

▲ BOTTLES AT MUSEU DEL PERFUM

11am–2pm. €5. They may have to turn the lights on for you at the back of the Regia perfume store, but there's no missing the exhibits as a rather cloying pong exudes from the room. It's a private collection of over five thousand perfume and essence bottles from Egyptian times onwards, and there are some exquisite pieces displayed, including Turkish filigree-and-crystal ware and bronze and silver Indian elephant flasks. More modern times are represented by scents made for Brigitte Bardot, Grace Kelly and Elizabeth Taylor, and if you're diligent enough to scan all the shelves you might be able to track down the perfume bottle designed by Salvador Dalí.

Modernisme

Modernisme, the Catalan offshoot of Art Nouveau, was the expression of a renewed upsurge in Catalan nationalism in the 1870s. Its most famous architectural exponent was **Antoni Gaudí i Cornet** (1852–1926), whose buildings are apparently lunatic flights of fantasy that at the same time are perfectly functional. His architectural influences were Moorish and Gothic, while he embellished his work with elements from the natural world. The imaginative impetus he provided to the movement was incalculable, inspiring other Catalan architects like **Lluís Domènech i Montaner** (1850–1923) – perhaps the greatest *modernista* architect – and **Josep Puig i Cadafalch** (1867–1957). It was in Domènech's café-restaurant at the Parc de la Ciutadella that a craft workshop was set up after the Universal Exhibition of 1888, giving Barcelona's *modernista* architects the opportunity to experiment with ceramic tiles, ironwork, stained glass and decorative stone carving. This combination of traditional methods with experiments in modern technology was to become the hallmark of *modernisme* – a marriage that produced some of the most fantastic and exciting modern architecture to be found anywhere in the world.

130

Dreta de l'Eixample

PLACES

DRETA DE L'EIXAMPLE

0   100 m

BARS & CLUBS
Barcelona City Hall 13
Les Gens Que J'aime 5

CAFÉS, TAPAS & RESTAURANTS

La Bodegueta	El Mussol	6 & 14
Casa Calvet 15	O'Nabo de Lugo	3
Ciudad Condal 11	TapaÇ 24	9
Forn de	Thai Gardens	10
Sant Jaume 7	Tragaluz	2
El Japonés 1	Valor	8
Laie Llibreria Café 12		

SHOPS

Antonio Miró	j	Mango	c & o
Armand Basi	h	Mango Outlet	p
Casa del Llibre	f	Muxart	a & i
Colmado Quilez	g	Purificacion	
Favorita	b	Garcia	m
Joaquín Berao	d	Zara	e & n
Mandarina Duck	k		

Casa Amatller

Fundació Amatller, Pg.
de Gràcia 41 ☎ 934 877
217, ⓦ www.amatller.org.
Tues–Sat 10am–8pm, Sun
10am–3pm. Free. Josep
Puig i Cadafalch's
striking Casa Amatller
(1900) was designed
for Antoni Amatller,
a Catalan chocolate
manufacturer, art
collector, photgrapher
and traveller. The facade
rises in steps to a point,
studded with coloured
ceramic decoration.
Inside the hallway the
ceramic tiles continue
along the walls, while
twisted stone columns

▲ LAMP AT CASA AMATLLER

are interspersed by dragon
lamps. All of this is further
illuminated by fine stained-glass
doors and an interior glass roof.
The ground floor now displays
temporary exhibitions under
the auspices of the Amatller
Foundation, while the shop here
sells Amatller chocolates, plus
modernista-related gifts.

Casa Batlló

Pg. de Gràcia 43 ☎ 932 160 306,
ⓦ www.casabatllo.es. Daily 9am–8pm,
access occasionally restricted. Visits
to main floor or attic and chimneys
€10 each, complete visit €16. Advance
sales from TelEntrada on ☎ 902 101
212, ⓦ www.telentrada.com. Perhaps
the most extraordinary creation
on the "Block of Discord" is
the Casa Batlló, designed for
the industrialist Josep Batlló
and finished in 1907. Antoni
Gaudí contrived to create an
undulating facade here that
Salvador Dalí later compared
to "the tranquil waters of a
lake". There's an animal aspect
at work too: the stone facade
hangs in folds, like skin, and,
from below, the twisted balcony

railings resemble malevolent
eyes. Self-guided audio tours
show you the main floor, the
patio and rear facade, the ribbed
attic and celebrated mosaic
roof-top chimneys. It's best to
reserve a ticket in advance (by
phone or in person), as this is
a very popular attraction – the
scrum of aimless visitors, audio-
stick glued to their ears, can be
a frustrating business at peak
times.

Fundació Antoni Tàpies

C/Aragó 255 ☎ 934 870 315, ⓦ www
.fundaciotapies.org. Tues–Sun
10am–8pm. €6. The definitive
collection of the work of
Catalan abstract artist Antoni
Tàpies i Puig is housed in
modernista architect Lluís
Domènech i Montaner's first
important building, the Casa
Montaner i Simon (1880). You
can't miss it – the foundation
building is capped by Tàpies'
own striking sculpture, *Núvol
i Cadira* ("Cloud and Chair":
1990), a tangle of glass, wire
and aluminium. The artist was
born in Barcelona in 1923 and

▲ ARTWORK AT FUNDACIÓ ANTONI TÀPIES

was a founding member (1948) of the influential avant-garde Dau al Set ("Die at Seven") grouping of seven artists. After a brief Surreal phase, Tàpies found his feet with an abstract style that matured in the 1950s, with underlying messages and themes signalled by the inclusion of everyday objects and symbols on the canvas. He has also continually experimented with unusual materials, like oil paint mixed with crushed marble, or employing sand, cloth or straw in his collages. Tàpies divides opinion, and you're either going to love or hate the gallery: changing exhibitions focus on selections of Tàpies' life's work, while three or four other exhibitions a year highlight works and installations by other contemporary artists.

Museu Egipci de Barcelona

C/de València 284 ☎ 934 880 188, ⓦ www.fundclos.com. Mon–Sat 10am–8pm, Sun 10am–2pm. €7. Barcelona's Egyptian Museum is an exceptional private collection of artefacts from ancient Egypt, ranging from the earliest kingdoms to the era of Cleopatra. It was founded by hotelier Jordi Clos – whose *Hotel Claris*, a block away, still has its own private museum for guests – and displays a remarkable gathering of over six hundred objects, from amulets to sarcophagi. The emphasis is on the shape and character of Egyptian society, and visitors are given a hugely detailed English-language guidebook covering every item. But the real pleasure here is a serendipitous wander, turning up items like a wood-and-leather bed of the First and Second Dynasties (2920–2649 BC), some examples of cat mummies of the Late Period (715–332 BC) or a rare figurine of a spoonbill (ibis) representing an Egyptian god. There are temporary exhibitions, a library and a good book and gift shop on the lower floor, as well as a terrace café upstairs. The museum also hosts a full programme of study sessions, children's activities and evening events – the reception desk or website can provide details.

Fundació Francisco Godia

C/de València 284 ☎ 932 723 180. Mon & Wed–Sat 10am–2pm & 4–7pm, Sun 10am–2pm. €4.50. The building next door to the Egyptian Museum houses the private art collection of aesthete and 1950s racing driver Francisco Godia. On the face of it, hardly a must-see, but in many ways it serves as a taster for the huge MNAC collections of medieval art, ceramics and modern Catalan art, while its small size makes it immediately more accessible. In hushed rooms, where the only sound is the hum of the air conditioning, lie selected Romanesque carvings, Gothic altarpieces and *modernista* and *noucentista* paintings, combined with a varied selection of ceramics from most of the historically important production centres in Spain. Not all of the collection can be shown at any one time, so pieces are rotated on occasion, while special exhibitions also run in tandem, to which there's usually no extra charge.

La Pedrera

Pg. de Gràcia 92, entrance on c/Provença ☎ 902 400 973, ⓦ www .fundaciocaixacatalunya.org. March–Oct daily 9am–8pm, Nov–Feb daily 9am–6.30pm. €8. La Pedrera de Nit, late June & July only, Fri & Sat 9–11.30pm; €12, advance sales from TelEntrada ☎ 902 101 212, ⓦ www .telentrada.com. Antoni Gaudí's weird apartment building at the top of Passeig de Gràcia is simply not to be missed – though you can expect queues whenever you visit. Built as the Casa Milà between 1905 and 1911 – but popularly known as La Pedrera, "the stone quarry" – its rippled facade, curving around the street corner in one smooth sweep, is said to have been inspired by the mountain of Montserrat, while the apartments themselves, whose balconies of tangled metal drip over the facade, resemble eroded cave dwellings. Indeed, there's not a straight line to be seen – hence the contemporary joke that the new tenants would only be able to keep snakes as pets. The self-guided visit includes a trip up to the extraordinary terrace to see at close quarters the enigmatic chimneys, as well as an excellent exhibition about Gaudí's life and work displayed under the brick arches of the attic. "El Pis" on the building's fourth floor recreates the design and style of a *modernista*-era bourgeois apartment. Perhaps the best experience of all is *La Pedrera de Nit*, when you can enjoy the rooftop and night-time cityscape with a complimentary *cava* and music – advance booking is essential.

La Pedrera is still split into private apartments and is administered by the Fundació Caixa de Catalunya. Through the grand main entrance of the building you can access the Fundació's first-floor **exhibition hall** (daily 10am–8pm; free; guided visits Mon–Fri at 6pm), which hosts temporary art shows of works by major international artists.

▼ PERIOD FURNITURE, LA PEDRERA

▲ PALAU ROBERT

Vinçon

Entrances at Pg. de Gràcia 96, c/Provença 273 and c/Pau Claris 175 ☎ 932 156 050, ⓦ www.vincon. com. Mon–Sat 10am–8.30pm. Right next to La Pedrera, the Vinçon store emerged in the 1960s as the country's pre-eminent purveyor of furniture and design. Pioneered by Fernando Amat, the "Spanish Terence Conran", the shop is filled to the brim with stylish and original household items. Apart from checking out the extraordinary furniture floor, which gives access to a terrace with views of La Pedrera, try and make time for *La Sala Vinçon* (open same hours as the store). This is Vinçon's exhibition hall and art gallery, which puts on shows of graphic and industrial design and contemporary furniture.

Palau Robert

Pg. de Gràcia 107 ☎ 932 388 091 or ☎ 012, ⓦ www.gencat.net/probert. Mon–Sat 10am–7pm, Sun 10am–2.30pm. Free. The information centre for the region of Catalunya hosts regularly changing exhibitions on all matters Catalan, from art to business. There are several exhibition spaces, both inside the main palace – built as a typical aristocratic residence in 1903 – and in the old coach house. The centre is also an important concert venue for recitals and orchestras, while the pretty gardens around the back are a popular meeting point for local nannies and their charges.

Casa Àsia

Avgda. Diagonal 373 ☎ 932 837 337, ⓦ www.casaasia.es. Tues–Sat 10am–8pm, Sun 10am–2pm. Free. Café open Mon–Sat 9am–9pm. The almost Gothic Palau Quadras (a Josep Puig i Cadafalch work of 1904) has a new lease of life as a cultural and arts centre for Asia and the Pacific Region. You can check the website for current exhibitions (usually free), but it's always worth calling in anyway as you pass, simply for a chance to see inside. There's a good café on the ground floor, a multimedia library and, best of all, the Jardi d'Orient roof terrace – take the elevator up for views of the neighbouring Casa de les Punxes and the Sagrada Família towers rising behind.

Casa de les Punxes

Avgda. Diagonal 416–420. No public access. Architect Josep Puig i Cadafalch's largest work, the soaring Casa Terrades, is more usually known as the Casa de les Punxes ("House of Spikes") because of its red-tiled turrets and steep gables. Built in 1903 for three sisters, and converted from three separate houses spreading around an entire corner of a block, the crenellated structure is almost northern European in style, reminiscent of a Gothic castle.

Palau Montaner

C/de Mallorca 278 ☎933 177 652, ⓦwww.rutadelmodernisme.com. Guided visits: Sat at 10.30am in English, plus 11.30am & 12.30pm, and Sun at 10.30am, 11.30am & 12.30pm in Spanish/Catalan. €5.

The Palau Montaner (1896) was built for a member of the Montaner i Simon publishing family – after the original architect quit, the *modernista* architect Lluís Domènech i Montaner took over halfway through construction, and the top half of the facade is clearly more elaborate than the lower part. Meanwhile, the period's most celebrated craftsmen were set to work on the interior, which sports rich mosaic floors, painted glass, carved woodwork and a monumental staircase. The building is now the seat of the Madrid government's delegation to Catalunya, but there are tours at the weekend which explain something of the house's history and show you the public rooms, grand dining room and courtyard. It's unusual to be able to get inside a private *modernista* house of the period, so it's definitely worth the effort.

Mercat de la Concepció

Between c/de Valencia and c/d'Aragó ☎934 575 329, ⓦwww.laconcepcio .com. Mon 8am–3pm, Tues–Fri 8am–8pm, Sat 8am–4pm; July & Aug closes at 3pm. Concepció market was inaugurated in

▼ CASA DE LES PUNXES

1888, its iron-and-glass tram-shed structure reminiscent of others in the city. Flowers, shrubs, trees and plants are a Concepció speciality (the florists on c/Valencia are open 24 hours a day), and there are a couple of good snack bars inside the market and a few outdoor cafés to the side. The market takes its name from the nearby church of **La Concepció** (entrance on c/Roger de Llúria), whose quiet cloister is a surprising haven of slender columns and orange trees. This was part of a fifteenth-century Gothic convent that once stood in the old town. It was abandoned in the early nineteenth century and then transferred here brick by brick in the 1870s, along with the Romanesque belfry from another old-town church.

Shops

Antonio Miró

C/Consell de Cent 349 ☎ 934 870 670, ⓦ www.antoniomiro.es. The showcase for Barcelona's most innovative designer, Antonio Miró, always good for classy men's suits in particular.

Armand Basi

Pg. de Gràcia 49 ☎ 932 151 421, outlets also at L'Illa and El Corte Inglés, ⓦ www.armandbasi.com. Colourful men's and women's clothes, jackets and jeans from the hot Spanish designer. There's also a full range of branded accessories – watches to fragrances – though the must-have items are the designer table- and kitchenware created with superchef Ferran Adrià.

Casa del Llibre

Pg. de Gràcia 62 ☎ 932 723 840, ⓦ www.casadellibro.com. This is Barcelona's biggest book emporium, strong on literature, humanities and travel, with lots of English-language titles and Catalan literature in translation.

Colmado Quilez

Rambla de Catalunya 63 ☎ 932 152 356. A dying breed now, this classic Catalan grocery has windows and shelves piled high with tins, preserves, bottles, jars and packets, plus a groaning *xarcuteria* counter.

Favorita

C/Mallorca 291 ☎ 934 765 721, ⓦ www.mueblesfavorita.com. Closed 3 weeks in Aug, also closed Sat July & Aug. A design showroom at the cutting edge of Barcelona style. The building (Casa Thomas) is by Domènech i Montaner, the interior filled with the very latest in furniture and household design.

Joaquín Berao

Rambla de Catalunya 74 ☎ 932 150 091, ⓦ www.joaquinberao.com. Avant-garde jewellery by a Madrid designer in a beautifully presented shop.

Mandarina Duck

Pg. de Gràcia 44 ☎ 932 720 364. Funky, colourful travel bags, backpacks, handbags and other carriers.

Mango

Pg. de Gràcia 8–10 ☎ 934 121 599 and Pg. de Gràcia 65 ☎ 932 157 530, plus others, ⓦ www.mango.com. Now available worldwide, Barcelona is where high-street fashion chain *Mango* began (and prices here are cheaper than in North America and other European countries). For last season's gear at unbeatable prices, make a beeline for Mango Outlet (c/Girona 37).

Muxart

C/Rosselló 230 ☎934 881 064,
and Rambla de Catalunya 47
☎934 677 423, ⓦwww.muxart
.com. Barcelona's top-class
shoe designer, selling gorgeous
footwear and handbags for men
and women.

Purificacion Garcia

Pg. de Gràcia 21 ☎934 872 292,
ⓦwww.purificaciongarcia.es. A
designer with real flair and an
eye for fabrics – Garcia's first
job was in a textile factory.
She's also designed clothes
for films, theatre and TV, and
her costumes were seen at
the opening ceremony of
the Barcelona Olympics. The
eponymous shop's a beauty,
with the more casual items
and accessories not particularly
stratospherically priced.

Zara

Pg. de Gràcia 16 ☎933 187 675,
Rambla de Catalunya 67 ☎932 160
868, plus others, ⓦwww.zara.com.
Trendy but cheap seasonal
fashion for men, women and
children from the Spanish chain.
The Passeig de Gràcia branch is
the flagship store.

Cafés

Forn de Sant Jaume

Rambla de Catalunya 50 ☎932 160
229. Mon–Sat 9am–9pm. Glittering
windows piled high with goodies
from this classic old *patisseria* and
bomboneria – croissants, cakes and
sweets, either to take away or eat
at the adjacent café.

Laie Llibreria Café

C/Pau Claris 85 ☎933 027 310,
ⓦwww.laie.es. Mon 9am–9pm,
Tues–Sat 9am–1am. The city's first
and best bookshop-café and a
great place to drop in on any
time. The buffet breakfast spread
is popular, and there are set
lunch and dinner deals, *à la carte*
dining, and magazines to browse.

Valor

Rambla de Catalunya 46 ☎934 876
246. Mon–Thurs 8.30am–1pm &
3.30–11pm, Fri–Sun 9am–midnight.
Ornate uptown chocolate
specialist, serving the gentlefolk
since 1881. A warming hot choc
and *xurros* (doughnut sticks)
sends you happily on your way
on a chilly morning.

Restaurants and tapas bars

La Bodegueta

Rambla Catalunya 100 ☎932 154 894.
Daily 8am–2am; closed mornings in
Aug. Long-established basement
bodega with *cava* and wine
by the glass, as well as good
ham, cheese, anchovies and
other tapas to soak it all up. In

Dine in style

For some of the city's fanciest Michelin-starred dining, head for the hotels. Currently making waves is Joan Roca's **Moo**, at the über-fashionable *Hotel Omm*,
while Martín Berasategui brings his highly rated Basque style to **Lasarte**, in the
Condes de Barcelona. At the glam waterfront *Arts Barcelona* it's Madrid-based chef
Sergi Arola lending his name to the designer tapas place **Arola**. Add Carles Gaig's
upscale Catalan restaurant **Gaig** into the mix (*Hotel Cram*), plus Ramon Freixa's
Actual (*Grand Hotel Central*), and you've got a cross section of some of the city's
most exciting cooking, right on the premises.

summer you can sit outside at the *rambla* tables.

Casa Calvet

C/de Casp 48 ☎ 934 124 012. Mon–Sat 1–3.30pm & 8.30–11.30pm. The restaurant takes its name from the building – nothing less than Antoni Gaudí's earliest commissioned town house, erected for a prominent local textile family in 1899. Although fairly conventional in style on the outside, the interior is a marvel of decoration, making for a truly glam night out. A seasonally changing, modern Catalan menu runs the gamut from simple (shrimp with home-made pasta and parmesan) to elaborate (duck livers with a balsamic vinegar reduction), and the desserts – some of which you have to order on arrival – are an artwork in themselves. From around €60; reservations advised.

Ciudad Condal

Rambla de Catalunya 18 ☎ 933 181 997. Daily 7.30am–1.30am. Breakfast sees the bar groan under the weight of a dozen types of crispy baguette sandwich, piled high on platters, supplemented by a cabinet of croissants and pastries, while the daily changing tapas selection ranges far and wide – *patatas bravas* to octopus. It's always reliable, and you can sit at the bar, in the rear dining room or on the summer terrace.

El Japonés

Ptge. de la Concepció 2 ☎ 934 872 592, ⊛ www.eljaponesdeltragaluz .com. Mon–Thurs & Sun 1.30–4pm & 8.30pm–midnight, Fri & Sat 1.30–4pm & 8pm–1am. Designer style – gunmetal grey interior, black-clad staff, sharp service – at moderate prices gives this minimalist Japanese restaurant the edge over its more traditional rivals. Tick your choices from the long menu and hand it to the waiter; average meal cost is around €20–25 a head.

El Mussol

C/Aragó 261 ☎ 934 876 151; branch at c/de Casp 19 ☎ 933 017 610. Mon–Sat 1pm–1am, Sun 1–4pm & 8pm–midnight. Big rustic dinner, known for their meat and vegetables *a la brasa* (on the grill), most of which run between €5 and €11. *Calçots* (big spring onions) are a spring

▼ UPTOWN TAPAS BAR

speciality, while snails (*cargols*) and wild mushrooms are on the menu all year round. It opens early for sandwich-and-croissant breakfasts for city workers.

O'Nabo de Lugo

C/de Pau Claris 169 ☎ 932 153 047. Mon–Sat 1–4pm & 8.30pm–midnight. *À la carte* meals in this renowned Galician seafood restaurant can easily top €60, but the budget-conscious can enjoy a three-course lunch at a fraction of the price. Thick, meaty broth usually figures, and simple standards like *botifarra* (Catalan sausage) and potatoes – for more choice (and for some fish), trade up to the €18 *menú especial*, still a pretty good deal.

TapaÇ24

C/Diputació 269 ☎ 934 880 977, ⓦ www.carlesabellan.com. Daily 12.30pm–midnight. Carles Abellan, king of pared-down designer cuisine at his restaurant *Comerç 24*, offers a simpler tapas menu at this retro basement bar-diner. There's a reassuringly traditional feel that's echoed in the menu – *patatas bravas*, Andalucian-style fried fish, *bombas* (meatballs), *chorizo* sausage and eggs. But the kitchen updates the classics too, so there's also *calamares romana* (fried squid) dyed black with squid ink or a burger with *foie gras*. Most tapas cost €6–14. A small streetside terrace fills quickly; downstairs there's a rush and bustle, and queues at night.

Thai Gardens

C/Diputació 273 ☎ 934 879 898. Daily 1.30–4pm & 8.30pm–midnight, until 1am at weekends. Barcelona's favourite Thai restaurant is an over-the-top experience of fountains and gilded elephants. Authenticity loses its way here

and there, but the weekday lunch deal is popular, while an English-language menu highlights things like a creamy prawn and vegetable curry or fiery lamb strips cooked in Thai basil. Most dishes are in the €7–17 range.

Tragaluz

Ptge. de la Concepció 5 ☎ 934 870 621, ⓦ www.grupotragaluz.com/tragaluz. Daily 1.30–4pm & 8.30pm–midnight, until 1am Thurs–Sat. Attracts beautiful people by the score, and the classy Mediterranean-with-knobs-on cooking, served under a glass roof (*tragaluz* means "skylight"), doesn't disappoint. Mains cost from €16–25, though cheaper eats are served downstairs courtesy of the *Tragarapid* menu (served daily 1pm–midnight), where things like blinis, fajitas or a club sandwich cater for those fresh off the *modernista* trail (La Pedrera is just across the way).

Bars

Les Gens Que J'aime

C/Valencia 286 ☎ 932 156 879. Daily 7pm–2.30am. It takes your eyes a while to adjust as you descend into the intimate *fin-de-siècle* interior of red velvet seats, dimmed lights and soulful mood music. As a refuge from the club scene, it's very pleasant for a relaxing drink.

Clubs

Barcelona City Hall

Rambla de Catalunya 2–4 ☎ 932 380 722, ⓦ www.ottozutz.com. Daily midnight–6am. Very popular dance joint – the handy location helps – which hosts some of the most varied club nights around, from 80s revival to electro.

Sagrada Família and Glòries

The easternmost reaches of the Eixample are dominated by the one building that is an essential stop on any visit to Barcelona – Antoni Gaudí's great church of the Sagrada Família. In many ways this has become a kind of symbol for the city, representing the glory of Catalan design and endeavour. Most visitors make a special journey out by metro to see the church and then head straight back into the centre, but it's worth diverting the few blocks south to the area known as Glòries for a further set of attractions, including the city's biggest flea market and Catalunya's flagship national theatre building.

Sagrada Familia

C/Mallorca 401, entrance on c/de la Marina ☎ 932 073 031, ⓦ www .sagradafamilia.org. Daily: April–Sept 9am–8pm; Oct–March 9am–6pm. €8, or €11.50 including guided tour; combination ticket with Casa Museu Gaudí at Parc Güell €9.

The overpowering church of the Sagrada Família ("Sacred Family") occupies an entire city block between c/de Mallorca and c/de Provença – the metro drops you right outside. Begun in 1882 on a modest scale, the project changed the minute that 31-year-old architect Antoni Gaudí took charge in 1884 – he saw in the Sagrada Família an opportunity to reflect his own deepening spiritual feelings. Gaudí spent the rest of his life working on the church and was adapting the plans ceaselessly right up to his untimely death. Run over by a tram on June 7, 1926, his death was treated as a Catalan national disaster, and all of Barcelona turned out for his funeral procession.

By the time of Gaudí's death only one facade of the Sagrada Família was complete. Although the building survived the Civil War, Gaudí's plans and models were destroyed in 1936 by the anarchists, who regarded the church as a conservative religious relic. Work restarted in the late 1950s amid great controversy, with some maintaining that the Sagrada Família should be left incomplete as a memorial to Gaudí, others that the architect intended it to be the work of several generations. As the project draws inexorably towards realization (current projections predict a completion date of around 2017), a fresh set of arguments has arisen as to how to wrap the whole thing up – whether to continue with the original grandiose design or to go for a quicker but more modest alternative.

Gaudí's plan was to build a church capable of seating over 10,000 people. Eight spires – symbolic of the apostles – rise to over 100m: Gaudí planned

to build four more and to add
a 170-metre tower topped
with a lamb (representing Jesus)
over the transept. A precise
symbolism also pervades the
facades, each of which is divided
into three porches devoted to
faith, hope and charity. Gaudí
made extensive use of human,
plant and animal models in
order to produce exactly the
likenesses he sought for the
building's sculptural groups.

In reality the place looks
like a giant building site, but
a recognizable church interior
is starting to take shape, and
if you take the **elevator** (€2)
up one of the towers around
the rose window, you'll be
rewarded by partial views of the
city through an extraordinary
jumble of latticed stonework,
ceramic decoration, carved
buttresses and sculpture. There's
also access to the crypt, where
a small museum (opening times
as for the church) traces Gaudí's
career through the history of the
church. Models, sketches and
photographs help to make some
sense of the continuing project,
and you can view the sculptors
and model-makers at work.

The **guided tours** run hourly
between April and October,
reduced to four daily from
Friday to Monday between
November and March.

Hospital de la Santa Creu i de Sant Pau

Centre del Modernisme, c/de Sant
Antoni Maria Claret 167 ☏ 933 177
652, ⓦ www.rutadelmodernisme.com.
Centre open daily 10am–2pm, free.
Tours daily at 10.15am and 12.15pm
in English, plus others in Spanish/
Catalan, €5. Lluís Domènech i
Montaner's innovative public
hospital (1901–10) is possibly
the one building that can touch
the Sagrada Família for harmony,
size and inventiveness. Craftsmen
adorned every centimetre with
sculpture, mosaics, stained glass
and ironwork, while much of
the actual business of running
a hospital was hidden away in
underground corridors, which
connect the buildings together.
The *modernista* hospital buildings
are now deemed to have served
their purpose; behind them
spreads the high-tech central
block of the new hospital. The
pavilions have been turned
over to educational and cultural

PLACES

Sagrada Família and Glòries

▼ SAGRADA FAMÍLIA

SAGRADA FAMILIA & GLÒRIES

CAFÉS, TAPAS & RESTAURANTS
Alkimia	1
Bar Gaudí	3
Gorria	4
Piazzenza	2

SHOPS
Centre Comercial
Barcelona Glòries **a**

ACCOMMODATION
Hotel Eurostars Gaudí **A**

use (a Museum of Medicine is mooted), and include the Centre del Modernisme, where you can find out about and buy the city's **Ruta del Modernisme** package. You can also sign up here for informative guided tours of the complex, which can tell you more about the 600-year history of the hospital.

▲ MOSAIC AT HOSPITAL DE LA SANTA CREU I DE SANT PAU

Casa Macaya

Pg. de Sant Joan 108. Just four blocks from the Sagrada Família, Josep Puig i Cadafalch's palatial Casa Macaya (1898–1900) is a superbly ornamental town house with a Gothic-inspired courtyard and canopied staircase from which griffins spring. It's rich in imaginative exterior carvings by craftsman Eusebi Arnau, who included an angel holding a camera and a tiny figure riding a bicycle among the more orthodox medieval symbols. The house is now in use as an exhibition space.

Els Encants

C/Dos de Maig ☎ 932 463 030, ⓦ www.encantsbcn.com. Mon, Wed, Fri & Sat 9am–6pm; plus Dec 1–Jan 5 Sun 9am–3pm. An absolute must for flea-market addicts, the open-air Els Encants – properly the Mercat Fira de Bellcaire – takes up the entire

block below c/Consell de Cent. You name it, you can buy it: old sewing machines, cheese graters, photograph albums, cutlery, lawnmowers, piles of clothes, shoes and CDs, antiques, furniture and out-and-out junk. Go in the morning to see it at its best. Haggling is *de rigueur*, but you're up against the experts.

Plaça de les Glòries Catalanes

Barcelona's major avenues all meet at the glorified traffic-circle named for and dedicated to the Catalan "glories", from architecture to literature. Glòries, as it's known, is at the centre of the city's latest wave of regeneration. By 2012, the traffic is to be tunnelled underground, thus opening up a grand pedestrianized park which will contain a cultural centre to house the city's municipal museum collections. Meanwhile, signature building on the roundabout is Jean Nouvel's cigar-shaped **Torre Agbar**, a remarkable aluminium-and-glass tower inspired by the rocky protuberances of Montserrat. At 142m high, it's the third-largest building in the city. **Avinguda Diagonal** shoots off to the southeast, with its tram service running down to the Diagonal Mar district, while across Gran Via de

▼ CASA MACAYA

Casa Macaya

les Corts Catalanes the play and park areas of **Parc del Clot** show what can be done in an urban setting within the remains of a razed factory site.

Teatre Nacional de Catalunya

Pl. de les Arts 1 ☎ 933 065 700, ⓦ www.tnc.es. Box office open Tues–Fri 3–8pm, Sat 3–9.30pm, Sun 3–6pm. Catalunya's National Theatre was specifically conceived as a venue to promote Catalan productions, and features a repertory programme of translated classics (such as Shakespeare in Catalan), original works and productions by guest companies from elsewhere in Europe. The building itself makes a dramatic statement, designed by Ricardo Bofill and presenting the neighbourhood with a soaring glass box encased within a Greek temple on a raised dais, surrounded by manicured lawns. There are guided building and backstage **tours** for anyone interested in learning more (currently Tues & Thurs; €3; reservations required).

L'Auditori

C/Lepant 150 ☎ 932 479 300, ⓦ www.auditori.org. Museu de la Música, c/Padilla 155 ☎ 932 563 650, ⓦ www.museumusicabcn.cat. Mon & Wed–Fri 11am–9pm, Sat, Sun & hols 10am–7pm. €4, first Sun of the month free. The city's main contemporary concert hall, built in 1999, is home to the Orquestra Simfònica de Barcelona i Nacional de Catalunya (OBC), whose weekend concert season runs from September to May. Many other concerts take place here year-round, including chamber pieces, music for children and performances under the auspices of the annual Contemporary Music Festival. The city's music museum is based here as well, presenting a unique collection of historic instruments plus all sorts of music-related exhibitions, activities and events.

Plaza de Toros Monumental and Museo Taurino

Gran Via de les Corts Catalanes 749 ☎ 932 455 804. Museum: Mon–Sat 10.30am–2pm & 4–7pm, Sun 11am–1pm; €4. Bullfights: April–Sept, usually Sun at 7pm; €20–100. The city's only surviving bullring provides a taste of Andalucia with its brick facade, Moorish egg-shaped domes, polychromatic

▲ PLAZA DE TOROS MONUMENTAL AND MUSEO TAURINO

decoration and *sol y sombra* ("sun and shade") seating sections. It's not a pastime with much of a following in Barcelona, and as the city authorities are minded to ban bullfighting altogether, its days may be numbered – tellingly, the ring is one part of the city where not a word of Catalan is seen. Bullfight costumes, posters, photographs and the stuffed heads of vanquished bulls occupy the small museum (enter at corner with c/de la Marina), while an overhead walkway outside the ring provides a view into the bull pens.

Shops

Centre Comercial Barcelona Glòries

Avgda. Diagonal 208, at Pl. de les Glòries Catalanes ☎ 934 860 404, ⓦ www.lesglories.com. Huge 230-store mall with all the national high-street fashion names (H&M, Zara, Bershka, Mango) as well as children's wear, toys and games, ice-cream parlours, a dozen bars, cafés and restaurants and a seven-screen cinema complex.

Cafés

Bar Gaudí

Mercat de la Sagrada Família, c/de Padilla 255; no phone. Tues–Thurs 7am–2pm & 5.30–8.30pm, Fri 7am–8.30pm, Sat 7am–3pm. Only two blocks east of the Sagrada Família – and not a tourist in sight. Browse the stalls and pick up your picnic lunch, or make straight for the stand-up market bar, which has pastries, sandwiches and tapas at local prices, and an internal courtyard with a small children's playground.

Restaurants and tapas bars

Alkimia

C/Indústria 79 ☎ 932 076 115. Mon–Fri 1.30–3.30pm & 8.30–11pm; closed 2 weeks in Aug. Ask Barcelona foodies which is the best Catalan new-wave restaurant in town and once they've all stopped bickering, this is the one they'll probably plump for. "Alchemy" is what's promised by the name, and that's what chef Jordi Vilà delivers in bitingly minimalist style – think *pa amb tomàquet* (Catalan bread rubbed with tomato and olive oil), only liquidized and served in a shot glass. It's a Michelin-starred operation, so reservations are vital and the bill might reach €100 a head.

Gorría

C/de la Diputacio 421 ☎ 932 451 164, ⓦ www.restaurantegorria.com. Mon–Sat 1–3.30pm & 9–11.30pm; closed Aug & Easter. This elegant family-owned restaurant serves the finest seasonal Basque cuisine, like *pochas de Sanguesa* (a sort of white-bean stew), clams and hake in *salsa verde*, or wood-grilled lamb and suckling pig. Prices are on the high side (around €50 a head), but this is traditional regional Spanish cooking of the highest order.

Piazzenza

Avgda. Gaudí 27–29 ☎ 934 363 817. Daily 1pm–1am; closed 2 weeks in Aug. A reliable standby just five minutes' walk from the Sagrada Família. There are tapas, drinks and pizzas, served outdoors in summer, and you can eat for around €15. It's a pretty buzzy place at night, just as popular with locals as tourists.

Esquerra de l'Eixample

The long streets west of Rambla de Catalunya as far as Barcelona Sants train station – making up the Esquerra de l'Eixample – are perhaps the least visited on any city sightseeing trip. With all the major architectural highlights found on the Eixample's eastern (or right-hand) side, the Esquerra (left-hand side) was intended by its nineteenth-century planners for public buildings and institutions, many of which still stand. However, the Esquerra does have its moments of interest – not least in an eye-catching public park or two – while it's here that some of the city's best bars and clubs are found, particularly in the gay-friendly streets of the so-called Gaixample district, near the university.

Universitat de Barcelona

Gran Via de les Corts Catalanes 585, at Pl. de la Universitat. Built in the 1860s, the Neoclassical university building is now mainly used for ceremonies and administration purposes, but no one minds if you stroll through the main doors. There's usually an exhibition in the echoing main hall, while beyond lie two fine arcaded courtyards and extensive gardens. The traditional student meeting point is the *Bar Estudiantil*, outside in Plaça Universitat, where you can usually grab a pavement table.

▼ UNIVERSITY CLOISTERS

Escola Industrial

Corner of c/del Comte d'Urgell and c/del Rossello. The Battló textile mill underwent major refurbishment in 1908 to emerge as the Escola Industrial. It occupies four entire Eixample blocks, with later academic buildings added in the 1920s, including a chapel by Joan Rubió i Bellvér, who worked with Antoni Gaudí. Students usually fill the courtyards, and you're free to take a stroll through to view the highly decorative buildings.

Museu i Centre d'Estudis de l'Esport

C/de Buenos Aires 56–58 ☎ 934 192 232. June to mid-Sept Mon–Fri 8am–3pm, otherwise Mon–Fri 10am–2pm & 3–7pm. Free. Built as the Casa Companys in 1911 by Josep Puig

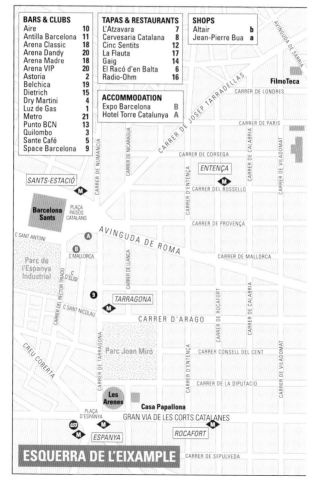

BARS & CLUBS	
Aire	10
Antilla Barcelona	11
Arena Classic	18
Arena Dandy	20
Arena Madre	18
Arena VIP	20
Astoria	2
Belchica	19
Dietrich	15
Dry Martini	4
Luz de Gas	1
Metro	21
Punto BCN	13
Quilombo	3
Sante Café	5
Space Barcelona	9

TAPAS & RESTAURANTS	
L'Atzavara	7
Cervesaria Catalana	8
Cinc Sentits	12
La Flauta	17
Gaig	14
El Racó d'en Balta	6
Radio-Ohm	16

SHOPS	
Altair	b
Jean-Pierre Bua	a

ACCOMMODATION	
Expo Barcelona	B
Hotel Torre Catalunya	A

FilmoTeca

AVINGUDA DE SARRIA
CARRER DE LONDRES
CARRER DE JOSEP TARRADELLAS
CARRER DE PARIS
SANTS-ESTACIÓ
CARRER DE NICARAGUA
CARRER DE NUMANCIA
CARRER DE CORSEGA
ENTENÇA
CARRER D'ENTENÇA
CARRER DE CALABRIA
CARRER DE VILADOMAT
CARRER DEL ROSSELLO
Barcelona Sants
PLAÇA PAÏSOS CATALANS
CARRER DE PROVENÇA
C SANT ANTONI
AVINGUDA DE ROMA
C MALLORCA
CARRER DE MALLORCA
Parc de l'Espanya Industrial
C D'ELISI
CARRER DE LLANÇA
CARRER DE ROCAFORT
CARRER DE CALABRIA
CARRER DEL RECTOR TRIADO
C SANT NICOLAU
TARRAGONA
CARRER D'ARAGO
CREU COBERTA
CARRER DE TARRAGONA
Parc Joan Miró
CARRER D'ENTENÇA
CARRER CONSELL DEL CENT
CARRER DE VILADOMAT
Les Arenes
Casa Papallona
CARRER DE LA DIPUTACIO
PLAÇA D'ESPANYA
GRAN VIA DE LES CORTS CATALANES
ESPANYA
ROCAFORT
CARRER DE SEPULVEDA

ESQUERRA DE L'EIXAMPLE

i Cadafalch, the little cream-coloured house contains probably the most unassuming sporting "Hall of Fame" found anywhere in the world. In a couple of quiet, wood-panelled rooms photographs of 1920s Catalan rally drivers and footballers are displayed alongside a varied collection of memorabilia, from a signed waterpolo ball used in the 1992 Olympics to Everest

mountaineer Carles Vâlles' ice pick.

FilmoTeca

Avgda. de Sarrià 33 ☎934 107 590, ⓦwww.gencat.cat/cultura/icic /filmoteca. Run by the Catalan government, the *FilmoTeca* has an excellent cinema programme, showing three or four different films (often foreign, and usually in their original language,

marked "V.O.") every day.
There's a children's club (*sessió
infantil*) on Sunday, and a decent
café attached to the cinema.
Tickets are €2.70, or you can
buy a discounted pass for €18
allowing entry to ten films. A
new cinema building is being
constructed in the Raval for
the FilmoTeca, but for the time
being it will still be based at
Avinguda de Sarrià.

Parc de l'Espanya Industrial

C/de Sant Antoni. Daily 10am–dusk.
Basque architect Luis Peña
Ganchegui's urban park lies a
two-minute walk around the
southern side of Barcelona
Sants station. Built on the site
of an old textile factory, it has a
line of red-and-yellow-striped
concrete lighthouses at the top
of glaring white steps with an
incongruously classical Neptune
in the water below. Altogether,
six sculptors are represented here,
and, along with the boating lake,
café kiosk, playground and sports
facilities provided, the park takes
a decent stab at reconciling local
interests with the mundane
nature of the surroundings.

Parc Joan Miró

C/de Tarragona. Daily 10am–dusk. Parc
Joan Miró was laid out on the
site of the nineteenth-century
municipal slaughterhouse. It

features a bare, raised piazza
whose only feature is Joan
Miró's gigantic mosaic sculpture
Dona i Ocell ("Woman and
Bird"), towering above a shallow
reflecting pool. The rear of the
park is given over to games areas
and landscaped sections of palms
and firs, with a kiosk café and
some outdoor tables found in
among the trees. The children's
playground here is one of the
best in the city, with a climbing
frame and aerial runway as well
as swings and slides.

Les Arenes

Pl. d'Espanya. The traditional
bullring backing Parc Joan
Miró is undergoing a massive
Richard Rogers-inspired refit,
to convert it into a leisure and
retail complex with enormous
roof terrace, while retaining
the circular Moorish facade of
1900. Also spared the wrecker's
ball is the six-storey *modernista*
Casa Papallona (1912), on the
eastern side of Les Arenes on
c/de Llança. It's one of the city's
favourite house facades, crowned
by a huge ceramic butterfly.

Shops

Altaïr

Gran Via de les Corts Catalanes 616
☎ 933 427 171, ⊛ www.altair.es.

There's a massive selection
of travel books, guides,
maps and world music in
Barcelona's travel superstore,
plus a programme of travel-
related talks and exhibitions.

Jean-Pierre Bua

Avgda. Diagonal 469 ☎ 934 397
100, ⊛ www.jeanpierrebua
.com. The city's high
temple for fashion victims:
a postmodern shrine for
Yamamoto, Gaultier,

▼ ALTAÏR BOOKSHOP

Miyake, Galliano, McQueen, McCartney, Westwood, Miró and other international stars.

Restaurants and tapas bars

L'Atzavara

C/Muntaner 109 ☎934 545 925. Mon–Sat 1–4pm. This lunch-only spot is a bit more gourmet than many similar vegetarian places. For a fixed price you choose from half a dozen starters and soups, and three or four mains and puds, and even with drinks and coffee it should come to well under €15.

Cervesaria Catalana

C/Mallorca 236 ☎932 160 368. Daily 9am–1am. A place that is serious about its tapas and beer – the counters are piled high, supplemented by a blackboard list of daily specials, while the walls are lined with bottled brews from around the world.

Cinc Sentits

C/Aribau 58 ☎933 239 490, ⓦwww .cincsentits.com. Mon 1.30–3.30pm, Tues–Sat 1.30–3.30pm & 8.30–11pm. Dishes are assembled with flair in this renowned contemporary "tasting kitchen", and though some find the whole experience a bit overly formal there's no doubting the skill in the "Five Senses" kitchen. Wild fish with black-olive compote and citrus caramel is a typical offering, with most mains costing €20–25, though various tasting menus (from €65) are the best way to get the measure of the place.

La Flauta

C/d'Aribau 23 ☎933 237 038. Mon–Sat 8am–1am. One of the city's best-value lunch menus sees diners queuing for tables early – get there before 2pm to avoid the rush. It's a handsome bar-restaurant of dark wood and deep colours, and, while the name recognizes the house speciality gourmet sandwiches (a *flauta* is a crispy baguette), there's also tapas served all day and a changing *menú del dia* that follows the seasons.

Gaig

C/Aragó 214 ☎934 291 017, ⓦwww .restaurantgaig.com. Mon 9–11pm, Tues–Sat 1–3.30pm & 9–11pm; closed 3 weeks in Aug. The Gaig family restaurant was first founded in 1869 out in the Horta neighbourhood, but under fourth-generation family member, Carles Gaig, it has now found a sleek new downtown home at the *Hotel Cram*. It's had a towering reputation for years for quality reinterpretations of traditional Catalan dishes, so a typical *arròs* (rice) dish might combine *foie gras*, endive and citrus. When starters can cost €35, and the *menu degustació* is €90, you're talking about a true special-occasion place, and reservations are essential.

El Racó d'en Balta

C/Aribau 125 ☎934 531 044, ⓦwww.racodenbalta.com. Mon–Thurs 1–3.45pm & 9–11pm, Fri 1–3.45pm & 9–11.30pm, Sat 9–11.30pm; closed 1 week in Jan, 3 weeks in Aug and Easter. This a very funky place to eat, with a vibrant colour- and sculpture-splashed interior that pretty much defies description. The weekday lunch is a good deal, otherwise you can eat for around €25 from a Mediterranean market-led menu; at night the local hipsters lend the bar a certain style.

▲ BAR ESTUDIANTIL

Radio-Ohm

C/Muntaner 55 ☎ 934 513 609.
Mon–Sat 1–4pm & 9pm–midnight. A
few shops in this old electrical
retailers' district still survive
– this one's been given a new
lease of life as a Mediterranean-
fusion restaurant, but retains a
few nods to its old trade in the
lighting and decor. The set lunch
includes a help-yourself soup
and salad bar, while at night the
seasonally changing menu offers
three courses for €25.

Bars

Aire

C/de Valencia 236 ☎ 934 515 812,
ⓦ www.arenadisco.com. Thurs–Sat
11pm–3am. The hottest, most
stylish lesbian bar in town is a
surprisingly relaxed place for a
drink and a dance to pop, house
and retro sounds. Gay
men are welcome too.

Belchica

C/Villaroel 60 ☎ 625 814
001. Tues–Sat 6pm–3am,
Sun & Mon 6pm–2am.
Barcelona's first
Belgian beer bar, which
guarantees a range of
decent brews. It's an
enjoyable locale, playing
electronica, new jazz,
lounge, reggae and
other left-field sounds.

Dietrich

C/Consell de Cent 255
☎ 934 517 707. Daily 6pm–
2.30am. Cornerstone of
the Gaixample scene is
this fashionable music
bar and "teatro-café" –
tranquilo during the
week, but ever more
hedonistic as the
weekend wears on,
with drag shows,
acrobats and dancers
punctuating the DJ sets.

Dry Martini

C/d'Aribau 166 ☎ 932 175 072.
Mon–Thurs 1pm–2.30am, Fri & Sat
1pm–3am, Sun 6.30pm–2.30am.
White-jacketed bartenders, dark
wood and brass fittings, a self-
satisfied air – it could only be
Barcelona's legendary uptown
cocktail bar. To be fair, though,
no one mixes drinks better and
the regulars aren't all the one-
dimensional business types you
might expect.

Punto BCN

C/Muntaner 63–65 ☎ 934 536
123, ⓦ www.arenadisco.com. Daily
6pm–2.30am. Gaixample classic
that attracts a lively crowd
for drinks, chat and music.
Wednesday happy hour is a
blast, while Friday night is
party night.

▼ MIXING MARTINIS IN DRY MARTINI

Quilombo

C/d'Aribau 149 ☎ 934 395 406.
Mon–Thurs & Sun 9pm–3am, Fri & Sat
7.30pm–3.30am. Unpretentious
music bar that's rolled with the
years (since 1971), featuring live
guitarists, South American bands
and a clientele that joins in
enthusiastically.

Sante Café

C/d'Urgell 171 ☎ 933 237 832. Mon–
Thurs 8am–3am, Fri & Sat 5pm–3am;
closed Aug. A minimalist sort
of place that's more of a café
during the day, but chills out at
night, with DJs guesting at the
weekend.

Clubs

Antilla Barcelona

C/Aragó 141–143 ☎ 934 514 564,
ⓦ www.antillasalsa.com. Daily
10.30pm–5am, weekends until
6am. Caribbean tunes galore:
rumba, son, salsa, merengue,
mambo – you name it.
There are live bands, killer
cocktails, and dance classes
most nights.

Arena Madre

C/Balmes 32 ☎ 934 878 342, ⓦ www
.arenadisco.com. The "mother"
club (Mon–Sat 12.30–5am,
Sun 7.30pm–5am) sits at the
helm of *Arena*'s gay empire, all
within a city block (pay for one,
get in to all), which includes
the high-disco antics of *Arena
Classic* (c/de la Diputació 233;
Fri & Sat 12.30–6am), more of
the same plus dance, r&b, pop
and rock at the more mixed
Arena VIP (Grand Via de les
Corts Catalanes 593; Fri & Sat
1–6am), and the best in house at
Arena Dandy (same address and
hours).

Astoria

C/de Paris 193 ☎ 934 144 799,
ⓦ www.grupocostaeste.com. Tues–Sat
9pm–3am. A once-decayed
cinema, now restyled as a very
handsome restaurant, lounge-
bar and club. You don't have to
pay to get in (always a bonus)
and the restaurant runs from
9pm until midnight, after which
you're looking at jazz, funk and
chill-out sounds.

Luz de Gas

C/Muntaner 246 ☎ 932 097 711,
ⓦ www.luzdegas.com. Smart venue
popular with a slightly older
crowd, with live music (local
rock, blues, soul, jazz and covers)
every night around midnight.
Foreign acts appear regularly
too, mainly jazz-blues types but
also old soul acts and up-and-
coming rockers.

Metro

C/Sepúlveda 158 ☎ 933 235 227,
ⓦ www.metrodiscobcn.com. Daily
midnight–5am. A gay institution
in Barcelona, with cabaret
nights and other events
midweek, and extremely
crowded club nights at
weekends in its two rooms
playing either current dance
and techno or retro disco.

Space Barcelona

C/Tarragona 141–147 ☎ 934 268 444,
ⓦ www.spacebarcelona.com. Fri &
Sat midnight–6am, Sun 9pm–3am.
With the Balearic beat big in
Barcelona, it was no surprise
when offshoots of the actual
Ibiza clubs appeared on the
scene. This was the first Space
launched outside the island
and it's a thumpingly young,
extremely posey joint. Sunday
night is the current pick of the
gay club nights.

Gràcia and Parc Güell

Gràcia was a village for much of its early existence, before being annexed as a suburb of the city in the late nineteenth century. It's traditionally been a stronghold of the liberal intelligentsia, though Gràcia also has a genuine local population that still lends it an attractive small-town atmosphere. Consequently, its annual summer festival, the Festa Major every August, has no neighbourhood peer. Much of the pleasure here is serendipitous – wandering the narrow, gridded streets, catching a film, or otherwise taking time out from the rigours of city-centre life. However, no one should miss the opportunity to visit nearby Parc Güell, an extraordinary flight of fancy by architectural genius Antoni Gaudí. To get to Gràcia take the FGC train from Plaça de Catalunya to Gràcia station, or the metro to either Diagonal, to the south, or Fontana, to the north. From any of the stations, it's around a 500-metre walk to Gràcia's main square, Plaça del Sol, hub of the neighbourhood's renowned nightlife.

Casa Vicens

C/de les Carolines 24. No public access. Antoni Gaudí's first major private commission (1883–85) took inspiration from the Moorish style, covering the facade of the house in linear green-and-white tiles with a flower motif. The decorative iron railings are a reminder of Gaudí's early training as a metalsmith, and to further prove his versatility – and demonstrate how Art Nouveau cuts across

▼ PLAÇA DE LA VIRREINA

art forms – Gaudí designed much of the mansion's original furniture, too.

Plaça de la Virreina

This pretty square, backed by the much-restored parish church of Sant Joan, is one of Gràcia's favourites, with the *Virreina Bar* and others providing a place to rest and admire the handsome houses, most notably Casa Rubinat (1909), at c/de l'Or 44, the last major work of Francesc Berenguer. Children and dogs, meanwhile, scamper around the small drinking fountain.

Plaça de Rius i Taulet

The thirty-metre-high clock tower in the heart of Gràcia was a rallying point for nineteenth-century radicals – whose twenty-first-century counterparts prefer to meet for brunch at the square's popular café *terrassas*.

Parc Güell

C/d'Olot. Daily: March & Oct 10am–7pm; April & Sept 10am–8pm; May–Aug 10am–9pm; Nov–Feb 10am–6pm. Free. Gaudí's Parc Güell (1900–14) was his most ambitious project after the Sagrada Família, conceived as a "garden city", of the type popular at the time in England. In the end, only two houses were actually built, and the park was officially opened to the public instead in 1922. Laid out on a hill, which provides fabulous views back across the city, the park is an almost hallucinatory expression of the imagination. Pavilions of contorted stone, giant decorative lizards, meandering rustic viaducts, a vast Hall of Columns, carved stone trees – all combine in one manic swirl of ideas and excesses. Perhaps the most famous element is the long, meandering ceramic bench that snakes along the edge of the terrace above the columned hall. The displays at the **Centre d'Interpretació** (daily 11am–3pm; €2), at the main park entrance, provide useful background information on the whole project.

The most direct route to Parc Güell is on bus #24 from Plaça de Catalunya, Passeig de Gràcia or c/Gran de Gràcia, which drops you at the eastern side gate by the car park. From Metro Vallcarca, walk a few hundred metres down Avinguda de l'Hospital Militar until you see the mechanical escalators on your left, ascending Baixada de la Glòria – follow these to the western side park entrance (15min in total). From Metro Lesseps, turn right along Travessera de Dalt and then left up steep c/Larrard, which leads (10min) straight to the park's main entrance on c/Olot. There's a small café in the park, and several others along c/Larrard.

▼ GAUDÍ'S DESK AT CASA MUSEU GAUDÍ

Casa Museu Gaudí

Parc Güell ☏ 932 193 811, ⓦ www.casamuseugaudi.org. Daily: April–Sept 10am–8pm; Oct–March 10am–6pm. €4, combination ticket with Sagrada Família €9. One of Gaudí's collaborators, Francesc Berenguer, designed and built a turreted house within Parc Güell for the architect (though he only lived in it intermittently). This now contains a

▲ CHILLIDA SCULPTURE IN PARC DE LA CREUETA DEL COLL

diverting collection of some of the furniture Gaudí designed for other projects – a typical mixture of wild originality and brilliant engineering – as well as plans and objects related to the park and to Gaudí's life. There's an inkling of his personality, too, in the displayed religious texts and pictures, along with a silver coffee cup and his death mask, made at the Santa Pau hospital where he died.

Parc de la Creueta del Coll

Pg. de la Mare de Deu del Coll 89. Daily 10am–dusk. Parc de la Creueta del Coll was laid out around a small artificial lake on the site of an old quarry. There's a stand of palm trees, a café kiosk, and concrete promenades under the sheer quarry walls, and you're greeted at the top of the park steps by an Ellsworth Kelly metal spike. Meanwhile, suspended by steel cables over a water-filled quarry corner is a massive concrete claw by the Basque artist Eduardo Chillida. Bus #28 from Plaça de Catalunya, up Passeig de Gràcia, stops just 100m from the park steps, or you can walk up Passeig de la Mare de Deu del Coll from Metro Vallcarca in about twenty minutes (there's a neighbourhood map at the metro station).

Shops

Camisería Pons

C/Gran de Gràcia 49 ☎ 932 177 292. Originally a *modernista* shirt shop, this has been transformed into a showcase for Spanish fashion designers.

A Casa Portuguesa

C/Verdi 58 ☎ 933 683 525, ⊛ www .acasaportuguesa.com. Tues & Wed 5–10pm, Thurs & Fri 5–11pm, Sat & hols 11am–3pm & 5–11pm. A sleek deli-cum-café-gallery on Gràcia's buzziest street that's a showcase for the food, wine and culture of Portugal. It's a great place to pop in for a coffee after trawling the designer and streetwear stores of Carrer Verdi – they make Portuguese specialities daily (including the famous *pasteis de Belém*, little custard tarts), and have a full programme of wine tastings, food festivals and other events.

Contribucions

C/Riera de Sant Miquel 30 ☎ 932 187 140. Uptown fashion bargain-seekers come straight to Gràcia's well-known discount outlet for Spanish and Italian designer labels.

Hibernian Books

C/Montseny 17 ☎ 932 174 796, ⊛ www.hibernian-books.com. Barcelona's best secondhand English bookstore has around 30,000 titles in stock – you can part-exchange, and there are always plenty of giveaway bargains available.

GRÀCIA

SHOPS
Camisería Pons   c
A Casa Portuguesa   a
Contribucions   d
Hibernian Books   b

BARS & CLUBS
Le Baignoire   5
Café del Sol   6
Canigó   5
Otto Zutz   1
Puku Café   3
Salambo   2

TAPAS & RESTAURANTS
Flash, Flash   9
Habibi   12
Jean Luc Figueras   13
Nou Candanchu   10
Samsara   7
La Singular   11
Sureny   8
Taverna El Glop   4

Restaurants and tapas bars

Flash, Flash

C/de la Granada del Penedès 25
℗ 932 370 990, ⓦ www.grup7portes
.com. Daily 1pm–1.30am, bar open
11am–2am. Tortillas (most around
€6) served any time you like,
any way you like, from plain
and simple to elaborately
stuffed, with sweet ones for
dessert. If that doesn't grab you,
there's a small menu of salads,
soups and burgers. Either way,
you'll love the original 1970s
white leatherette booths and
monotone cutouts – very *Austin
Powers*.

Habibi

C/Gran de Gràcia 7 ℗ 932 179 545.
Mon–Fri 1pm–1am, Sat 2–4.30pm
& 8pm–1am. Bright and breezy
North African dining room,
with a summer *terrassa*. The
Plat Habibi gives you a taste
of all the house specials
– from a minty *tabbouleh* to
chicken *schawarma*. Add a
fresh-squeezed juice (there's no
alcohol served), home-made
dessert and a mint tea, and
you're still unlikely to spend
more than €15.

Jean Luc Figueras

C/Santa Teresa 10 ℗ 934 152
877. Mon–Sat 1.30–3.30pm &
8.30–11.30pm; closed Aug. Gràcia
does posh as well as cool:
witness the Michelin-starred
Franco-Catalan cooking here,
that's of the very highest order
– reckon on at least €100 a
head. It's a very sophisticated
place that's an early port of
call for most dedicated foodies,
and the menu pitches and rolls
with the seasons and market
availability.

Nou Candanchu

Pl. Rius i Taulet 9 ☎ 932 377 362.
Mon, Wed, Thurs & Sun 7am–1am,
Fri & Sat until 3am. Sit beneath
the clock tower in summer and
choose from the wide selection
of dishes – tapas and hot
sandwiches, but also steak and
eggs, steamed clams and mussels,
or cod and hake cooked plenty
of different ways. It's managed
by an affable bunch of young
guys, and there's lots of choice
for €8–12.

Samsara

C/Terol 6 ☎ 932 853 688. Mon–Thurs
& Sun 8.30pm–1.30am, Fri & Sat
8.30pm–3am. Low tables, low
lighting, and painted concrete
walls hung with artworks and
photos provide the backdrop
for a laid-back place offering
contemporary tapas and
"platillos" (little plates). The
menu changes daily, but things
like brochettes of asparagus
tempura, mini hamburgers and
inventive salads are typical,
most costing €5–6. It's totally

▼ FLASH, FLASH

Gràcia – yes, that's a chillout
soundtrack and yes, there's a
projection screen above the bar.

La Singular

C/Francesc Giner 50 ☎ 932 375
098. Mon–Thurs 1.30–4pm &
9pm–midnight, Fri 1.30–4pm &
9pm–1am, Sat 9pm–1am. The
tiniest of kitchens turns out
refined Mediterranean food at
moderate prices (most dishes
€8–14) – think aubergine and
smoked fish salad or chicken
stuffed with dates and ham.
There's always something
appealing on the menu for
veggies too. It's a cornerstone
of the neighbourhood, with a
friendly atmosphere, but there
are only nine tables, so go early
or reserve.

Sureny

Pl. de la Revolució 17 ☎ 932 137
556. Tues–Sat 8.30pm–midnight,
Sun 1–3.30pm & 8.30pm–midnight.
Although a tapas place, it's
good for a relaxed meal as
you can dine at tables as well
as stand at the bar. It's
also more of a gourmet
experience than most tapas
bars, with a market-led
seasonally changing menu
(fresh fish, game, wild
mushrooms etc) that goes
well beyond sliced *chorizo*
and fried potatoes.

Taverna El Glop

C/Sant Lluís 24 ☎ 932 137 058,
ⓦ www.tavernaelglop.com. Daily
1–4pm & 8pm–1am.
The rusticity (stone-
flagged floors, baskets of
garlic) stops just the right
side of parody and the
lunch *menú del dia* is one
of the city's best deals;
otherwise expect to spend
around €15–25 a head
for grills and other tavern

▲ CAFÉ DEL SOL

specials prepared in front of you on the open kitchen ranges. At the weekend you may have to wait for a table.

Bars

La Baignoire

C/Verdi 6, no phone. Daily 8pm–2am, Fri & Sat until 3am. Cosy wine bar offering a small corner of sophistication – Ella Fitzgerald on the CD, a dozen good wines by the glass and cheesy nibbles.

Café del Sol

Pl. del Sol 16 ☎ 934 155 663. Daily 1pm–2.30am. The stalwart of the Plaça del Sol scene sees action day and night. On summer evenings, when the square is packed, the outdoor tables are at a premium, but even in winter this is a draw – the pubby interior has a back room and gallery, often rammed to the rafters.

Canigó

Pl. de la Revolució 10; no phone. Tues–Sun 11am–midnight.

Family-run neighbourhood bar now entering its third generation. It's not much to look at, but it's a friendly spot, packed out at weekends with a young, hip and largely local crowd meeting to chew the fat.

Puku Café

C/Guilleries 10 ☎ 933 682 573. Mon–Thurs & Sun 7pm–1am, Fri & Sat 7pm–3am. Come early and it's a relaxed place for a bite to eat and a drink, while at weekends it morphs into an equally chilled electro-lounge as "indietronica" DJs take the helm.

Salambo

C/Torrijos 51 ☎ 932 186 966. Mon, Wed, Thurs & Sun noon–1am, Fri & Sat noon–3am. Stylish neighbourhood drink-and-meet spot. The pre- and post-cinema crowd pops in for *cafetières* of coffee, sandwiches and meals, and there are lots of wines and *cava* by the glass. Upstairs, you can shoot pool.

Clubs

Otto Zutz

C/de Lincoln 15 ☎ 932 380 722, ⓦ www.grupo-ottozutz.com. Tues–Sat midnight–6am. It first opened in 1985, and has lost some of its glam cachet, but this three-storey former textile factory still has a shedload of pretensions. The sounds are basically hip-hop, r&b and house, and with the right clothes and face you're in (you may or may not have to pay, depending on how impressive you are, the day of the week, the mood of the doorstaff, etc).

Camp Nou, Pedralbes and Sarrià-Sant Gervasi

On the northwestern edge of the centre, the city's famous football stadium, Camp Nou, draws locals and visitors alike, both to the big game and to the FC Barcelona museum. The nearby suburb of Pedralbes, across Avinguda Diagonal, contains two interesting museums (of decorative art and ceramics), while a half-day's excursion can be made of the trip by walking from the museums, past an early Gaudí creation, to the calm cloister and celebrated art collection at the Gothic monastery of Pedralbes. You can complete the day by returning via Sarrià, just to the east, more like a small town than a suburb, with a pretty main street and market to explore. At night, the focus shifts southeast to neighbouring Sant Gervasi and the style bars in the streets north of Avinguda Diagonal.

Camp Nou and FC Barcelona

Avgda. Arístides Maillol ☎902 189 900, or ☎934 963 600 from outside Spain, ⊛www.fcbarcelona.com. Match tickets (€20–60) also from ServiCaixa ☎902 332 211, ⊛www.servicaixa .com. Ⓜ Collblanc/Maria Cristina. In

Barcelona, football is a genuine obsession, with support for the local giants FC (Futbol Club) Barcelona raised to an art form. "More than just a club" is the proud boast, and certainly during the dictatorship years the

▲ T-SHIRTS FOR THE FANS

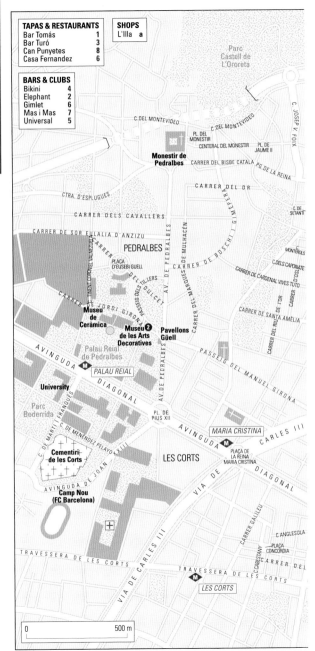

TAPAS & RESTAURANTS

Bar Tomás	1
Bar Turó	3
Can Punyetes	8
Casa Fernandez	6

SHOPS

L'Illa	a

BARS & CLUBS

Bikini	4
Elephant	2
Gimlet	6
Mas i Mas	7
Universal	5

0 — 500 m

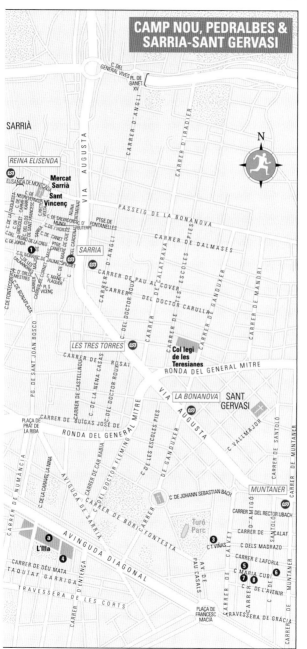

CAMP NOU, PEDRALBES &
SARRIÀ-SANT GERVASI

club stood as a Catalan symbol, around which people could rally. Arch-rivals, Real Madrid, on the other hand, were always seen as Franco's club. Moreover, unlike any other professional team, the famous "Blaugrana" (claret and blue) shirts remained unsullied by sponsors' names for a century – until, in a typically Catalan statement of intent, the Unicef logo was chosen. The swashbuckling team – European champions in 1992 and 2006, home to the great names of Cruyff, Maradona, Stoichkof and Ronaldinho – plays at the magnificent Camp Nou football stadium (not "Nou Camp", whatever your local football commentator might say). This was built in 1957, and enlarged for the 1982 World Cup semi-final to accommodate 98,000 spectators. It provides one of the best football-watching experiences in the world, and the matches can be an invigorating introduction to Catalan passions.

The **football season** runs from late August until early June, with games usually played on Sundays (though sometimes on other days). Tickets are usually relatively easy to come by, except for the biggest domestic games and major European ties. Football club members get priority (and FC Barcelona has the world's largest soccer club membership), but for most games tickets go on general sale up to a month before each match – you can buy them on the website, at the ticket office, or by calling ServiCaixa.

The stadium complex also boasts a great museum (see below) and hosts basketball, handball and hockey games with FC Barcelona's other professional teams, while there's also a public ice rink, stadium souvenir shop and café.

Museu del Futbol and stadium tour

Camp Nou, Avgda. Arístides Maillol, enter through Gates 7 & 9 ☎ 902 189 900, or ☎ 934 963 600 from outside Spain, ⓦ www.fcbarcelona.com. Museum Mon–Sat 10am–8pm, Sun 10am–3pm; tours until 1hr before museum closes. Museum only €7.50, museum and tour €11.50. Together, the Camp Nou stadium and football museum provide a splendid celebration of Spain's national sport. An all-inclusive ticket allows you on the self-guided tour, winding into the bowels of the stadium, through the changing rooms, out onto the pitch side and up to the press gallery and directors' box. The museum, meanwhile, is jammed full of silverware, memorabilia, paintings and sculpture, while displays and archive footage trace the history of the club back to 1901. Finally, you're directed into the FC Botiga Megastore, where you can buy anything from a replica shirt down to a branded bottle of wine.

Palau Reial de Pedralbes

Avgda. Diagonal 686. Ⓜ Palau Reial. The Palau Reial de Pedralbes – basically a large villa with pretensions – was originally built for the use of the royal family on their visits to Barcelona. It received its first such visit in 1926, but was never popular with the royals and within five years the king had abdicated anyway, so the palace somewhat lost its role. Franco kept it on as a presidential residence and it later passed to the city, which since 1990 has used its rooms to show off its fine ceramics and decorative arts collections in two separate museums: the Museu de Ceràmica, and the Museu de les Arts Decoratives (see below). The gardens (free entry) are a calm oasis, where – hidden in a bamboo thicket, to the left-centre of the facade – is the "Hercules fountain", an early work by Antoni Gaudí.

Museu de Ceràmica

Avgda. Diagonal 686 ☏ 932 805 024, ⓦ www.museuceramica.bcn.es. Tues–Sat 10am–6pm, Sun 10am–3pm. €3.50, free on first Sun of the month; ticket also valid for Museu de les Arts Decoratives and Museu Textil i d'Indumentària in La Ribera. The bulk of the exhibits ranges from the thirteenth to the nineteenth centuries, and includes splendid Moorish-influenced tiles and plates from the Aragonese town of Teruel, as well as a series of fifteenth- and sixteenth-century *socarrats* – decorated terracotta panels – from Paterno displaying demons and erotic scenes. Perhaps the most vivid examples of the work coming out of Barcelona and Lleida workshops of the time are the two extensive *azulejo* (tile) panels of 1710: one showing a Madrid bullfight, the other the feasting and dancing taking place at a party centred on the craze of the period – hot-chocolate-drinking.

Museu de les Arts Decoratives

Avgda. Diagonal 686 ☏ 932 805 024, ⓦ www.museuartsdecoratives.bcn.es. Tues–Sat 10am–6pm, Sun 10am–3pm. €3.50, free on first Sun of the month; ticket also valid for Museu de Ceràmica and Museu Textil i d'Indumentària in La Ribera. Arranged around the upper gallery of the Palau Reial's former throne room, the Decorative Arts Museum provides a fair old romp from Romanesque art through to contemporary Catalan design. Side rooms showcase the various periods under the spotlight, with displays of highly polished Baroque and Neoclassical furniture contrasting with the varied Art Deco and *modernista* holdings. The latter half of the gallery concentrates on Catalan *disseny* (design), from chairs to espresso machines, lighting to sink taps.

▼ EXHIBIT AT MUSEU DE LES ARTS DECORATIVES

Pavellons Güell

Avgda. de Pedralbes 7 ☎ 933 177 652, ⓦ www .rutadelmodernisme.com. Tours Mon, Fri, Sat & Sun at 10.15am & 12.15pm in English, plus 11.15am & 1.15pm in Spanish/ Catalan. €5. Ⓜ Palau Reial. As an early test of his capabilities, Antoni Gaudí was asked by his patron, Eusebi Güell, to rework the entrance, gatehouse and stables of the Güell summer residence (the house itself was later given to the royal family, and rebuilt as the Palau Reial). The resultant brick and tile buildings are frothy, whimsical affairs with more than a Moorish touch to them, though it's the gateway that's the most famous element. An extraordinary winged dragon of twisted iron snarls at the passers-by, its razor-toothed jaws spread wide in a fearsome roar. During the week you can't go any further than the gate, but it's well worth coinciding with the guided visits, especially to see inside Gaudí's innovative stables, now used as a library by the historical architectural department of the University of Coimbra.

▲ DRAGON GATES AT PAVELLONS GÜELL

Monestir de Pedralbes

Biaxada del Monestir ☎ 932 039 282, ⓦ www.museuhistoria.bcn.es. Tues–Sat 10am–5pm, Sun 10am–3pm. €5, free on first Sun of the month. Ⓜ Palau Reial and 20min walk, FGC Reina Elisenda and 10min walk, or 30min ride on bus #22 from Plaça de Catalunya or #64 from Ronda Sant Antoni. Founded in 1326 for the nuns of the Order of St Clare (whose members still reside here), this is in effect an entire monastic village preserved on the outskirts of the city; it's set within medieval walls and gateways that shut out completely the noise and clamour of the twenty-first century.

It took the medieval craftsmen a little over a year to prepare Pedralbes (from the Latin *petras albas*, "white stones") for its first community of nuns. The speed of the initial construction, and the subsequent uninterrupted habitation by the Order, helps explain the monastery's architectural harmony. The cloisters in particular are perhaps the finest in the city, built on three levels and adorned by the slenderest of columns. All around the cloisters are alcoves and rooms displaying the monastery's treasures – frescoes, paintings, memorabilia and religious artefacts – while the adjacent church retains some of its original fourteenth-century stained glass and the superb carved marble tomb of the foundation's sponsor, Elisenda de Montcada, wife of Jaume II, who died in 1364.

Sarrià

FGC Sarrià c/Mare de Deu de Núria exit, or bus #64 from Pl. Universitat or Pedralbes. Sarrià's narrow traffic-free main street – c/Major de Sarrià – shows aspects of the independent small town that Sarrià once was. At its northern end, at Plaça de Sarrià, the much-restored church of Sant Vincenç flanks the main Passeig de la Reina Elisenda de Montcada, across which lies the neighbourhood market, housed in a *modernista* red-brick building of 1911. Carrer Major de Sarrià runs downhill from here, past other surviving old-town squares, prettiest of which is **Plaça Sant Vicenç** (off c/Mañe i Flaquer), where there's a statue of the saint.

You also must not miss the *Bar Tomás*, just around the corner on c/Major de Sarrià, for the world's best *patatas bravas*.

Avinguda Diagonal

The uptown section of Avinguda Diagonal runs through the heart of Barcelona's flashest business and shopping district. Typical of the enterprises here is L'Illa, the giant shopping centre, whose 340-metre-long facade flanks the avenue – the stepped design is a prone echo of New York's Rockefeller Center. Smaller designer fashion stores are ubiquitous, particularly around **Plaça de Francesc Macià** and Avinguda Pau Casals – at the end of the latter, **Turó Parc** (daily 10am–dusk) is a good place to rest weary feet, with a small lake and a café-kiosk. Meanwhile, behind L'Illa, it's also worth seeking out **Plaça de la Concordia**, a surprising survivor from the past amidst the uptown tower blocks – the pretty little square is dominated by its church belltower and

▲ MERCAT SARRIÀ

ringed by local businesses (florist, pharmacy, hairdresser), with an outdoor café or two for a quiet drink.

Shops

L'Illa
Avgda. Diagonal 555–559 ☎934 440 000, ⓦwww.lilla.com. The landmark uptown shopping mall, stuffed full of designer fashion, plus Camper (shoes), FNAC (music and books), Sfera (cosmetics), Decathlon (sports), El Corte Inglés (department store), Caprabo (supermarket) and much more. You can get here by metro (Maria Cristina) or tram, or on the **Tomb Bus shopping line service** from Plaça de Catalunya, which visits other uptown stores as well (departures every 6–8min; tickets available on board).

Restaurants and tapas bars

Bar Tomás
C/Major de Sarrià 49 ☎932 031 077. Daily except Wed 8am–10pm; closed Aug. The best *patatas*

▼ PATATAS BRAVAS

bravas in town? Everyone points you here, to this utterly unassuming, white-Formica-table bar in the 'burbs for a taste of their unrivalled spicy fried potatoes with garlic mayo and *salsa picante*. They fry noon to 3pm and 6pm to closing, so if it's *bravas* you want, note the hours.

Bar Turó
C/del Tenor Viñas 1 ☎932 006 953. Mon–Sat 9am–midnight, Sun 9am–4.30pm. A reliable place for tapas, fresh pasta and home-made pizzas, right by Turó Parc. It's a modern bar with big windows that overlook a year-round street *terrassa*, and the food is pretty good value for uptown.

Can Punyetes
C/Marià Cubí 189 ☎932 009 159, ⓦwww.canpunyetes.com. Daily 1–4pm & 8pm–midnight. Traditional grillhouse-tavern – well, since 1981, anyway – that offers diners a taste of older times. Simple salads and tapas, open grills turning out *botifarra* (sausage), lamb chops, chicken and pork – accompanied by grilled country bread, white beans and char-grilled potato halves. It's cheap (everything under €10) and locals love it.

Casa Fernandez
C/Santaló 46 ☎932 019 308, ⓦwww.casafernandez.com. Daily 1pm–1.30am. The long kitchen hours are a boon for the bar-crawlers in this neck of the woods. It's a contemporary place featuring market cuisine, though they are

▲ GIMLET

specialists in – of all things – fried eggs, either served straight with chips or with Catalan sausage, foie gras or other variations.

Bars

Elephant

Pg. dels Til.lers ☎ 933 340 258, ⓦ www.elephantbcn.com. Thurs–Sat 11pm–4am. A gorgeous designer bar for gorgeous designer people. There's dancing, but mostly there's preening in a series of oriental-style gardens.

Gimlet

C/Santaló 46 ☎ 932 015 306. Daily 7pm–3am. This favoured cocktail joint is especially popular in summertime, when the streetside tables offer a great vantage point for watching the party unfold.

Mas i Mas

C/Marià Cubí 199 ☎ 932 094 502, ⓦ www.masimas.com. Mon–Thurs & Sun 7pm–2.30am, Fri & Sat 7pm–3am. Cornerstone of the uptown bar scene and, in their own words, "a cross between a cocktail bar and a dancehall". The music policy is blues, acid-jazz, hip-hop and r&b, and the crowd young and funky.

Universal

C/Marià Cubí 182 ☎ 932 013 596, ⓦ www.grupocostaeste.com. Mon–Thurs 10pm–3.30am, Fri & Sat 10pm–4.30am. A classic designer bar that's been at the cutting edge of Barcelona style since 1985. Be warned: they operate a strict door policy here, and if your face doesn't fit you won't get in.

Clubs

Bikini

C/Deu i Mata 105 ☎ 933 220 800, ⓦ www.bikinibcn.com. Wed–Sun midnight–5am; closed Aug. This traditional landmark of Barcelona nightlife (behind the L'Illa shopping centre) offers a regular diet of great gigs followed by club sounds, from house to Brazilian, according to the night.

Tibidabo and Parc del Collserola

The views from the heights of Tibidabo (550m), the peak that signals the northwestern boundary of the city, are legendary. On a clear day you can see across to Montserrat and the Pyrenees, and out to sea even as far as Mallorca. However, while many make the tram and funicular ride up to Tibidabo's amusement park and church, few realize that beyond stretches the Parc de Collserola, an area of peaks and wooded valleys roughly 17km by 18km, threaded by rivers, roads and hiking paths – one of Barcelona's best-kept secrets. You could walk into the park from Tibidabo, but it's actually better to start from the park's information centre, across to the east, above Vallvidrera, where hiking-trail leaflets are available. Meanwhile, families won't want to miss CosmoCaixa, the city's revamped science museum, which can easily be seen on the way to or from Tibidabo.

Parc d'Atraccions

Pl. del Tibidabo ☎ 932 117 942, ⓦ www .tibidabo.es. Days and hours vary (check website), but basically July, Aug & hols daily; rest of the year weekends only; possibly closed Jan & Feb. Park open from noon until 7–11pm depending on season. All rides €24, restricted rides €11, plus family/ discount tickets. The Funicular

▲ SAGRAT COR

del Tibidabo (see box, p.172) drops you right outside the gates of a wonderful amusement park, laid out around several levels of the mountaintop, connected by landscaped paths and gardens. The self-styled "magic mountain" is a mix of traditional rides and high-tech attractions, many of which take full advantage of the park's location to offer jaw-dropping perspectives over the city. For a real thrill, try the aeroplane ride, a Barcelona icon; the red plane has been spinning since 1928. And don't miss the Museu d'Autòmates, a collection of coin-operated antique fairground machines in working order. Summer weekends end with parades, concerts and a noisy *correfoc*, a theatrical fireworks display.

Sagrat Cor

Elevator operates daily 10am–2pm & 3–7pm. €1.50. Next to Tibidabo's amusement park, climb the shining steps of the Templo Expiatorio de España – otherwise known as the Sagrat Cor (Sacred Heart) – to the dramatic, wide balcony for some stunning views. The church is topped with a huge statue of Christ and, inside the church, an elevator (*ascensor*) takes you higher still, to just under the statue's feet, from where the city, surrounding hills and sea shimmer in the distance.

Torre de Collserola

Carretera de Vallvidrera al Tibidabo ☎ 934 069 354, ⓦ www .torredecollserola.com. Wed–Sun 11am–2.30pm & 3.30–7pm, July–Sept until 8pm. €5. Follow the road from the Tibidabo car park and it's only a few minutes' walk to Norman Foster's soaring communications tower. High above the tree line, this features a glass elevator that whisks you up ten floors (115m) for extensive views – 70km, they claim, on a good day.

Parc de Collserola

Centre d'Informació ☎ 932 803 552, ⓦ www.parccollserola.net. Daily 10am–3pm. FGC Baixada de Vallvidrera

Tibidabo and Parc del Collserola

Getting to Tibidabo

Reaching the heights of Tibidabo is half the fun, since you'll need to combine several forms of transport. It takes up to an hour, all told, from the city centre. First, take the FGC train (line 7) from Plaça de Catalunya station to **Avinguda Tibidabo** (the last stop). Emerging from the station escalators, cross the road to the tram/bus shelter at the bottom of the tree-lined avenue; the Bus Turístic stops here too. The **Tramvia Blau**, an antique tram service (mid-June to mid-Sept daily 10am–8pm; rest of year weekends & hols, plus Christmas and Easter weeks 10am–6pm; departures every 15–30min; €2.60 one-way, €3.90 return) then runs you up the hill to Plaça Doctor Andreu; there's a bus service instead out of season during the week. Here, you change to the **Funicular del Tibidabo**, with connections every 15min to Tibidabo at the top (operates when the Parc d'Atraccions is open; €2 one-way, €3 return). If the funicular isn't running, you can always take a taxi from Avinguda Tibidabo instead.

Alternatively, the special **Tibibus** runs direct to Tibidabo from Plaça de Catalunya, outside El Corte Inglés (June–Sept, Christmas & Easter daily every 30min; rest of the year, weekends & hols only, every hour; €2.30). For details of public transport, call ☎010 or check out ⊛www.tmb.net.

(on the Sabadell or Terrassa line from Pl. de Catalunya; 15min). The park information centre lies in oak and pinewoods, an easy ten-minute walk up through the trees from the FGC Baixada de Vallvidrera train station. There's a bar-restaurant here

with an outdoor terrace, plus an exhibition on the park's history, flora and fauna, while the staff hand out English-language leaflets detailing the various park walks. Some of the well-marked paths – like the oak-forest walk – soon gain height for marvellous views over the tree canopy, while others descend through the valley bottoms to springs and shaded picnic areas. Perhaps the nicest short walk from the information centre is to the Font de la Budellera (1hr return), a landscaped spring deep in the woods. If you follow the signs instead from the *font* to the Torre de Collserola (another 20min), you can return to Barcelona on the funicular from the nearby suburban village of Vallvidrera (daily 6am–midnight; every 6–10min), which connects to Peu del Funicular, an FGC train station on the line from Plaça de Catalunya.

CosmoCaixa

C/Teodor Roviralta 47–51 ☎932 126 050, ⊛www.cosmocaixa.com. Tues–Sun 10am–8pm. €3, 1st Sun of

▲ THE VIEW FROM MIRABLAU

the month free, children's activities
€2, planetarium €2. A dramatic
refurbishment in 2005 has
turned the city's science museum
into a must-see attraction,
certainly if you've got children
in tow. It's partly housed in a
converted *modernista* hospice,
but renovations added a stylish,
light-filled public concourse and
a huge underground extension
with four subterranean levels
where hands-on experiments
and displays investigate life,
the universe and everything,
"from bacteria to Shakespeare".
The two big draws are the 100
tonnes of "sliced rock" in the
Geological Wall and, best of all,
the Bosc Inundat – nothing
less than a thousand square
metres of real Amazonian
rainforest, complete with croc-
filled mangroves, anacondas
and giant catfish. Other levels
of the museum are devoted to
children's and family activities,
which tend to be held at
weekends and during school
holidays – pick up a schedule
when you arrive. There are also
daily shows in the planetarium
(in Spanish and Catalan only),
a great gift shop and a café-
restaurant with outdoor seating
beneath the restored hospital
facade. The easiest way to reach
CosmoCaixa is by FGC train
from Plaça de Catalunya to
Avinguda del Tibidabo station,
and then walk up the avenue,
turning left just before the ring
road (10min) – or the Tramvia
Blau or Bus Turistic can drop
you close by.

Bars

Mirablau

Pl. del Dr. Andrea, Avgda. Tibidabo
☎ 934 185 879. Daily 11am–5am.
Unbelievable city views from
a chic bar near the Tibidabo
funicular that fills to bursting
at times. By day, a great place
for coffee and views, by night a
rich-kid disco-tunes stomping
ground.

Montserrat

The mountain of Montserrat, with its weirdly shaped rock crags, vast monastery and hermitage caves, stands just 40km northwest of Barcelona. It's the most popular day-trip from the city, reached in around ninety minutes by train and then cable car or rack railway for a thrilling ride up to the monastery. Once there, you can visit the basilica and monastery buildings and complete your day with a walk around the woods and crags, using the two funicular railways that depart from the monastery complex.

Aeri de Montserrat

Montserrat Aeri ☎ 938 350 005, ⓦ www.aeridemontserrat.com. Departures every 15min, daily 9.25am–1.45pm & 2.20–6.45pm. For the cable-car service, get off the train from Barcelona at Montserrat Aeri station (52min). You may have to wait in line fifteen minutes or so, but then it's only a five-minute swoop up the sheer mountainside to a terrace just below the monastery – probably the most exhilarating ride in Catalunya. Returning to Barcelona, the line R5 trains depart hourly from Montserrat Aeri (from 9.37am).

▼ AERI DE MONTSERRAT

Getting to Montserrat

To reach the Montserrat cable-car/rack-railway stations, take the **FGC train** (line R5, direction Manresa), which leaves daily from **Plaça d'Espanya** (M*Espanya) at hourly intervals from 8.36am. A desk and information board at **Plaça d'Espanya** station details all fare options, including return through-tickets from Barcelona (around €16) either for the train/cable car or train/rack railway. There are also two combination tickets available: the **Transmontserrat** (€21), which includes all transport services, including unlimited use of the mountain funiculars; and the **Totmontserrat** (€35), which includes the same, plus monastery museum entry and a cafeteria lunch. Both tickets are also available at the Plaça de Catalunya tourist office. Many pilgrims still **walk up to Montserrat** – the traditional footpath (part of the route to Santiago de Compostela) runs from Monistrol de Montserrat and takes around two hours (you can download route details from the monastery visitor centre website).

Cremallera de Montserrat

Monistrol de Montserrat ☎ 902 312 020, ⓦ www.cremallerademontserrat .com. Departures every hour, daily 7.35am–6.38/8.38pm (later services at weekends April–Oct, plus daily July–Sept). The alternative approach to the monastery is by the Montserrat rack railway, which departs from Monistrol de Montserrat station (the next stop after Montserrat Aeri, another 4min), and takes twenty minutes to climb to the monastery, via Monistrol-Vila. The original rack railway on Montserrat ran between 1892 and 1957, and this modern replacement recreates the majestic engineering that allows the train to climb 550m in 4km. Returning to Barcelona, the line R5 trains depart hourly from Monistrol de Montserrat (from 9.33am).

Monestir de Montserrat

Visitor centre ☎ 938 777 701, ⓦ www .montserratvisita.com. Mon–Fri 9am– 5.45pm, Sat until 7pm. Walking maps and accommodation advice available. Legends hang easily upon the monastery of Montserrat. Fifty years after the birth of Christ, St Peter is said to have deposited an image of the Virgin (known as La Moreneta), carved by St Luke, in one of the mountain caves. The icon was lost in the early eighth century after being hidden during the Moorish invasion, but reappeared in 880, accompanied by the customary visions and celestial music. A chapel was built to house it, and in 976 this was superseded by a Benedictine monastery, set at an altitude of nearly 1000m. Miracles abounded and the Virgin of Montserrat soon became the chief cult-image of Catalunya and a pilgrimage centre second in Spain only to Santiago de Compostela – the main pilgrimages to Montserrat take place on April 27 and September 8.

The monastery's various buildings – including hotel, post office, souvenir shop, bar, patisserie and supermarket – fan out around an open square, and there are extraordinary mountain views from the terrace as well as from various other vantage points scattered around the complex. There are plenty of places to eat, but all are relatively pricey and none particularly inspiring. Best views are from the *Restaurant*

▲ MONTSERRAT

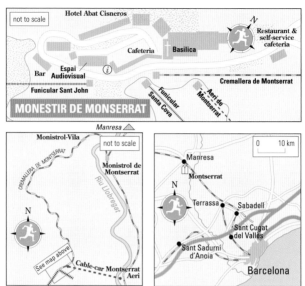

Hotel Abat Cisneros

not to scale

Restaurant &
self-service
cafeteria

Basilica

Cafeteria

Bar Espai
Audiovisual

Cremallera de Montserrat

Funicular Sant John

MONESTIR DE MONSERRAT

Funicular Santa Cova

Aeri de Montserrat

Manresa △

Monistrol-Vila

not to scale

Monistrol de
Montserrat

CREMALLERA DE MONTSERRAT

Riu Llobregat

N

See map above
Cable-car Montserrat
Aeri

Barcelona ▽

0   10 km

Manresa

Montserrat

N

Terrassa   Sabadell

Sant Cugat
del Vallès

Sant Sadurní
d'Anoia

Barcelona

de Montserrat, in the cliff-edge
building near the car park
– the self-service cafeteria, one
floor up, is where you eat with
the all-inclusive *Tot Montserrat*
ticket.

Basilica

Basilica daily 7.30am–8pm. Access
to La Moreneta 8–10.30am & noon–
6.30pm. Free. Of the religious
buildings, only the Renaissance
basilica, dating largely from

▼ CANDLES AT MONTSERRAT

1560 to 1592, is open to
the public. **La Moreneta**,
blackened by the smoke of
countless candles, stands above
the high altar – reached from
behind, by way of an entrance
to the right of the basilica's
main entrance. The approach
to this beautiful icon reveals
the enormous wealth of the
monastery, as you queue along
a corridor leading through the
back of the basilica's rich side
chapels. Signs at head height
command "SILENCE" in
various languages, but nothing
quietens the line which waits to
kiss the image's hands and feet.

The best time to be here
is when Montserrat's world-
famous **boys' choir** sings
(Mon–Fri at 1pm, Sun at noon
& 6.45pm; *not* Sat and *not*
during school holidays from
late June to mid-Aug). The
boys belong to the Escolania,
a choral school established in
the thirteenth century and

▲ SANT JOAN HERMITAGE

unchanged in musical style since its foundation.

Museu de Montserrat

Mon–Fri 10am–5.45pm, Sat & Sun 9am–7pm. €6.50. Near the entrance to the basilica, the monastery museum presents a few archeological finds brought back by travelling monks, together with painting and sculpture dating from the thirteenth century, including works by Caravaggio, El Greco, Tiepolo, Picasso, Dalí, Monet and Degas. Religious items are in surprisingly short supply, as most of the monastery's valuables were carried off by Napoleon's troops, who sacked the complex in 1811. The ticket also gets you in the **Espai Audiovisual** (Mon–Fri 9am–5.45pm, Sat & Sun 9am–7pm), near the information office, which tells you something of the life of a Benedictine community.

Mountain walks

Funicular departures every 20min, daily 10am–6pm, weekends only Oct–March. Santa Cova €2.70 return, Sant Joan €6.60 return, combination ticket €7.50. Following the mountain tracks to the caves and hermitages, you can contemplate what Goethe wrote in 1816: "Nowhere but in his own Montserrat will a man find happiness and peace." The going is pretty good on all the tracks and the signposting is clear, but you do need to remember that you are on a mountain. Take water if you're hiking far and keep away from the edges.

Two separate funiculars run from points close to the cable-car station. One drops to the path for **Santa Cova**, a seventeenth-century chapel built where the Moreneta icon is said to have been found. It's an easy walk of less than an hour there and back. The other funicular rises steeply to the hermitage of **Sant Joan**, from where it's a tougher 45 minutes' walk to the **Sant Jeroni** hermitage, and another 15 minutes to the Sant Jeroni summit at 1236m. Several other walks are also possible from the Sant Joan funicular, perhaps the nicest being the circuit around the ridge that leads in 45 minutes all the way back down to the monastery.

Sitges

The seaside town of Sitges, 36km south of Barcelona, is definitely the highlight of the local coast – a great weekend escape for young Barcelonans, who have created a resort very much in their own image. It's also a noted gay holiday destination, with an outrageous annual Carnival (Feb/March) and a summer nightlife to match. During the heat of the day, though, the tempo drops as everyone hits the beach. Out of season Sitges is delightful: far less crowded, and with a temperate climate that encourages promenade strolls and old-town exploration.

The beaches

There are clean sands either side of the old town headland, though these become extremely crowded in high season. For more space it's best to keep walking west from Passeig de la Ribera along the palm-lined promenade of Passeig Marítim, past a series of eight interlinked beaches that runs a couple of kilometres down the coast as far as the *Hotel Terramar*. There are breakwaters, beach bars, restaurants, showers and watersports facilities along the way, with the more notorious gay nudist beaches found at the far end – for these, keep on past *L'Atlantida* disco to the *Sun Beach Garden* beach bar (10min) and the small coves beyond.

Església Parroquial

Pl. del Baluard ☎ 938 940 374. Church usually open for Mass. The knoll overlooking the town beaches and marina is topped by the landmark Baroque parish church dedicated to Sant Bartolomeu, whose annual festival is celebrated in town in the last week of August. The views from the terrace sweep up and down the coast, while behind in the narrow streets of the old town you'll find a series of old whitewashed mansions, as well as the town hall and the brick Mercat Vell (Old Market), the latter now an exhibition hall.

▼ SITGES BEACH

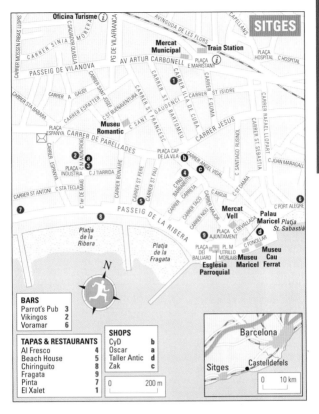

Museu Cau Ferrat

C/Fonollar ☎ 938 940 364. June–Sept
Tues–Sat 9.30am–2pm & 4–7pm,
Sun 10am–3pm; Oct–May Tues–Sat
9.30am–2pm & 3.30–6.30pm, Sun
10am–3pm. €3.50. Artists were
drawn to the town in the late
nineteenth century by its light
and views, and Sitges flourished
as an important *modernista* centre
under the patronage of artist and
writer Santiago Rusiñol (1861–
1931). His former house and
workshop contains a massive
jumble of his own paintings, as
well as sculpture, painted tiles,
drawings and various collected
odds and ends – like the
decorative ironwork Rusiñol

brought back in bulk from the
Pyrenees. The museum also
contains works by the artist's

▼ SITGES AT NIGHT

Sitges information

Trains to Sitges (€2.60 each way) leave Passeig de Gràcia or Barcelona Sants stations every twenty minutes, more frequently at peak times (destination Vilanova/ St Vicenç), and it's a thirty- to forty-minute ride depending on the service. There's also a direct bus from Barcelona airport with Monbus (ⓦ www.monbus.org), which takes 40 minutes, and an hourly **nightbus** (11pm–4am) between Sitges (Pg. de Vilafranca, by the tourist office) and Barcelona (Ronda Universitat).

There's a summer **tourist information kiosk** (mid-June to mid-Sept daily 9am–1pm & 5–9pm) outside the train station, while the town's main **Oficina Turisme** (c/Sinia Morera 1, behind Oasis shopping centre ☎ 938 109 340, ⓦ www .sitgestour.com; mid-June to mid-Sept daily 9am–8pm; mid-Sept to mid-June Mon–Fri 9am–2pm & 4–6.30pm) is five minutes' walk away. Several places in town advertise **bikes for rent** from around €15–20 a day – ask at the tourist office or look for flyers.

A **combination ticket** (€6.40, valid one month) is available for all three museums – note that **Monday** isn't the best day to come, as the museums and many restaurants are closed.

friends and contemporaries (including Picasso).

Palau and Museu Maricel

C/Fonollar ☎ 938 940 364. Museum open June–Sept Tues–Sat 9.30am–2pm & 4–7pm, Sun 10am–3pm; Oct–May Tues–Sat 9.30am–2pm & 3.30–6.30pm, Sun 10am–3pm. €3.50. The museum in this lovely mansion near the church contains minor art works, medieval to modern,

and maintains an impressive collection of Catalan ceramics and sculpture. In July and August (usually two evenings a week), the main part of the mansion itself is open for guided tours, a short classical music concert and drinks – ask at the tourist office for the current schedule.

Museu Romàntic

C/Sant Gaudenci 1 ☎ 938 942 969. June–Sept Tues–Sat 9.30am–2pm & 4–7pm, Sun 10am–3pm; Oct–May Tues–Sat 9.30am–2pm & 3.30–6.30pm, Sun 10am–3pm. €3.50, access by guided tour only every hour. Occupying the stately rooms of Can Llopis, a bourgeois house of 1793, the so-called "Romantic Museum" aims to show the lifestyle of a rich Sitges family in the nineteenth century by displaying a wealth of period furniture and possessions, from divans to dolls. Other handsome mansions in town were largely built in the nineteenth century by successful local merchants (known as "Americanos") returned from Cuba and Puerto Rico – a walk along the seafront promenade reveals the best of

▼ A SITGES MANSION

them, adorned with wrought-iron balconies, stained-glass windows and ceramic decoration.

Mercat Municipal

Avgda. Artur Carbonell ☎938 940 466. Mon–Thurs 8am–2pm, Fri & Sat 8am–2pm & 5.30–8.30pm. The town market is a great place to put together a beach picnic. Stalls offer cooked and cured meats, marinaded olives, cheese, anchovies, fresh bread, home-made crisps and fruit.

Shops

CyD

C/Major 60. The one-stop shop for men's designer shirts in limited-edition styles – classic whites to vibrant colours.

Oscar

Pl. de l'Industria 2. Closed Mon. Swim, beach and clubwear for the very well-toned man about town.

Taller Antic

C/Fonollar. A treasure trove of Art Nouveau jewellery and nineteenth-century design pieces, from perfume bottles and picture frames to ornamental clocks and letter-openers.

Zak

C/Major 34. Designer labels for men and women, and some gorgeously over-the-top accessories, come together in this breezy boutique, where the shop window is always a picture.

Restaurants and tapas bars

Al Fresco

Cafe, c/Major 33 ☎938 113 307, closed Mon. Restaurant, c/Pau Barrabeitg 4 ☎938 940 600, dinner only, closed Mon & Tues. The café on the main shopping street is a crisp, white space open for breakfast, lunch and light Mediterranean-style meals. The associated restaurant of the same name is just around the corner and down the steps, serving fancier Catalan fusion meals, with mains (char-grilled tuna, lamb tagine, oven-baked monkfish) for around €17–25.

Beach House

C/Sant Pau 34 ☎938 949 029, ⓦwww.beachhousesitges.com. Easter–Oct only, daily 9am–2am. The Australian chef-owners have created a highly relaxed restaurant, with a *table d'hôte* menu (€25) that changes every day and offers four courses of the best in Asian–Med fusion food. Breakfast and gourmet sandwiches are available until 4pm, an open-air terrace adds a touch of seaside romance, while "after-beach" happy-hour cocktails are served daily (4–8pm).

Chiringuito

Pg. de la Ribera ☎938 947 596. Daily 10am–10pm, reduced hours in winter. Claims to be Spain's oldest beach bar, serving grilled sardines, fried baby squid and calamari, sandwiches and tapas at budget prices on the prom.

Fragata

Pg. de la Ribera 1 ☎938 941 086, ⓦwww.restaurantefragata.com. Daily 1–4pm & 8–11pm. Typical of the new wave of classy seafood places in town, serving inventive fish, shellfish, rice and *fideuà* (noodle) dishes at moderate to expensive prices. Catch-of-the-day choices like monkfish casserole, tuna with an olive-and-pistachio crumb,

▲ PARROT'S PUB

or grilled local prawns cost from €17 to €25.

Pinta

Pg. de la Ribera 58–59 ☎938 947 871. Daily 1–4pm & 8pm–midnight. Every restaurant along the front does a paella with a promenade view, but this is better than most, with an enormous fish and seafood menu and a shady terrace. The lunchtime *menú del dia* (not available weekends) is a bargain at €12.50, though a full meal including drinks can be had for around €35.

El Xalet

C/Illa de Cuba 35 ☎938 110 070, ⓦwww.elxalet.com. May–Oct, dinner only, closed Tues. Dine around the pool in the magical courtyard of a nineteenth-century villa, shaded by a spreading tree canopy. It's set well away from the seafront crowds and the fresh Mediterranean cuisine is very good value, especially the €20 set dinner, where you might be served a seasonal salad followed by seared tuna.

Bars

Parrot's Pub

Pl. de l'Industria ☎938 947 881. Daily 9pm–2am. The stalwart of the gay bar scene in Sitges. Take a seat under the plastic raffia parasols and watch the parade, or check with the locals on the current club scene.

Vikingos

C/Marqués de Montroig 7–9 ☎938 949 687, ⓦwww.losvikingos.com. Mon–Thurs & Sun 11am–1am, Fri & Sat 11am–2am. Long-standing party-zone bar with an enormous air-conditioned interior and streetside terrace. Drinks, snacks or full meals served from morning to night.

Voramar

C/Port Alegre 55 ☎938 944 404. Daily 6pm–2am. This charismatic seafront bar features a few choice pavement tables and a panelled and carved interior that has the feel of an English pub. A mixed crowd of drinkers sinks ice-cold beers or the house cocktails.

The Sitges gay scene

The gay scene is frenetic and ever-changing, but the bulk of the nightlife is centred on Plaça de l'Industria. Summer, of course, sees one long non-stop party in the bars and clubs, but **carnival time** (February/March) is also notoriously riotous. Bar doors stand wide open, bands play, drag queens swan around the streets, and processions, beach parties and masked balls go on until dawn.

Accommodation

Hotels

Finding a vacancy in a good hotel in Barcelona can be very difficult, and you're advised to book well in advance between Easter and the end of October. Prices are relatively high, too. The absolute cheapest double rooms in a simple family-run pension, sharing an outside shower, cost around €45, though €60 a night is more realistic. For air conditioning, a TV and an elevator to your room there's a fair amount of choice around the €80–100 mark, while up to €180 gets you the run of decent hotels in most city areas. For Barcelona's most fashionable hotels, count on €250–400 a night.

Prices given below are for the cheapest available double/twin room in high season, including the seven percent **tax** (IVA) that is added to all accommodation bills. Some places offer discounts in winter (Nov, Jan & Feb), or for longer stays, while the larger hotels often have special rates in August (when business travel is scarce) or at weekends. **Breakfast** isn't usually included (even in very expensive places), unless specifically stated in the reviews. **Credit cards** are accepted almost everywhere, even in very modest places (though American Express isn't always). There's a lot of street noise in Barcelona, so bring earplugs if you're at all concerned.

On the Ramblas

Benidorm Ramblas 37 ☏ 933 022 054, ⓦ www.hostalbenidorm.com. Refurbished pension opposite Plaça Reial that offers real value for money, hence the tribes of young tourists. Rooms available for one to five

---

Reservation agencies

You can book accommodation at the city tourist offices (Turisme de Barcelona), but only in person on the day or online – they do not have an advance telephone reservation service. Alternatively, contact one of the reservation agencies listed below. As well as finding hotels, some specialize in apartment rentals (starting at around €90–110 a night for a studio sleeping two), but make sure you understand all the costs – seasonal premiums, cleaning charges, utility bills and taxes can all push up the headline figure.

Barcelona Apartment Rentals UK ☏ 0117/907 5060, ⓦ www.barcelonaapartmentrentals.co.uk. A small range of quality apartments, mainly in the Eixample (some near the Sagrada Família) and Gràcia.

Barcelona On-Line Barcelona ☏ 902 887 017 or 933 437 993/4, ⓦ www .barcelona-on-line.es. Commission-free reservations for hotels, pensions and apartments.

My Favourite Things Barcelona ☏ 637 265 405, ⓦ www.myft.net. Tour and accommodation agency with an eye for unusual and offbeat accommodation, from boutique hotels to private bed and breakfasts. No commission.

Turisme de Barcelona Offices in Barcelona at Pl. de Catalunya; Pl. de Sant Jaume; Barcelona Sants; Barcelona Airport ☏ 932 853 833, ⓦ www.hotelsbcn .com. Same-day, commission-free accommodation bookings in person, by phone, or on the website.

ACCOMMODATION

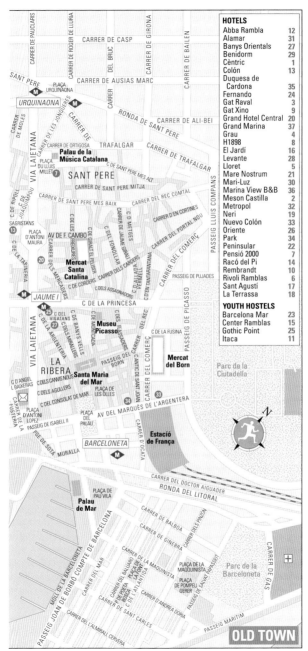

HOTELS

Abba Rambla	12
Alamar	31
Banys Orientals	27
Benidorm	29
Cèntric	1
Colón	13
Duquesa de Cardona	35
Fernando	24
Gat Raval	3
Gat Xino	9
Grand Hotel Central	20
Grand Marina	37
Grau	4
H1898	8
El Jardí	16
Levante	28
Lloret	5
Mare Nostrum	21
Mari-Luz	30
Marina View B&B	36
Meson Castilla	2
Metropol	32
Neri	19
Nuevo Colón	33
Oriente	26
Park	34
Peninsular	22
Pensió 2000	7
Racó del Pi	14
Rembrandt	10
Rivoli Ramblas	6
Sant Agustí	17
La Terrassa	18

YOUTH HOSTELS

Barcelona Mar	23
Center Ramblas	15
Gothic Point	25
Itaca	11

OLD TOWN

people, all with bathtubs or showers, and a balcony with a Ramblas view if you're lucky (and prepared to pay a bit more). From €65.

H1898 Ramblas 109 ☏ 935 529 552, ⊛ www.nnhotels.com. The former HQ of the Philippines Tobacco Company has been given a boutique refit, adding four grades of rooms (the standard is "Classic") in deep red, green or black, all beautifully appointed. Public areas reflect the period – 1898 – but there are some stunningly updated spaces, like the neo-colonial lobby-lounge, while facilities include outdoor pool and spa, gym, bar and restaurant. Some suites even have their own pool-Jacuzzi and garden. Same-day rates from €150, otherwise from €250.

Lloret Ramblas 125 ☏ 933 173 366, ⊛ www.hlloret.com. Gilt mirrors, old paintings and wrinkled leather sofas in the lounge speak of a faded glory for this one-star hotel, though some rooms, bathrooms and tile floors have been upgraded. But it's a fine building in a good location, and many rooms have Ramblas-facing balconies – as does the dining room, where breakfast is available (not included). From €85.

Mare Nostrum Ramblas 67 ☏ 933 185 340, ☏ 934 123 069. Comfortable double or triple/family rooms with satellite TV and a/c – nothing flashy, but modern, well kept and double-glazed against the noise. Some come with balconies and street views. Simple breakfast included. €66; en suite €75.

Oriente Ramblas 45 ☏ 933 022 558, ⊛ www.husa.es. If you're looking for somewhere traditional on the Ramblas, this historic three-star is your best bet – mid-nineteenth-century style in the grand public rooms and tastefully updated bedrooms, some with Ramblas views. Be warned, this is the noisy end of the street. From €100.

Rivoli Ramblas Ramblas 128 ☏ 933 026 643, ⊛ www.rivolihotels.com. The elegant, soundproofed rooms in this stylish four-star hotel are variously furnished (Art Deco to contemporary), but all come with spacious bathrooms, while the front ones have classic Ramblas views. There's a lovely rooftop terrace and bar, and guests can use the rooftop deck and small pool at the sister hotel, the Ambassador, across the Ramblas in the Raval. From €200.

Barri Gòtic

Alamar c/Comtessa de Sobradiel 1 ☏ 933 025 012, ⊛ www.pensioalamar .com. If you don't mind sharing a bathroom, then this simply furnished pension makes a convenient base. Twelve rooms (including five singles) have basin and double-glazing (no TVs); most also have little balconies. Space is tight, but there's a friendly welcome, laundry service and use of a kitchen. No credit cards. €45.

Colón Avgda. Catedral 7 ☏ 933 011 404, ⊛ www.hotelcolon.es. Splendidly situated four-star hotel, right opposite the cathedral – rooms at the front throw open their windows to balconies with superb views. It's an old-money kind of place, with faithful-retainer staff and huge public salons. "Superior" rooms have an Edwardian lounge area and highly floral decor, though other rooms are more contemporary. Check the website for best rates, otherwise from €200.

Fernando c/de Ferran 31 ☏ 933 017 993, ⊛ www.hfernando.com. Rooms at these prices fill quickly and, as a bonus, they're also light, modern and well kept by friendly people. All come with basin, shower and TV (some singles share bathroom facilities), while dorm accommodation is available on the top floor in rooms that sleep four to eight, some with attached bathroom. All accommodation is a few euros cheaper outside July and Aug. Rooms €70; dorms €25.

El Jardí Pl. Sant Josep Oriol 1 ☏ 933 015 900, ⊛ www.hoteljardi-barcelona. com. The location sells this place – overlooking the charming Plaça del Pi – which explains the steepish prices for rooms that, though smart and modern, can be a bit bare and even poky. But the bathrooms have been nicely done, and some rooms (the top ones have terraces) look directly onto the square. You can have breakfast here (not included), but the Bar del Pi in the square is a better bet. From €85; terrace or balcony €100.

Levante Bxda. Sant Miquel 2 ☏ 933 179 565, ⊛ www.hostallevante.com. A budget favourite with fifty rooms – singles, doubles, twins, triples – on two rambling floors. Some rooms are much better than others (with newer pine furniture, en-suite bathrooms and balconies), and the comings and goings aren't to everyone's liking (tranquilo it isn't), but prices are reasonable. Six apartments also available nearby, sleeping five to seven people. €56; en suite €65; apartments from €30 per person per night.

Mari-Luz c/de la Palau 4, 2° ☎933 173 463, ✆www.pensionmariluz.com. This old mansion, on a quieter than usual Barri Gòtic street, has a mix of inexpensive private rooms and small dorms, some with attached bathroom. Renovations have smartened up the rooms and added a/c, someone's been to IKEA for furniture, and there are laundry facilities, a small kitchen and wifi. It's a tight squeeze when full, but there's a personal touch lacking in many similar places. Their restored apartments a few minutes' walk away in the Raval offer more space. Dorms €15–24, rooms from €35.

Metropol c/Ample 31 ☎933 105 100, ✆www.hesperia-metropol.com. Slightly off the beaten old-town track – consequently, prices are better value than similar three-star places on the nearby Ramblas, with online rates a particularly good deal. The lobby is a masterpiece of contemporary design, while rooms are understated but comfortable – street noise isn't too bad, either, and there's wifi access throughout. From €120.

Neri c/de Sant Sever 5 ☎933 040 655, ✆www.hotelneri.com. A delightful eighteenth-century palace close to the cathedral houses this stunning boutique hotel of just 22 individually styled rooms and suites. Swags of flowing material, rescued timber, subdued colours, granite-toned bathrooms and lofty proportions provide a common theme. In the public areas Catalan designers have created eye-catching effects, like a boa constrictor sofa and a tapestry that falls four floors through the central atrium. A beamed library and stylish roof terrace provide a tranquil escape, while breakfast is served bento-box style in the contemporary Mediterranean restaurant (or out in the courtyard in summer). From €285.

Racó del Pi c/del Pi 7 ☎933 426 190, ✆www.h10.es. Some imagination went into the conversion of this old-town mansion, and the result is a stylish three-star hotel in a great location. Rooms – some with balconies over the street – have wood floors and granite-and-mosaic bathrooms. There's a glass of *cava* on check-in and although breakfast is extra there's free coffee and pastries during the day in the bar. Low-season last-minute rates as low as €100, otherwise from €150.

Rembrandt c/Portaferrissa 23 ☎933 181 011, ✆www.hostalrembrandt.com. A clean, safe, old-town budget pension that has been smartened up over the years by friendly English-speaking owners who request "pin-drop silence" after 11pm. Simple tile-floored rooms have a balcony or little patio, while larger ones are more versatile and can sleep up to four. Low-season rates shave up to €10 off the prices. Apartments are also available nearby, offering en-suite single and double rooms with balcony, a/c, satellite TV and daily housekeeping. €55; en suite €65; apartment rooms €70–100.

Port Vell

Duquesa de Cardona Pg. de Colom 12 ☎932 689 090, ✆www .hduquesadecardona.com. Step off the busy harbourfront highway into this soothing four-star haven, remodelled from a sixteenth-century mansion. The rooms are calm and quiet, decorated in earth tones and immaculately appointed. Not all the "classic" (ie, standard) rooms have views, but everyone has access to the stylish roof-deck overlooking the harbour – it's great for sundowner drinks and boasts (if that's the word) probably the city's smallest outdoor pool. From €180.

Grand Marina World Trade Centre, Moll de Barcelona ☎936 039 000, ✆www .grandmarinahotel.com. Five-star comforts on eight floors overlooking the port. Most of the rooms have enormous marble bathrooms with Jacuzzi baths with a separate dressing area. Public areas draw gasps, with commissioned works by Catalan artists and a rooftop pool with fantastic views. Winter-season and other special rates sometimes bring the price down to under €200; otherwise, from €350.

Marina View B&B Pg. de Colom ☏609 206 493, ⓦ www.marinaviewbcn.com. A classy, personally run place in a great location – the two front rooms have terrific harbour views. There's far more of a hotel feel here than simple B&B, with the five rooms featuring stylish linen, bold colours, excellent bathrooms, mini-bars (with normal drinks prices), hospitality trays, satellite TV and wifi access – then again, these aren't exactly run-of-the-mill B&B prices. Breakfast is included (served in the room). Advance reservations are essential (contact for directions), two-night minimum stay usually required. €112; harbour views €127.

El Raval

Abba Rambla Rambla de Raval 4 ☏935 055 400, ⓦ www.abbaramblahotel.com. Three-star style on the Raval's up-and-coming rambla. Public areas, including the bar, are pretty cool and contemporary, rooms less so, though they all have wall-mounted flat-screen TVs and decent bathrooms. Rooms, bar and coffee shop all face the rambla, and there's wifi throughout. From €105.

Cèntric c/Casanova 13 ☏934 267 573, ⓦ www.hostalcentric.com. A good upper-budget choice, just a couple of minutes' walk from the Raval. Most rooms feature new panelling and furniture, and plenty of light; cheaper ones on the upper floors (no elevator) share bathrooms, while some of the more expensive ones also have a/c. There's a sunny terrace at the rear and Internet access. €60; en suite from €80.

Gat Raval c/Joaquín Costa 44, 2° ☏934 816 670, ⓦ www.gataccommodation. com. Boutique style on a budget, with each lime-green room broken down to fundamentals – folding chair, wall-mounted TV, and signature back-lit street photograph/artwork that doubles as a reading light. Only six of the 24 rooms are en suite, but communal facilities are good, and there's Internet access, free tea and coffee, and staff on duty 24/7. €70; en suite €80.

Gat Xino c/Hospital 149–155 ☏933 248 833, ⓦ www.gataccommodation .com. Sister hotel to Gat Raval, where the same style applies but all the rooms are en

suite and breakfast is included, served in a cheery internal patio area. Four suites have much more space, bigger bathrooms and less street noise (and one has a terrace). From €85; suite €110; terrace suite €130.

Grau c/Ramelleres 27 ☏933 018 135, ⓦ www.hostalgrau.com. A really friendly pension, with attractive, colour-coordinated rooms on several floors (no elevator); renovated superior rooms also have balconies, a/c, new bathrooms and a touch of modern Catalan style. There's a little rustic-chic lounge area, wireless Internet access, and breakfast available weekdays in the adjacent bar (included in Jan & Feb). Six small private apartments in the same building (sleeping 2 to 5, available by the night) offer a bit more independence, and prices out of season for all rooms drop by quite a bit. €70; en suite from €90; apartments from €95.

Meson Castilla c/Valldonzella 5 ☏933 182 182, ⓦ www.mesoncastilla.com. A throwback to 1950s rural Spain, with every inch carved, painted and stencilled, from the grandfather clock in reception to the wardrobe in your room. Large, a/c rooms (some with terraces) are filled with country furniture; there's a vast rustic dining room (buffet breakfast included); and – best of all – a lovely tiled rear patio on which to relax in the sun. Special offers (Nov–Feb & July–Aug) bring rates down to around €100, otherwise €135; terrace room €150.

Peninsular c/de Sant Pau 34 ☏933 023 138, ⓦ www.hotelpeninsular.net. The interesting old building which houses this hotel originally belonged to a priestly order, which explains the slightly cell-like quality of the rooms. There's nothing spartan about the attractive galleried inner courtyard though (around which the rooms are ranged), hung with dozens of tumbling houseplants, while breakfast (included) is served in the arcaded dining room. €75.

Sant Agusti Pl. Sant Agusti 3 ☏933 181 658, ⓦ www.hotelsa.com. Barcelona's oldest hotel occupies a former seventeenth-century convent building, with balconies overlooking a restored square and name-sake church. It's of three-star standard, with appealing rooms that have been modernized and air-conditioned – the best are located right in the attic (supplement charged), from where there are rooftop views. Breakfast included. From €155.

La Terrassa c/Junta del Comerç 11 ☎933 025 174, ⓦwww.laterrassa-barcelona.com. All 45 rooms on various floors of this popular budget pension (there's an elevator) have built-in closets, modern shower rooms, effective double-glazing, ceiling fans and central heating. They are fairly plain, and "basic interior" rooms don't have much natural light, but the better exterior rooms face either the street or a sunny courtyard, and some are more spacious than others. Interior rooms from €50; exterior €55; large exterior €75.

Sant Pere

Grand Hotel Central Via Laietana 30 ☎932 957 900, ⓦwww.grandhotel-central.com. It might be on one of the city's noisiest thoroughfares, but the soundproofing does its job handsomely in this wham-glam designer hotel. Spacious, ever-so-lovely rooms hit all the right buttons – hardwood floors, massage-showers, flat-screen TVs, MP3 players – and up on the roof there are amazing views from the sundeck and infinity pool. Meanwhile, the chic hotel restaurant, Actual, showcases the new-wave Catalan cooking of chef Ramón Freixa. From €200.

Pensió 2000 c/Sant Pere Més Alt 6, 1° ☎933 107 466, ⓦwww.pensio2000.com. As close to a traditional family-style bed-and-breakfast as Barcelona gets – seven huge rooms in a welcoming mansion apartment strewn with books, plants and pictures. A third person could easily share most rooms (€20 extra), while a choice of breakfasts (not included) is served either in your room or on the internal patio. €55; en suite €70.

La Ribera

Banys Orientals c/de l'Argenteria 37 ☎932 688 460, ⓦwww.hotelbanys orientals.com. Funky boutique hotel with 43 minimalist rooms and some more spacious duplex suites nearby. Hardwood floors, crisp white sheets, sharp marble bathrooms and urban-chic decor – not to mention bargain prices for this sort of style

– make it a hugely popular choice. The attached restaurant, Senyor Parellada, is a great find too. €105; suites €135.

Nuevo Colón Avgda. Marquès de l'Argentera 19, 1° ☎933 195 077, ⓦwww.hostalnuevocolon.com. In the hands of the same friendly family for over seventy years, with 26 spacious rooms painted yellow and kitted out with directors' chairs, good beds and double glazing. Front rooms are very sunny, as is the lounge and terrace, all with side views to Ciutadella park. There are also three self-catering apartments available (by the night) in the same building, which sleep up to six. €45; en suite €65; apartments €150.

Park Avgda. Marquès de l'Argentera 11 ☎933 196 000, ⓦwww.parkhotel barcelona.com. A classy update for this elegant, modernist 1950s building starts with the chic bar and lounge, and runs up the feature period stairway to rooms in fawn and brown with parquet floors, marble bathrooms and beds with angular reading lights. It's pricey for a three-star hotel but there's real style here, augmented by the new-wave Abac restaurant on the premises. From €150.

Port Olímpic

Arts Barcelona c/Marina 19–21 ☎932 211 000, ⓦwww.ritzcarlton.com/hotels/barcelona. See map on p.123. The city benchmark for five-star designer luxury. Service and standards are first-rate, and the classy rooms feature floor-to-ceiling windows with fabulous views of the port and sea. Stunning duplex apartments have their own perks (24hr butler service, personal Mini Cooper), and dining options range from the terrace restaurant to Michelin-starred chef Sergi Arola's contemporary tapas place Arola (closed Mon & Tues). Seafront gardens encompass an open-air pool and hot tub, while the jaw-dropping Six Senses spa occupies the two top floors. Special rates start at around €200, otherwise from €400.

Montjuïc

AC Miramar Pl. Carles Ibáñez 3° ☎932 811 600, ⓦwww.hotelacmiramar.com. See map on p.112. Quite the grandest location in the city for a hotel, with views to knock your socks off. The remodelled Miramar – first built for the 1929 International Exhibition – now has 75 super-stylish rooms wrapped around the kernel of the original building, all with sweeping vistas. From the architecture books in the soaring lobby to the terrace-Jacuzzi that comes with each room, you're clearly in designer heaven; the wifi access, plasma TVs, i-pod connections and stunning pool, garden and deck come as no surprise. True, you're not in the city centre, but it's only a 10min taxi ride from most downtown destinations. From €250.

Eixample

Australia Ronda Universitat 11, 4° ☏ 933 174 177, ✆ www.residenciaustralia.com. A very welcoming budget pension – the owner is into her third decade looking after visitors, and treats everyone kindly. Three of the four rooms have basins and balconies, and share two nice bathrooms; the other is a suite with private bathroom, a/c and coffee-making machine. There's wifi throughout, while some studio-apartments (Studios Pelayo) are available nearby. €45–60, suite €65–85; apartments from €95.

Claris c/Pau Claris 150 ☏ 934 876 262, ✆ www.derbyhotels.es. Very select five-star-deluxe hotel, from the incense-scented marble lobby complete with authentic Roman mosaics to the hugely appealing rooms ranged around a soaring, water-washed atrium. And how many other hotels have their own private antiquities museum? The staff couldn't be more accommodating and breakfast is served until 1pm. There's also a rooftop terrace pool for those idle moments, a great bar and an excellent restaurant, East 47, named for its original Warhols. From €350.

HOTELS	
Australia	9
Claris	4
Condes de Barcelona	2
D'Uxelles	8
Eurostars Gaudi	6
Girona	14
Goya	12
Inglaterra	11
Majestic	3
Omm	1
Prestige	5
San Remo	15
thefiverooms	13
YOUTH HOSTELS	
Alternative Creative Youth Home	10
Centric Point	7

Condes de Barcelona Pg. de Gràcia 73–75 ☎ 934 450 000, ⊛ www .condesdebarcelona.com. Straddling two sides of c/Mallorca, the Condes is fashioned from two former palaces, its rooms all turned out in contemporary style, some with Jacuzzi and balcony, some with views of Gaudí's La Pedrera. Best deal are those on the south side, seventh-floor exterior, with fantastic private terraces but charging standard room rates. There's also a pretty roof terrace and plunge pool, while Michelin-starred Basque chef Martín Berasategui is at the helm in the acclaimed Lasarte restaurant. From €250.

D'Uxelles Gran Via de les Corts Catalanes 688 ☎ 932 652 560, ⊛ www .hotelduxelles.com. The elegant nineteenth-century town-house rooms feature wrought-iron bedsteads, antique mirrors, typical tiled floors and country-decor bathrooms; some also have balconies and little private patios (it's quietest at the back of the building). Prices are highly reasonable, and extra beds can be placed in many rooms – a few rooms are also available in another building at Gran Via 667. €100.

Eurostars Gaudí c/Consell de Cent 498–500 ☎ 932 320 288, ⊛ www .eurostarshotels.com. See map on **p.142.** An excellent-value four-star choice within walking distance of the Sagrada Família. The hotel doesn't overdo the Gaudí theme, staff are really helpful and the comfortable rooms feature contemporary furniture, black-out curtains and flat-screen TV. Junior suites on the eighth floor boast a terrace with loungers and views of the Gaudí church. From €110; suites €120–200.

Expo Barcelona c/Mallorca 1–23 ☎ 936 003 020, ⊛ www.expogrupo.com. See map on **p.148.** Bright, spacious rooms at a good-value four-star hotel – each has a sliding window onto a capacious terrace and the best have views across to Montjuïc. There's also a rooftop pool, a good buffet breakfast, and the metro right on the doorstep (it's just a minute from Sants station). From €90.

Girona c/Girona 24, 1° ☎ 932 650 259, ⊛ www.hostalgirona.com. Delightful and friendly family-run pension with a wide range of cosy, traditional rooms (some sharing a bathroom, others with a shower or full bath) – the best and biggest have a/c and balconies, though you can expect some noise. Room prices vary considerably, but from €50; full en suite €75.

Goya c/de Pau Claris 74, 1° ☎ 933 022 565, ⊛ www.hostalgoya.com. Refurbishment has raised the game at this boutique-style pension, now offering a dozen fabulous rooms in Hostal Goya and seven more on the floor below in Goya Principal (formerly the owners' own apartment), all stylishly decorated and with excellent bathrooms. There's a fair range of options (not all rooms are en suite), with the best rooms opening onto a balcony or (in Goya Principal) directly onto a terrace. There are comfy sitting areas, and free coffee and tea available, on both floors. €70; en suite from €80; balcony/terrace from €90.

Inglaterra c/Pelai 14 ☎ 935 051 100, ⊛ www.hotel-inglaterra.com. The boutique little sister to the Majestic has an excellent location, and harmoniously toned rooms with snazzy bathrooms. Space is at a premium but some rooms have cute private terraces, others street-side balconies (and very effective double-glazing). Best of all is the romantic roof-terrace – and guests can use the Majestic's pool. Three-nights-for-two offers run Dec–Feb and July–Aug, and there are other special rates on the website; otherwise from €129.

Majestic Pg. de Gràcia 68 ☎ 934 873 939, ⊛ www.hotelmajestic.es. Traditional grande-dame hotel, first opened in 1918, though refitted in contemporary style and muted colours to provide a tranquil city-centre base. Big-ticket original art adorns the public areas (it's known for its art collection), and the rooms – larger than many in this price range – have been pleasantly refurbished. The absolute clincher is the rooftop pool and deck, with amazing views over to the Sagrada Família. The Drolma restaurant is excellent too, while the high quoted room rates can almost always be beaten, either simply by asking or by checking the website. From €350.

Omm c/Rosselló 265 ☎ 934 454 000, ⊛ www.hotelomm.es. Barcelona's most fashionable restaurant group, Tragaluz, has entered the hotel game with the designer experience that is Omm – minimalist, open-plan rooms in muted colours, a studiously chic bar, the Michelin-starred Moo restaurant, terrace, pool and Spaciomm "relaxation centre", not to mention fearsomely handsome staff. It's not to everyone's taste – it's probably fair to say that the less annoyed you are by the website, the more you'll like the hotel. From €300.

Prestige Pg. de Gràcia 62 ☏ 932 724 180, ☻ www.prestigepaseodegracia .com. A sharp redesign of a 1930s Eixample building has added achingly fashionable minimalist rooms, an Oriental-style internal patio garden and the Zeroom, a lounge with wireless Internet and style library. It's almost a parody of itself it's so cool, but the staff keep things real and are very helpful. "Functional" (ie standard) rooms are a bit less impressive (no views), so upgrade if you can. From €250.

San Remo c/Ausias Marc 19, 2° ☏ 933 021 989, ☻ www.hostalsanremo.com. As pensions go, the doubles aren't a bad size for the money and the small tiled bathrooms are pretty good for this price range. There's a/c and double glazing, but even so you'll get more peace at the back – though the internal rooms aren't nearly as appealing as those with balconies. The seven rooms include one decently priced single. €65.

the5rooms c/Pau Claris 72, 1° ☏ 933 427 880, ☻ www.thefiverooms.com. The luxury B&B concept has suddenly taken off in Barcelona, and the impeccably tasteful "five rooms" set the standard. The owner's fashion background is evident in gorgeous contemporary-styled rooms that are spacious and light-filled, with original artwork above each bed, exposed brick walls and terrific bathrooms. Despite the high-spec surroundings, the feel is house-party rather than hotel – breakfast is served whenever you like, drinks are always available, and Jessica is happy to sit down and talk you through her favourite bars, restaurants and galleries. Two apartments are also available (sleeping up to 4). €135–165.

Torre Catalunya Avgda. Roma 2–4 ☏ 936 006 999, ☻ www.expogrupo.com. See map on p.148. The landmark four-star-deluxe hotel outside Sants station towers over the surrounding buildings – which means the large, light rooms have sweeping views from all sides. Rooms above the twelfth floor are superior in terms of views and services, but all are elegantly turned out in earth tones and feature huge beds, flat-screen TVs and very good bathrooms. Breakfast is a buzz – an extensive buffet on the 23rd floor, accompanied by panoramic views; there's also a spa with indoor pool, and guests can use the sister Expo hotel's outdoor pool. From €100, superior from €125.

Youth hostels

The number of **hostels** in Barcelona has expanded rapidly in recent years. Some traditional backpacker dives survive here and there, but they have largely been superseded by purpose-built modern hostels with en-suite dorm rooms as well as private rooms. They compare well in price with budget rooms in the very cheapest pensions, and Internet access, kitchens,

common/games rooms and laundry facilities are standard. Always use the lockers or safes provided (for which there's sometimes a small charge). You need an International Youth Hostel Federation (IYHF) card for a couple of the hostels, but you can join on check-in. Rates below indicate the low-season/high-season range, and some places offer discounts for multi-night stays.

Alternative Creative Youth Home
Ronda Universitat, Eixample ☏ 635 669
021, ✆ www.alternative-barcelona.com.
See map on p.192. A self-selecting art-
and-counterculture crowd make their way to
this highly individual hostel – you don't even
find out the exact address until you book,
and once there you can expect a stylishly
refurbished space with wireless Internet,
projection lounge and cool music. The regular hostel stuff is well designed, if on the
small side, with a maximum of 24 people
spread across 3 small dorms. There's a
walk-in kitchen, lockers and laundry, and
plenty of information from city-savvy staff.
€20–30.

Barcelona Mar c/de Sant Pau 80, El
Raval ☏ 933 248 530, ✆ www
.youthostel-barcelona.com. See map on
p.187. Large hostel with mixed dorms – in
6-, 8-, 10-, 14- or 16-bedded rooms – on
the fringe of the Rambla de Raval. Beds are
ship's-bunk style, with a little curtain for
privacy. It's a good location for night owls,
and a secure place, with 24hr reception.
€18–25 including breakfast.

Center Ramblas c/Hospital 63, El Raval
☏ 934 124 069, ✆ www.center-ramblas
.com. See map on p.187. Very popular
200-bed hostel in a prime location 100m
from the Ramblas and well equipped with
3- to 10-bed dorms, lounge, bar and
travel library. Open 24hr. IYHF membership
required. No credit cards. Under-25s €16–
20; over 25s €20–25; breakfast included.

Centric Point Pg. de Gràcia 33, Eixample ☏ 932 312 045, ✆ www
.centricpointhostel.com. See map on
p.192. The flashiest hostel in the city with
450 beds spread across several floors of a

refurbished *modernista* building in a swish
midtown location near the Gaudí houses
and boutiques. Private twins, doubles, triples and quads available, all with wardrobe,
shower room, balcony and views; dorms (all
en suite) sleep up to 12. Facilities are first-
rate, including a roof terrace with spectacular views. Dorms €18–25; rooms €70–110;
breakfast included.

Gothic Point c/Vigatans 5, La Ribera
☏ 932 687 808, ✆ www.gothicpoint.com.
See map on p.187. A grand downstairs
communal area shows off the building's
dramatic proportions, and there's a great
roof terrace. Rooms have 14 bunks and
attached bathrooms, and each bed gets
its own bedside cabinet and reading light.
Tours and bike rental available; free Internet; open 24hr. €18–25; breakfast included.

Ithaca c/Ripoll 21, Barri Gòtic ☏ 933 019
751, ✆ www.itacahostel.com. See map
on p.187. Bright and breezy house close to
the cathedral with spacious rooms with balconies. Dorms are mixed, though you can
also reserve a private room or apartment
(sleeps up to six), and with a hostel capacity
of only 30 it doesn't feel at all institutional.
No TV lounge, but there's a kitchen, book
exchange service, and coffee and breakfast
available. Dorm €20; room €55; apartment
from €100.

Sea Point Pl. del Mar 1–4, Barceloneta
☏ 932 312 045, ✆ www.seapointhostel
.com. See map on p.74. Neat little modern bunk rooms sleeping 6 or 7, with an
integral shower-bathroom in each one. The
attached café, where you have breakfast,
looks right out onto the boardwalk and palm
trees. Open 24hr; free Internet. €18–25;
breakfast included.

Essentials

Arrival

Whatever your point of arrival, it's easy to get to central Barcelona. In most cases, you can be off the plane, train or bus and in your hotel room within the hour.

By air

Barcelona's **airport** at El Prat de Llobregat (☎902 404 704, ⓦ www .aena.es) is 12km southwest of the city. Easyjet uses Terminal A, British Airways and Iberia Terminal B. There's a tourist office in each terminal, handling hotel bookings; there are also ATMs, exchange facilities and car rental offices.

A metered **taxi** to the centre costs €20–25, including the airport surcharge (and note other surcharges for travel after 9pm, at weekends or for luggage in the boot). Far cheaper is the convenient **airport train** (6am–11.44pm; journey time 19min; €2.60; info on ☎902 240 202), which runs every thirty minutes to Barcelona Sants (see "By rail and road" below) and continues on to Passeig de Gràcia (best stop for Eixample, Plaça de Catalunya and the Ramblas) and Estació de França (for La Ribera). There are metro stations at each of these stops too. City travel passes (*targetes*) and the Barcelona Card are valid on the airport train service.

Alternatively, the **Aerobús** service (Mon–Sat 6am–1am; €3.75; departures every 6–15min) stops in the city at Plaça d'Espanya, Plaça Universitat, Plaça de Catalunya, Passeig de Gràcia and Barcelona Sants. It takes around thirty minutes to reach Plaça de Catalunya, though allow longer in rush hour.

By rail and road

The national rail service is operated by RENFE (fare and timetable information on ☎902 240 202, ⓦ www.renfe.es). The city's main station is **Barcelona Sants**, 3km west of the centre, with a metro station (called ⓂSants Estació) that links directly to the Ramblas (ⓂLiceu), Plaça de Catalunya and Passeig de Gràcia. Some Spanish intercity services and international trains also stop at **Estació de França**, 1km east of the Ramblas and close to ⓂBarceloneta.

Regional and local commuter train services are operated by FGC (☎932 051 515, ⓦ www.fgc.es), with stations at **Plaça de Catalunya**, at the top of the Ramblas (for trains from coastal towns north of the city); **Plaça d'Espanya** (Montserrat); and **Passeig de Gràcia** (Catalunya provincial destinations).

The main bus terminal is the **Estació del Nord** (☎902 260 606, ⓦ www .barcelonanord.com; ⓂArc de Triomf) on Avinguda Vilanova (main entrance on c/Ali-Bei), three blocks north of Parc de la Ciutadella. Some intercity and international services also make a stop at the bus terminal behind Barcelona Sants station. Either way, you're only a short metro ride from the city centre.

With a car, the best advice is to head straight for a signposted central **car park** (from around €2 per hr), which include those at Plaça de Catalunya, Plaça Urquinaona, Arc de Triomf, Passeig de Gràcia, Plaça dels Angels/ MACBA and Avinguda Paral.lel. It can be tough to find **street parking**, especially in the old town (where it's nearly all residents' parking only). Elsewhere in the city, the ubiquitous Área Verde (Green Zone) meter-zones are for pay-and-display parking, usually with a one- or two-hour maximum stay (€2.80 per hr).

Information

The city's tourist board, **Turisme de Barcelona** (℡ 807 117 222 from within Spain, ℡ 932 853 834 from abroad, 🕸 www.barcelonaturisme.com), has useful offices at the airport and Barcelona Sants. The main city office is in **Plaça de Catalunya** (daily 9am–9pm; Ⓜ Catalunya), down the steps in the southeast corner of the square, where there's a money exchange and tours service, and separate accommodation desk. There's also an office in the Barri Gòtic at **Plaça de Sant Jaume**, entrance at c/Ciutat 2 (Mon–Fri 9am–8pm, Sat 10am–8pm, Sun & hols 10am–2pm; Ⓜ Jaume I), and staffed information booths dotted across the city at major attractions, including on the Ramblas.

For information about travelling in the wider province of Catalunya, you need the Centre d'Informació de Catalunya at **Palau Robert**, Pg. de Gràcia 107, Eixample, Ⓜ Diagonal (℡ 012 from within Catalunya, ℡ 902 400 012 from abroad, 🕸 www.gencat.net/probert; Mon–Sat 10am–7.30pm, Sun & hols 10am–2.30pm).

For anything else you might need to know, try the city's ℡ **010 telephone** enquiries service (Mon–Sat 8am–10pm; some English-speaking staff available). They'll be able to help with questions about transport, public services and other matters.

Events, concerts, exhibitions and festivals are covered in full at the walk-in office of the Institut de Cultura at the **Palau de la Virreina**, Ramblas 99, Ⓜ Liceu (℡ 933 017 775, 🕸 www.bcn.es/cultura; Mon–Sat 10am–8pm, Sun 11am–3pm). Pick up their free "Cultural Agenda" (in English), a monthly what's-on listings guide. Otherwise, the most useful **listings magazine** is the paperback-book-sized, Spanish-language *Guia del Ocio* (out every Thursday; 🕸 www.guiadelociobcn.es), available at any newspaper kiosk. There's also the free monthly English-language magazine *Barcelona Connect* (🕸 www.barcelonaconnect.com), which you can pick up at outlets all over the city.

Barcelona on the Internet

The city tourist office website (🕸 www.barcelonaturisme.com) is a good place

---

Discount cards

If you're going to do a lot of sightseeing, you can save yourself money by buying one of the widely available discount cards.

• **Barcelona Card** (2 days €25, 3 days €25, 4 days €34 or 5 days €40; full details on 🕸 www.barcelonaturisme.com). Free public transport, plus museum and attraction discounts. Available at tourist offices, points of arrival and other outlets.

• **Articket** (€20; valid six months; 🕸 www.articketbcn.org). Free admission into seven major art galleries (including Picasso museum, MNAC, MACBA, and Tàpies and Miró foundations). Buy it at participating galleries, or at Plaça de Catalunya, Plaça de Sant Jaume or Barcelona Sants tourist offices.

• **Ruta del Modernisme** (€12; valid one year; 🕸 www.rutadelmodernisme.com). Excellent English-language guidebook, map and discount-voucher package that covers 115 *modernista* buildings (including Sagrada Família and La Pedrera), plus other benefits. It's also packaged with *Let's Go Out*, a guide to *modernista* bars and restaurants (total package €18), with both available from the three Centre del Modernisme desks listed on the website, including at the main Plaça de Catalunya tourist office.

to start and, along with those operated by the city hall (Ajuntament; ⓦwww.bcn.es) and local government (Generalitat; ⓦwww.gencat.es), has a full English-language version. From these three alone you'll be able to find out about museum opening hours, bus routes, local politics, all-night pharmacies, festivals, sports, theatres and much, much more. The sites listed below offer more specialized information.

ⓦ**www.barcelona-online.com** Packed with information in English on Barcelona, with punchy reviews and links to scores of other useful websites.

ⓦ**www.barcelonareporter.com** Daily updated news and views from the city in English.

ⓦ**www.gaudiclub.com** The best first stop for Antoni Gaudí and his works, with plenty of links to other sites.

ⓦ**www.lecool.com** Hip cultural agenda and city guide, available online or as a weekly graphic email.

ⓦ**www.rutadisseny.com** Designer guide to the city's most cutting-edge shops, bars, restaurants and buildings, with maps, reviews and walking itineraries.

City transport and tours

Barcelona's excellent integrated transport system comprises the metro, buses, trams and local trains, plus a network of funiculars and cable cars. Detailed **transport information** is available by telephone (☎010) and in English on the Internet (ⓦwww.tmb.net or ⓦwww.emt-amb.com). There's an invaluable free public transport map (*Guia d'Autobusos Urbans de Barcelona*), available at TMB customer service centres at Barcelona Sants station, and Diagonal, Sagrada Família and Universitat metro stations. The map and ticket information is also posted at major bus stops and all metro and tram stations. There's no need to rent a car to see anything in the city, while day-trips to Sitges and Montserrat are best undertaken by public transport.

Tickets and travel passes

On all the city's public transport you can buy a **single ticket** every time you ride (€1.30), but it's much cheaper to buy a **targeta** – a discount ticket card. They are available at metro, train and tram stations, but not on the buses. The best general deal is the **T-10** ("tay day-oo" in Catalan) *targeta* (€7.20), valid for ten separate journeys, with changes between methods of transport allowed within 75 minutes. The card can also be used by more than one person at a time – validate it the same number of times as there are people travelling.

Other useful (single-person) *targetes* include: the **T-Dia** ("tay dee-ah"; 1 day's unlimited travel; €5.50), plus combos up to the **5-Dies** (5 days; €21.60); the **T-50/30** (50 trips within a 30-day period; €29.80); or the **T-Mes** (1 month; €46.25). Prices given above are for passes valid as far as the Zone 1 city limits, which in practice is everywhere you're likely to want to go except Montserrat and Sitges. For trips to these and other out-of-town destinations, it's best to buy a specific ticket.

The metro

The quickest way of getting around Barcelona is by metro. Entrances are marked with a red diamond sign with an "M". Its **hours of operation** are Monday to Thursday, plus Sunday and public holidays 5am to midnight; Friday, Saturday and the day before a public holiday 5am to 2am (a trial period in 2007 extended Sat night and public holiday eve hours to an all-night service, which may become permanent). The system is perfectly safe, though many of the train carriages are heavily graffitied. Buskers and beggars are common, zipping from one carriage to the next at stations.

Buses, trams and trains

Most **buses** operate daily, roughly from 4 or 5am until 10.30pm. **Night buses** (*autobusos nocturns* or simply *Nitbus*) fill in the gaps on all the main routes, with services every twenty to sixty minutes from around 10pm to 4am. The **tram** system (ⓦwww.trambcn.com) runs along the uptown part of Avinguda Diagonal to suburban destinations in the northwest – a useful stop is at L'Illa shopping centre – while line T4 operates from Ciutadella-Vila Olímpica (metro connection) to Diagonal Mar and the Fòrum site.

The FGC **commuter train line** has its main stations at Plaça de Catalunya and Plaça d'Espanya. You'll use this going to Sarrià, Vallvidrera, Tibidabo and Montserrat, and details are given in the text where appropriate. The national rail service, RENFE, runs all the other services out of Barcelona, with local lines designated as **Rodiales/Cercanías**. The hub is Barcelona Sants station, with services also passing through Plaça de Catalunya (heading north) and Passeig de Gràcia (south).

Funiculars and cable cars

Several **funicular railways** still operate in the city, most notably to Montjuïc and Tibidabo. Summer (and year-round weekend) visits to Tibidabo also involve a ride on the antique tram, the **Tramvia Blau**. There are two **cable-car** (*telefèric*) rides you can make: from Barceloneta across the harbour to Montjuïc, and

then from the top station of the Montjuïc funicular right the way up to the castle.

Taxis

Black-and-yellow **taxis** are relatively inexpensive and plentiful. Most short journeys across town run to around €7. There are taxi ranks outside major train and metro stations, in main squares, near large hotels and at places along the main avenues. To call a taxi in advance (few of the operators speak English, and you'll be charged an extra €3 or €4), try: **Barna Taxis** ⓣ933 577 755; **Fono-Taxi** ⓣ933 001 100; **Radio Taxi** ⓣ933 033 033; **Servi-Taxi** ⓣ933 300 300; or **Taxi Amic** ⓣ934 208 088.

City tours

The number of available tours is bewildering, and you can now see the sights on anything from a Segway to a hot-air balloon. Look out for flyers, or ask at the tourist office. Highest profile are still the two tour-bus operators with daily board-at-will, open-top services (1 day €20, 2 days €26), which can drop you outside every attraction in the city. The choice is between **Barcelona Tours** (ⓦwww.barcelonatours.es) or the **Bus Turístic** (ⓦwww.barcelonaturisme.com), with frequent departures from Plaça de Catalunya and many other stops – tickets are available on board.

Advance booking is advised (at Pl. de Catalunya tourist office) for **Barcelona Walking Tours'** two-hour historical Barri Gòtic tour (daily all year, in English at 10am). There are also "Picasso", "Modernisme" and "Gourmet" walking tours on selected days.

The guides at **My Favourite Things** (ⓣ637 265 405, ⓦwww.myft.net) reveal Barcelona in a new light, particularly on the signature tour "My Favourite Fusion", which gives an insider's view of the city. Tours (in English, flexible departures, call for information) cost €26 per person and last around four hours, and there's always time for diversions, workshop visits and café stops. Altogether more idiosyncratic is **Follow the Baldie** (details and contacts through website, ⓦwww.followthebaldie.com), with whom you can variously tour anarchist Barcelona, track tarantulas near Sitges or stagger from bar to tavern in rural Catalunya.

There are city bike tours most days of the year (from €22) with a growing number of operators, including **Fat Tire Bike Tours** (☎933 013 612, ⓦwww.fattirebiketoursbarcelona.com) and **Bike Tours Barcelona** (☎932 682 105, ⓦwww.biketoursbarcelona.com). For youth-oriented tours and activities, from bar crawls to cooking classes, contact **Barcelona Vibes** (☎933 103 747, ⓦwww.barcelonavibes.com) – you can find out more, and book tours at the travellers' bar in the Barri Gòtic, the **Travel Bar**, c/Boqueria 27, ⓂLiceu (☎933 425 252, ⓦwww.travelbar.com).

To see Barcelona from the sea, go with **Las Golondrinas** (☎934 423 106, ⓦwww.lasgolondrinas.com), whose daily sightseeing boats depart (at least hourly June–Sept; less frequently Oct–May) from the quayside opposite the Columbus statue, at the bottom of the Ramblas (ⓂDrassanes), and visit either the port (35min; €5), or port and local coast (1hr 30min; €10.50).

Catamaran Orsom (☎934 410 537, ⓦwww.barcelona-orsom.com) has two daily afternoon departures (€12.50) from the same quayside – there's a ticket kiosk there, or phone and reserve the day before. The catamaran also has a summer evening jazz cruise (daily June, July & Aug; €14.90).

Festivals and events

Almost any month you visit Barcelona you'll coincide with a festival, event or holiday. The best are picked out below, but for a full list check out the Ajuntament (city hall) website ⓦwww.bcn.es.

Festes de Santa Eulàlia
The depths of winter are interrupted by a burst of festivities around **February 12** in honour of the young Barcelona girl who suffered a beastly martyrdom at the hands of the Romans. The saint parades with other *gegants* (giants), and there are concerts, fireworks and *sardana* dancing.

Carnaval/Carnestoltes
In the week before Lent (**Feb or March**) there are costumed parades, concerts, street barbecues and other traditional carnival events in every city neighbourhood. Sitges, down the coast, has the best and most outrageous celebrations.

Dia de Sant Jordi
St George's Day (**April 23**) celebrates Catalunya's patron saint, with hundreds

of book and flower stalls down the Ramblas, on Passeig de Gràcia and in Plaça de Sant Jaume.

Primavera Sound
The city's hottest music festival (usually the last few days of **May/early June**) attracts top international names in the rock, indie and electronica world.

Marató de l'Espectacle
Every **June** it's time for the annual Entertainment Marathon (ⓦwww.marato.com), a nonstop, two-day festival of local theatre, dance, mime, cabaret, music and children's shows, which takes place at the Mercat de les Flors theatre.

Verbena/Dia de Sant Joan
The "eve" and "day" of St John (**June 23/24**) herald probably the wildest celebrations in the city, with a "night of fire" involving bonfires and fireworks (particularly on Montjuïc), drinking and dancing, and watching the sun come up on the beach. The day itself (June 24) is a public holiday.

Celebrating Catalan-style

Central to any traditional Barcelona festival is the parade of **gegants**, five-metre-high giants with papier-mâché or fibreglass heads, who dance cumbersomely to the sound of flutes and drums. Also typically Catalan is the **correfoc** ("fire-running"), where brigades of drummers, dragons and demons with firework-flaring tridents cavort in the streets. Guaranteed to draw crowds are the teams of **castellers** – "castle-makers" – who pile person upon person, feet on shoulders, to see who can construct the highest tower. It's an art that goes back over 200 years – ten human storeys is the record.

Sónar

Sónar (**W** www.sonar.es), Europe's biggest and most cutting-edge electronic music and multimedia art festival, presents three days of brilliant noise and spectacle every **June**. Experience DJs, VDJs, gigs, conferences, exhibitions and installations at venues across the city.

Festival de Barcelona

Starting in the last week of **June** (and running throughout July and into August), the city's main performing arts festival (**W** www.barcelonafestival.com) incorporates theatre, music and dance, some of it free, much of it performed at Montjuïc's Teatre Grec.

Summercase Barcelona

The sound of summer is this huge annual rock and indie showcase of bands at the Parc del Fòrum (with simultaneous gigs in Madrid). It's held over a weekend in **July** (and there's a Wintercase edition too in November).

Festa Major de Gràcia

A **mid- to late-August** extravaganza (**W** www.festamajordegracia.cat) of music, dancing, decorated floats and streets, noisy fireworks, parades of giants and devils, and human castle-building takes place in the streets and squares of Barcelona's most vibrant neighbourhood. The festivities last a week – don't miss them if you're in town.

Festa de la Mercè

The city's main festival – dedicated to Our Lady of Mercy – is celebrated for several days around **September 24** (with the 24th a public holiday). There are live bands and traditional dancing outside the cathedral and in central squares, plus a parade of costumed giants and fire-running devils, a breathtaking firework display choreographed to music and human tower competitions. During the week the concurrent BAM alternative music festival puts on free rock, world and fusion gigs at emblematic old-town locations and at Parc del Fòrum.

Festival Internacional de Jazz

The annual jazz festival (**W** www .the-project.net) in **October/November** attracts big-name solo artists and bands to the clubs, as well as smaller-scale street concerts.

Christmas

For more than two hundred years the Christmas season has seen a special market and crafts fair, the **Fira de Santa Llúcia** (Dec 1–22), outside the cathedral. Browse for gifts, or watch the locals snapping up Christmas trees, nativity figures and traditional decorations.

New Year

At **Cap d'Any** (New Year's Eve) there are mass gatherings in Plaça de Catalunya and other main squares. You're supposed to eat 12 grapes in the last 12 seconds of the year for 12 months of good luck. The Three Kings (who traditionally distribute seasonal gifts to Spanish children) arrive by sea at the port at about 5pm on January 5 and undertake the **Cavalcada de Reis**, riding into town, throwing sweets as they go. The traditional gift-giving is the next day (Jan 6).

Directory

AIRPORT Trains to the airport depart every 30min from Barcelona Sants (5.20am–10.50pm; €2.60) – you can also catch the train at Estació de França or Passeig de Gràcia. Aerobús runs every 6–15min from Pl. de Catalunya, Pg. de Gràcia or Pl. d'Espanya (Mon–Sat 6am–1am; €3.75).

BANKS AND EXCHANGE Normal banking hours are Monday to Friday from 8.30am to 2pm. Outside these hours you can use an exchange office, including those at the airport (daily 7.30am–10.45pm), Barcelona Sants (daily 8am–8pm), El Corte Inglés (Mon–Sat 10am–9.30pm), and the Pl. de Catalunya tourist office (Mon–Sat 9am–9pm, Sun 9am–2pm). However, by far the easiest way to get money is to use your bank debit card to withdraw cash from an ATM, found all over the city, including the airport and major train stations. You can usually withdraw up to €200 a day, and instructions are offered in English once you insert your card.

BIKE RENTAL Rental costs from around €5 an hour, €15–20 per day. Try: Barcelona Bici, Pl. de Catalunya, ⓂCatalunya ☎932 853 832, ⓦwww.barcelonaturisme.com; Barnabike, Pg. Sota la Murralla 3, mBarceloneta ☎932 690 204, ⓦwww.barnabike .com; Biciclot, Pg. Marítim 33–35, Port Olímpic, ⓂCiutadella-Vila Olímpica ☎932 219 778, ⓦwww.biciclot.net; Un Coxte Menys/Bicicleta Barcelona, c/Esparteria 3, La Ribera ⓂBarceloneta ☎932 682 105, ⓦwww.bicicletabarcelona.com; and many others.

CINEMA Films at most of the larger cinemas and multiplexes (including the Maremàgnum screens at Port Vell) are shown dubbed into Spanish or Catalan. However, several cinemas do show original-language (versión original or "V.O.") foreign films, and are listed in the week's Guia del Ocio. Tickets cost around €7, while most cinemas have discounted entry one night (usually Mon or Wed), costing

around €5. Many also feature late-night weekend screenings (madrugadas), at 12.30 or 1am. Best art-house cinema is the Generalitat's Filmoteca, while every July there's a giant-screen open-air cinema at Montjuïc castle (Mon, Wed & Fri nights; ⓦwww.salamontjuic.com).

CONSULATES Australia, Pl. Gala Placidia 1-3, Gràcia, ⓂDiagonal/FGC Gràcia ☎934 909 013, ⓦwww.embaustralia .es; Britain, Avgda. Diagonal 477, Eixample, ⓂHospital Clinic ☎933 666 200, ⓦwww .ukinspain.com; Canada, c/Elisenda de Pinós 10, Sarrià, FGC Reina Elisenda ☎932 042 700, ⓦwww.canada-es.org; Republic of Ireland, Gran Via Carles III 94, Les Corts, mMaria Cristina/Les Corts ☎934 915 021; New Zealand, Trav. de Gràcia 64, Gràcia, FGC Gràcia ☎932 090 399; USA, Pg. de la Reina Elisenda 23, Sarrià, FGC Reina Elisenda ☎932 802 227, ⓦwww.embusa.es.

CRIME To avoid petty crime: sling bags across your body, not off one shoulder; don't carry wallets in zipped or back pockets; and don't hang bags on the back of a café chair. Make photocopies of your passport, leaving the original and any tickets in the hotel safe. You most need to be on your guard when on public transport, or on the crowded Ramblas and the medieval streets to either side – keep a hand on your wallet or bag if it appears you're being distracted.

DISABLED TRAVELLERS Barcelona's airport and Aerobús are fully accessible to travellers in wheelchairs. The metro is more problematic since only lines 1 and 2 are easily accessible, with elevators at major stations (including Pl. de Catalunya, Universitat, Pg. de Gràcia and Sagrada Família) from the street to the platforms. However, all city buses have been adapted for wheelchair use, with automatic ramps/steps and a designated wheelchair space inside. Best single source of information is the AccessibleBarcelona website

Fly less – stay longer!

Rough Guides believes in the good that travel does, but we are deeply aware of the impact of travel on climate change. We recommend taking fewer trips and staying for longer. If you can avoid travelling by air, please use an alternative, especially for journeys of under 1000km/600miles. And always offset your travel at ⓦwww.roughguides.com/climatechange.

(🌐www.accessiblebarcelona.com), which reviews accessible city sights, hotels, bars and restaurants, and offers wheelchair-friendly guided tours. The Institut Municipal de Persones amb Discapacitat (🌐www .bcn.es/imd) also has information (in Catalan and Spanish) on most aspects of life and travel in the city. If you're coming for the showpiece attractions, note that only MNAC, Fundació Joan Miró, Fundació Antoni Tàpies, La Pedrera, Caixa Forum, CosmoCaixa, Museu d'Història de Catalunya and Palau de la Música are fully accessible; most old-town attractions, including the Museu Picasso, have steps or other impediments to access. The city information line – ☎010 – also has accessibility information for hotels, restaurants, museums, bars and stores.

EMERGENCY SERVICES Call ☎112 for ambulance, police and fire services; ☎061 for an ambulance.

GAY AND LESBIAN For up-to-date information and other advice, contact the lesbian and gay city telephone hotline on ☎900 601 601 (Mon–Fri 6–10pm only). Ca la Dona (c/de Casp 38, Eixample ☎934 127 161, 🌐www.caladona.org; ⓂUrquinaona), a women's centre with library and bar, is used for meetings of feminist and lesbian organizations; information available to callers. General listings magazine *Guia del Ocio* can put you on the right track for bars and clubs, though there's also a good free magazine called *Nois* (🌐www.revistanois .com), widely available in bars and clubs, which carries an up-to-date review of the scene. For full listings and other links, the Web portal 🌐www.gaybarcelona.net is extremely useful. The annual lesbian and gay pride march is on the nearest Saturday to June 28.

HOSPITALS The following central hospitals have 24hr accident and emergency services: Centre Perecamps, Avgda. Drassanes 13–15, El Raval, ⓂDrassanes ☎934 410 600; Hospital Clínic i Provincial, c/Villaroel 170, Eixample, ⓂHospital Clínic ☎932 275 400; Hospital del Mar, Pg. Marítím 25–29, Vila Olímpica, ⓂCiutadella-Vila Olímpica ☎932 483 000; Hospital de la Santa Creu i de Sant Pau, c/Sant Antoni Maria Claret, Eixample, ⓂHospital de Sant Pau ☎932 919 000.

INTERNET ACCESS There are Internet places all over Barcelona, and competition has driven prices down to around €1 per hour. There's also wireless access in many bars, restaurants and public places.

LEFT LUGGAGE Barcelona Sants office (daily 7am–11pm; €3–4.50 a day). Lockers at Estació de França, Passeig de Gràcia station and Estació del Nord (all 6am–11.30pm; €3–4.50 a day).

LOST PROPERTY The main lost property office (*objectes perduts*) is at c/de la Ciutat 9, Barri Gòtic, ⓂJaume I (Mon–Fri 9.30am–1.30pm; ☎010). You could also try the transport office at ⓂUniversitat station.

MAIL The main post office (*Correus*) is on Pl. d'Antoni López, at the eastern end of Pg. de Colom, in the Barri Gòtic (Mon–Sat 8.30am–10pm, Sun noon–10pm; ☎902 197 197, 🌐www.correos.es; ⓂBarceloneta/Jaume I). There's a poste restante/general delivery service here (*llista de correus*), plus express post, fax service and phone-card sales. Each city neighbourhood also has a post office, though these have far less comprehensive opening hours and services. For stamps it's much easier to visit a tobacconist (look for the brown-and-yellow *tabac* sign), found on virtually every street. Use the yellow on-street *postboxes* and put your mail in the flap marked *províncies i estranger* or *altres destins*.

MARKETS Opening hours and locations for all Barcelona's neighbourhood markets are detailed on the useful city website 🌐www .bcn.cat/mercatsmunicipals. Don't miss the Boqueria, Santa Caterina, Sant Antoni and Barceloneta, each with a style of its own.

MONEY Spain's currency is the euro (€), with notes issued in denominations of 5, 10, 20, 50, 100, 200 and 500 euros, and coins in denominations of 1, 2, 5, 10, 20 and 50 cents, and 1 and 2 euros.

NEWSPAPERS AND MAGAZINES Foreign newspapers and magazines are available from the stalls down the Ramblas, on Pg. de Gràcia, on Rambla de Catalunya, around Pl. de Catalunya and at Barcelona Sants. Or try FNAC at El Triangle on Pl. de Catalunya, which stocks a big selection of British, European and American newspapers and magazines.

PHARMACIES Usual hours are 9am to 1pm and 4 to 8pm. At least one in each neighbourhood is open 24hr (and marked as such), or phone ☎010 for information on those open out of hours. A list of out-of-hours pharmacies can also be found in the window of each pharmacy store.

POLICE The easiest place to report a crime is at the Guàrdia Urbana (municipal police) station at Ramblas 43, opposite Pl. Reial, ⓂLiceu ☎933 441 300 (open 24hr; English spoken). If you've had something stolen, you need to go in person for the insurance report to the Policía Nacional office at c/Nou de la Rambla 80, El Raval, ⓂParal. lel ☎932 902 849 (take your passport).

PUBLIC HOLIDAYS Official holidays are: Jan 1 (Cap d'Any, New Year's Day); Jan 6 (Epifanía, Epiphany); Good Friday & Easter Monday; May 1 (Dia del Treball, May Day/Labour Day); June 24 (Dia de Sant Joan, St John's Day); Aug 15 (L'Assumpció, Assumption of the Virgin); Sept 11 (Diada Nacional, Catalan National Day); Sept 24 (Festa de la Mercè, Our Lady of Mercè, Barcelona's patron saint); Oct 12 (Día de la Hispanidad, Spanish National Day); Nov 1 (Tots Sants, All Saints' Day); Dec 6 (Dia de la Constitució, Constitution Day); Dec 8 (La Imaculada, Immaculate Conception); Dec 25 (Nadal, Christmas Day); Dec 26 (Sant Esteve, St Stephen's Day).

TAXES Local sales tax (IVA) is seven percent in hotels and restaurants, and sixteen percent in shops. Quoted prices should always make it clear whether or not tax is included (it usually is).

TELEPHONES Public telephones accept coins, credit cards and phone cards (the latter available in various denominations in tobacconists, newsagents and post offices). The cheapest way to make an international call is to go to a *locutorio* (phone centre); these are scattered throughout the old city, particularly in the Raval and Ribera. You'll be assigned a cabin to make your calls, and afterwards pay in cash.

TICKETS You can buy concert, sporting and exhibition tickets with a credit card using the ServiCaixa (☎902 332 211, ⓌÑwww.servicaixa.com) automatic dispensing machines in branches of La Caixa savings bank. It's also possible to order tickets by phone or online through *ServiCaixa* or TelEntrada (☎902 101 212, Ⓦwww.telentrada.com). In addition, there's a concert ticket desk in the FNAC store, El Triangle, Plaça de Catalunya (ⓂCatalunya). For advance tickets for all Ajuntament-sponsored concerts, visit the Palau de la Virreina, Ramblas 99.

TIME Barcelona is one hour ahead of the UK, six hours ahead of New York and Toronto, nine hours ahead of Los Angeles, nine hours behind Sydney and eleven hours behind Auckland. This applies except for brief periods during the changeovers to and from daylight saving (in Spain the clocks go forward in the last week in March, back again in the last week of Oct).

TIPPING Locals leave only a few cents or round up the change for a coffee or drink, and a euro or two for most meals. Anything beyond is considered excessive, though fancy restaurants may specifically indicate that service is not included, in which case you will be expected to leave ten to fifteen percent. Taxi drivers usually get around five percent.

Budget Barcelona

Here's how to keep costs to a minimum in Barcelona:

• Eat your main meal of the day at lunchtime, when the *menú del dia* offers fantastic value.

• Buy a public transport travel pass, which will save you around forty percent on every ride.

• Visit museums and galleries on the first Sunday of the month, when admission is usually free.

• Purchase one of the useful city discount cards or packages.

• Drink and eat *inside* cafés – there's usually a surcharge for terrace service.

• Take any student/youth/senior citizen cards you're entitled to carry, as they often attract discounts on museum, gallery and attraction charges.

• Take advantage of the discount nights at the cinema (Mon and sometimes Wed) and theatre (Tues).

• Go to the Ramblas, Boqueria market, La Seu, Santa María del Mar, Parc de la Ciutadella, Parc de Collserola, Port Vell, Port Olímpic, city beaches, Diagonal Mar and Fòrum site, Olympic stadium, Els Encants flea market, Caixa Forum and Parc Güell – all free.

Chronology

Chronology

c230 BC ▶ Carthaginians found the settlement of "Barcino", probably on the heights of Montjuïc.

218–201 BC ▶ Romans expel Carthaginians from Iberian peninsula in Second Punic War. Roman Barcino is established around today's Barri Gòtic.

304 AD ▶ Santa Eulàlia – the city's patron saint – is martyred by Romans for refusing to renounce Christianity.

c350 AD ▶ Roman city walls built, as threat of invasion grows.

415 ▶ Visigoths sweep across Spain and establish temporary capital in Barcino (later "Barcelona").

711 ▶ Moorish conquest of Spain. Barcelona eventually forced to surrender (719).

801 ▶ Barcelona re-taken by Louis the Pious, son of Charlemagne. Frankish counties of Catalunya become a buffer zone, known as the Spanish Marches.

878 ▶ Guifré el Pelós (Wilfred the Hairy) declared first Count of Barcelona, founding a dynastic line that was to rule until 1410.

985 ▶ Moorish sacking of city. Sant Pau del Camp – city's oldest surviving church – built after this date.

1137 ▶ Dynastic union of Catalunya and Aragón established.

1213–1276 ▶ Reign of Jaume I, "the Conqueror", expansion of empire and beginning of Catalan golden age.

1282–1387 ▶ Barcelona at centre of an aggressively mercantile Mediterranean empire. Successive rulers construct most of Barcelona's best-known Gothic buildings.

1348 ▶ Black Death strikes, killing half of Barcelona's population.

1391 ▶ Pogrom against the city's Jewish population.

1410 ▶ Death of Martí el Humà (Martin the Humane), last of Catalan count-kings. Beginning of the end of Catalan influence in the Mediterranean.

1469 ▶ Marriage of Ferdinand of Aragón and Isabel of Castile.

1479 ▶ Ferdinand succeeds to Catalan-Aragón crown, and Catalunya's fortunes decline. Inquisition introduced to Barcelona, leading to forced flight of the Jews.

1493 ▶ Christopher Columbus received in Barcelona after triumphant return from New World. Shifting of trade routes away from Mediterranean and across Atlantic further impoverishes the city.

1516 ▶ Spanish crown passes to Habsburgs and Madrid is established as capital of Spanish empire.

1640–1652 ▶ Uprising known as "War of the Reapers" declares Catalunya an independent republic. Barcelona besieged and surrenders to Spanish army.

1714 ▶ After War of Spanish Succession, Spanish throne passes to Bourbons. Barcelona finally subdued on September 11 (now Catalan National Day); Ciutadella fortress built, Catalan language banned and parliament abolished.

1755 ▶ Barceloneta district laid out – gridded layout is early example of urban planning.

1778 ▶ Steady increase in trade; Barcelona's economy improves.

1814 ▶ After Peninsular War (1808–1814), French finally driven out, with Barcelona the last city to fall.

1848 ▶ Rapid expansion and industrialization.

1850 ▶ Plaça Reial – emblematic old-town square – laid out.

1859 ▶ Old city walls demolished and Eixample district built to accommodate growing population.

1882 ▶ Work begins on Sagrada Família; Antoni Gaudí takes charge two years later.

1888 ▶ Universal Exhibition held at Parc de la Ciutadella. *Modernista* architects start to make their mark.

1893 ▶ First stirrings of anarchist unrest. Liceu opera house bombed.

1901 ▶ Pablo Picasso's first public exhibition held at *Els Quatre Gats* tavern.

1909 ▶ Setmana Trágica (Tragic Week) of rioting. Many churches destroyed.

1922 ▶ Parc Güell opens to the public.

1926 ▶ Antoni Gaudí run over by a tram; Barcelona stops en masse for his funeral.

1929 ▶ International Exhibition held at Montjuïc.

1936–1939 ▶ Spanish Civil War. Barcelona at heart of Republican cause, with George Orwell and other volunteers arriving to fight. City eventually falls to Nationalists on January 26, 1939.

1939–1975 ▶ Spain under Franco. Generalitat president Lluís Companys executed and Catalan language banned. Emigration encouraged from south to dilute Catalan identity. Franco dies in 1975.

1977 ▶ First democratic Spanish elections for 40 years.

1978–1980 ▶ Generalitat re-established and Statute of Autonomy approved. Conservative nationalist government elected.

1992 ▶ Olympics held in Barcelona. Massive rebuilding projects transform Montjuïc and the waterfront.

1995 ▶ MACBA (contemporary art museum) opens, signals regeneration of El Raval district.

1997–2004 ▶ Joan Clos is city's mayor, while left-wing coalition replaces the nationalists in Catalan government (2003). Diagonal Mar hosts Universal Forum of Cultures (2004).

2006 ▶ New statute of autonomy agreed with Spain. Clos replaced by Jordi Hereu as mayor. Ambitious building projects continue to change Barcelona. FC Barcelona are European football champions for second time.

Language

Catalan

In Barcelona Catalan (Català) has more or less taken over from Castilian (Castellano) Spanish as the language on street signs and maps. On paper it looks like a cross between French and Spanish and is generally easy to read if you know those two. Few visitors realize how important Catalan is to those who speak it: never commit the error of calling it a dialect. Despite the preponderance of the Catalan language you'll get by perfectly well in Spanish as long as you're aware of the use of Catalan in timetables, on menus, and so on. However you'll generally get a good reception if you at least try communicating in the local language.

Pronunciation

Don't be tempted to use the few rules of Spanish pronunciation you may know – in particular the soft Spanish Z and C don't apply, so unlike in the rest of Spain the city is not Barthelona but Barcelona, as in English.

A as in hat if stressed, as in alone when unstressed.

E varies, but usually as in get.

I as in police.

IG sounds like the "tch" in the English scratch; lleig (ugly) is pronounced "yeah-tch".

O a round full sound, when stressed, otherwise like a soft U sound.

U somewhere between the U of put and rule.

Ç sounds like an English S; plaça is pronounced "plassa".

C followed by an E or I is soft; otherwise hard.

G followed by E or I is like the "zh" in Zhivago; otherwise hard.

H is always silent.

J as in the French "Jean".

L.L is best pronounced (for foreigners) as a single L sound; but for Catalan speakers it has two distinct L sounds.

LL sounds like an English Y or LY, like the "yuh" sound in million.

N as in English, though before F or V it sometimes sounds like an M.

NY corresponds to the Castilian Ñ.

QU before E or I sounds like K, unless the U has an umlaut, (Ü) in which case, and before A or O, as in quit.

R is rolled, but only at the start of a word; at the end it's often silent.

T is pronounced as in English, though sometimes it sounds like a D; as in viatge or dotze.

V at the start of a word sounds like B; in all other positions it's a soft F sound.

W is pronounced like a B/V.

X is like SH or CH in most words, though in some, like exit, it sounds like an X.

Z is like the English Z in zoo.

Words and phrases

Basics			
Si, No, Val	Yes, No, OK	Hola, Adéu	Hello, Goodbye
Si us plau, Gràcies	Please, Thank you	Bon dia	Good morning
		Bona tarde/nit	Good afternoon /night

Fins després	See you later
Ho sento	Sorry
Perdoni	Excuse me
(No) Ho entenc	I (don't) understand
Parleu anglès?	Do you speak English?
On? Quan?	Where? When?
Què? Quant?	What? How much?
Aquí, Allí/Allá	Here, There
Això, Allò	This, That
Obert, Tancat	Open, Closed
Amb, Sense	With, Without
Bo(na), Dolent(a)	Good, Bad
Gran, Petit(a)	Big, Small
Barat(a), Car(a)	Cheap, Expensive
Vull (pronounced "vwee")	I want
Voldria	I'd like
Vostès saben?	Do you know?
No sé	I don't know
Hi ha(?)	There is (Is there?)
Què és això?	What's that?
Té…?	Do you have…?
Avui, Demà	Today, Tomorrow

Accommodation

Té alguna habitació?	Do you have a room?
…amb dos llits/ llit per dues persones	…with two beds/ double bed
…amb dutxa/ bany	…with shower/bath
Per a una persona (dues persones)	It's for one person (two people)
Per una nit (una setmana)	For one night (one week)
Esta bé, quant és?	It's fine, how much is it?
En té de més bon preu?	Don't you have anything cheaper?

Directions and transport

Per anar a…?	How do I get to…?
A la dreta, A l'esquerra, Tot recte	Left, Right, Straight on
On és…?	Where is…?
…l'estació de autobuses	…the bus station
…l'estació	…the train station
…el banc més a prop	…the nearest bank
…l'oficina de correus	…the post office
…la toaleta	…the toilet
De on surt el autobús a…?	Where does the bus to…leave from?
Aquest tren va a Barcelona?	Is this the train for Barcelona?
Voldria un bitlet (d'anar i tornar) a…	I'd like a (return) ticket to…
A quina hora surt (arriba a)?	What time does it leave (arrive in)?

Numbers

un(a)	1
dos (dues)	2
tres	3
quatre	4
cinc	5
sis	6
set	7
vuit	8
nou	9
deu	10
onze	11
dotze	12
tretze	13
catorze	14
quinze	15
setze	16
disset	17
divuit	18
dinou	19
vint	20
vint-i-un	21
trenta	30
quaranta	40
cinquanta	50
seixanta	60
setanta	70
vuitanta	80
novanta	90
cent	100
cent un	101
dos-cents (dues-centes)	200
cinc-cents	500
mil	1000

Days of the week

dilluns	Monday
dimarts	Tuesday
dimecres	Wednesday
dijous	Thursday
divendres	Friday
dissabte	Saturday
diumenge	Sunday

Menu reader

Basic words

Esmorzar	To have breakfast
Dinar	To have lunch
Sopar	To have dinner
Ganivet	Knife
Forquilla	Fork
Cullera	Spoon
Taula	Table
Ampolla	Bottle
Got	Glass
Carta	Menu
Sopa	Soup
Amanida	Salad
Entremesos	Hors d'oeuvres
Truita	Omelette
Entrepà	Sandwich
Torrades	Toast
Tapes	Tapas
Mantega	Butter
Ous	Eggs
Pa	Bread
Olives	Olives
Oli	Oil
Vinagre	Vinegar
Sal	Salt
Pebre	Pepper
Sucre	Sugar
El compte	The bill
Sóc vegetarià/ vegetariana	I'm a vegetarian

Cooking terms

Assortit	Assorted
Al forn	Baked
A la brasa	Char-grilled
Fresc	Fresh
Fregit	Fried
A la romana	Fried in batter
All i oli	Garlic mayonnaise
A la plantxa	Grilled
En escabetx	Pickled
Rostit	Roast
Salsa	Sauce
Saltat	Sautéed
Remenat	Scrambled
Del temps	Seasonal
Fumat	Smoked
A l'ast	Spit-roasted
Guisat	Stewed
Al vapor	Steamed
Farcit	Stuffed

Fish and seafood/Peix i marisc

Anxoves/Seitons	Anchovies
Calamarsets	Baby squid
Cloïses	Clams
Cranc	Crab
Sipia	Cuttlefish
Lluç	Hake
Llagosta	Lobster
Rap	Monkfish
Musclos	Mussels
Pop	Octopus
Gambes	Prawns
Navalles	Razor clams
Salmó	Salmon
Bacallà	Salt cod
Sardines	Sardines
Llobarro	Sea bass
Llenguado	Sole
Calamars	Squid
Peix espasa	Swordfish
Tonyina	Tuna

Meat and poultry/Carn i aviram

Embotits	Charcuterie
Pollastre	Chicken
Xoriço	Chorizo sausage
Pernil serrà	Cured ham
Llonganissa	Cured pork sausage
Costelles	Cutlets/chops
Ànec	Duck
Pernil dolç	Ham
Xai/Be	Lamb
Fetge	Liver
Llom	Loin of pork
Mandonguilles	Meatballs
Porc	Pork
Conill	Rabbit
Salsitxes	Sausages
Cargols	Snails
Bistec	Steak

Vegetables/Verdures i llegums

Carxofes	Artichokes
Alberginia	Aubergine/eggplant
Faves	Broad/lima beans
Cigrons	Chickpeas
Carbassó	Courgette/zucchini
All	Garlic
Mongetes	Haricot beans
Llenties	Lentils

Xampinyons	Mushrooms
Cebes	Onions
Patates	Potatoes
Espinacs	Spinach
Tomàquets	Tomatoes
Bolets	Wild mushrooms

Fruit/Fruita

Poma	Apple
Plàtan	Banana
Raïm	Grapes
Meló	Melon
Taronja	Orange
Pera	Pear
Maduixes	Strawberries

Desserts/Postres

Pastis	Cake
Formatge	Cheese
Macedonia	Fruit salad
Flam	Crème caramel
Gelat	Ice cream
Arròs amb llet	Rice pudding
Tarta	Tart
Yogur	Yoghurt

Catalan specialities

Amanida Catalana Salad served with sliced meats (sometimes cheese)

Arròs a banda Rice with seafood, the rice served separately

Arròs a la marinera Paella: rice with seafood and saffron

Arròs negre "Black rice", cooked in squid ink

Bacallà a la llauna Salt cod baked with garlic, tomato and paprika

Botifarra (amb mongetes) Grilled Catalan pork sausage (with stewed haricot beans)

Calçots Large char-grilled spring onions, eaten with romesco sauce (see below), available February/March

Canelons Cannelloni, baked pasta with ground meat and béchamel sauce

Conill all i oli Rabbit with garlic mayonnaise

Crema Catalana Crème caramel, with caramelized sugar topping

Escalivada Grilled aubergine/eggplant, pepper/capsicum and onion

Espinacs a la Catalana Spinach cooked with raisins and pine nuts

Esqueixada Salad of salt cod with peppers/capsicums, tomatoes, onions and olives, a summer dish

Estofat de vedella Veal stew

Faves a la Catalana Stewed broad beans, with bacon and *botifarra*, a regional classic

Fideuà Short, thin noodles (the width of vermicelli) served with seafood, accompanied by *all i olli*

Fuet Catalan salami

Llenties guisades Stewed lentils

Mel i mató Curd cheese and honey, a typical dessert

Pa amb tomàquet Bread (often grilled), rubbed with tomato, garlic and olive oil

Pollastre al cava Chicken with *cava* (champagne) sauce

Pollastre amb gambes Chicken with prawns

Postres de músic Cake of dried fruit and nuts

Salsa Romesco Spicy sauce (with chillis, nuts, tomato and wine), often served with grilled fish

Samfaina Ratatouille-like stew (onions, peppers/capsicum, aubergine/eggplant, tomato), served with salt cod or chicken

Sarsuela Fish and shellfish stew

Sipia amb mandonguilles Cuttlefish with meatballs

Suquet de peix Fish and potato casserole

Xató Mixed salad of olives, salt cod, preserved tuna, anchovies and onions

Drinks

Cervesa	Beer
Vi	Wine
Xampan/Cava	Champagne
Cafè	Coffee
Cafè sol	Espresso
Cafè Americà	Large black coffee
Cafè amb llet	Large white coffee
Cafè tallat	Small white coffee
Descafeinat	Decaf
Te	Tea
Xocolata	Drinking chocolate
Granissat	Crushed ice drink
Llet	Milk
Orxata	Tiger nut drink
Aigua	Water
Aigua mineral	Mineral water
…(amb gas)	…(sparkling)
…(sense gas)	…(still)

Travel store

Available from all good bookstores D: Rough Guide DIRECTIONS

For more information go to www.roughguides.com

Listen Up!

"You may be used to the Rough Guide series being comprehensive, but nothing will prepare you for the exhaustive Rough Guide to World Music . . . one of our books of the year."

Sunday Times, London

Rough Guide Music Titles

The Beatles • Blues • Bob Dylan • Classical Music
Elvis • Frank Sinatra • Heavy Metal • Hip-Hop
iPods, iTunes & music online • Jazz • Book of Playlists
Led Zeppelin • Opera • Pink Floyd • Punk • Reggae
Rock • The Rolling Stones • Soul and R&B • World
Music Vol 1 & 2 • Velvet Underground

BROADEN YOUR HORIZONS

NOTES

NOTES

NOTES

NOTES

NOTES

small print & **Index**

A Rough Guide to Rough Guides

In 1981, Mark Ellingham, a recent graduate in English from Bristol University, was travelling in Greece on a tiny budget and couldn't find the right guidebook. With a group of friends he wrote his own guide, combining a contemporary, journalistic style with a practical approach to travellers' needs. That first Rough Guide was a student scheme that became a publishing phenomenon. Today, Rough Guides include recommendations from shoestring to luxury and cover hundreds of destinations around the globe, including almost every country in the Americas and Europe, more than half of Africa and most of Asia and Australasia. Millions of readers relish Rough Guides' wit and inquisitiveness as much as their enthusiastic, critical approach and value-for-money ethos. The guides' ever-growing team of authors and photographers are spread all over the world.

In the early 1990s, Rough Guides branched out of travel, with the publication of Rough Guides to World Music, Classical Music and the Internet. All three have become benchmark titles in their fields, spearheading the publication of a range of more than 350 titles under the Rough Guide name, including phrasebooks, waterproof maps, music guides from Opera to Heavy Metal, reference works as diverse as Conspiracy Theories and Shakespeare, and popular culture books from iPods to Poker. Rough Guides also produce a series of more than 120 World Music CDs in partnership with World Music Network.

Visit www.roughguides.com to see our latest publications.

Rough Guide travel images are available for commercial licensing at www.roughguidespictures.com

Publishing information

This second edition published June 2008 by Rough Guides Ltd, 80 Strand, London WC2R 0RL. 345 Hudson St, 4th Floor, New York, NY 10014, USA.

Distributed by the Penguin Group
Penguin Books Ltd, 80 Strand, London WC2R 0RL
Penguin Group (USA), 375 Hudson Street, NY 10014, USA
14 Local Shopping Centre, Panchsheel Park, New Delhi 110017, India
Penguin Group (Australia), 250 Camberwell Road, Camberwell, Victoria 3124, Australia
Penguin Group (Canada), 10 Alcorn Avenue, Toronto, ON M4V 1E4, Canada
Penguin Group (NZ), 67 Apollo Drive, Mairangi Bay, Auckland 1310, New Zealand
Typeset in Bembo and Helvetica to an original design by Henry Iles.

Cover concept by Peter Dyer.

Printed and bound in China
© Jules Brown/Rough Guides, 2008

No part of this book may be reproduced in any form without permission from the publisher except for the quotation of brief passages in reviews.
240pp includes index

A catalogue record for this book is available from the British Library

ISBN 978-1-85828-280-0

The publishers and authors have done their best to ensure the accuracy and currency of all the information in Barcelona DIRECTIONS, however, they can accept no responsibility for any loss, injury, or inconvenience sustained by any traveller as a result of information or advice contained in the guide.

1   3   5   7   9   8   6   4   2

Help us update

We've gone to a lot of effort to ensure that the second edition of Barcelona DIRECTIONS is accurate and up-to-date. However, things change – places get "discovered", opening hours are notoriously fickle, restaurants and rooms raise prices or lower standards. If you feel we've got it wrong or left something out, we'd like to know, and if you can remember the address, the price, the phone number, so much the better.

Please send your comments with the subject line "Barcelona DIRECTIONS Update" to ✉mail@roughguides.com. We'll credit all contributions and send a copy of the next edition (or any other Rough Guide if you prefer) for the very best emails.
Have your questions answered and tell others about your trip at ✇community.roughguides.com

Rough Guide credits

Text editors: Sarah Eno and Lucy White
Layout: Pradeep Thapliyal
Photography: Chris Christoforou
Cartography: Katie Lloyd-Jones and Ed Wright

Picture editor: Emily Taylor
Proofreader: Jan McCann
Production: Rebecca Short
Cover design: Chloë Roberts

SMALL PRINT

The author

Jules Brown first visited Barcelona in 1985. Apart from this book he has also written half-a-dozen other Rough Guides, and contributed as researcher to and editor of many others. But he's beginning to think he's left it too late to play for Huddersfield Town.

Acknowledgements

From the photographer:
A special thank you to my dear friends Izqui & Babi for sharing their home with me so generously. To Uri Baba, an amazing friend and photographer. To Santy Belleza, my beautiful friend, saghabo belleza! To Ivan the great, an amazing guide and a great cook. Thanks also to Mark Thomas. Shiny smiles, Chris Christoforou.

Readers' letters

Thanks to: Phil Agre, Elise Butt, Susan Clark, Frederic Echivard, Kathryn Gutteridge, Peter Henshaw, Chloe Hiddleston, Bradley Lynch, Diana Papaioannou, Jordi París, Sally Darnell, Sarah Salmon, Susan Truce and Kate Ward.

Index

Maps are marked in colour

NOTES